Beautiful
CRESCENT
A History of New Orleans

Best Wishes
Betsy Swanson

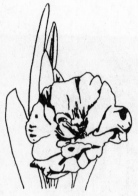

Oleander,
City Flower

Seal of the City

City Flag

The Spanish brought the oleander from Cuba after the fires of 1788 and 1794 had devastated plant life in New Orleans. The city adopted the oleander as the city flower in June 1923. The seal, adopted in 1805 and redesigned in 1852, shows a pair of Indians, the region's first inhabitants; recumbent Father Mississippi; and an alligator from the swamplands. Mayor Martin Behrman accepted the flag on February 9, 1918.

Beautiful CRESCENT

A History of New Orleans

By Joan B. Garvey and Mary Lou Widmer

Edited and updated by Kathy Chappetta Spiess
and Karen Chappetta

Foreword by Barbara Robichaux

PELICAN PUBLISHING COMPANY
GRETNA 2017

First edition, 1982
Second edition, 1984
Third edition, 1988
Fourth edition, 1989
Fifth edition, 1991
Sixth edition, 1992
Seventh edition, 1994
First Pelican edition, 2013
Second Pelican printing, 2014
Third Pelican printing, 2016
Second Pelican edition, 2017

Library of Congress Cataloging-in-Publication Data

Garvey, Joan B., 1929-2016
  Beautiful crescent: a history of New Orleans / by Joan B. Garvey and Mary Lou
Widmer ; foreword by Barbara Robichaux. — 2nd Pelican ed. / edited and updated
by Kathy Chappetta Spiess and Karen Chappetta.
    p. cm.
  Includes bibliographical references and index.
    ISBN 978-1-4556-2341-9 (pbk. : alk. paper) — ISBN 978-1-4556-2342-6
(ebook) 1. New Orleans (La.)—History. I. Widmer, Mary Lou, 1926- II. Spiess,
Kathy Chappetta. III. Chappetta, Karen. IV. Title.
  F379.N557G37 2017
  763'35—dc23

Printed in the United States of America
Published by Pelican Publishing Company, Inc.
1000 Burmaster Street, Gretna, Louisiana 70053

To Mom and Dad—we miss you both—and to our brother and sisters for your never-ending support

Contents

Foreword

Beautiful Crescent, long heralded as "the tour guide's handbook," gives us a glimpse of New Orleans through the eyes of the people who founded and molded her into the city she is today. This uncluttered, informative, yet entertaining history results in a greater understanding of who we are and how our customs came about to make our city totally unique. This updated volume of *Beautiful Crescent* is a gift to visitors and locals alike and invaluable to all students of New Orleans. We applaud you!

Barbara Robichaux
President
Tour Guides Association of
Greater New Orleans, Inc.

Preface

History is a story, and as a story, differs with the storyteller. The storyteller's point of view becomes the attitude with which the history is related. For this reason, the following chronology is *a* history of New Orleans, not *the* history of New Orleans.

We maintain that there is no definitive history, only stories told with more or less documentation. Opinions cannot be documented, nor importance decided, except through a personal approach. Our approach is a "people approach." We have tried to view the city through the people who came here, some to stay, some to make their mark and then move on. We hope to share with you our view of the development of New Orleans in this narrative.

Joan B. Garvey
Mary Lou Widmer
Authors

It is truly a pleasure to be associated with *Beautiful Crescent: A History of New Orleans.* In 2009, we met with Mary Lou Widmer, one of the authors of this book. After many discussions and negotiations, we obtained the rights and the responsibility of keeping this magnificent book of New Orleans history alive.

We have always considered ourselves knowledgeable about New Orleans and her history. Yet it wasn't until we began the process of updating this book line by line that we realized how little we really knew about the city of New Orleans.

In addition, while reading and researching the distant and recent pasts, it became apparent that the attitudes, customs, and general doggedness of New Orleanians to celebrate life and to overcome adversity and disaster and get on with the business of life are engraved in our civic psyche. Long ago, newcomers to the Louisiana colony said with regard to the laissez-faire attitude of the people here, "it was caused by the humidity." Whether it is in the humidity or in the water, after reading this book and understanding the motives of Bienville, Iberville, and everyone else who formed a community in New Orleans, it is no wonder we have been able to rise above disaster and celebrate the city that we all love.

All New Orleanians and visitors to the area would benefit from becoming familiar with the history of New Orleans, and we don't believe there is any book with which it is better to do that than through the pages of *Beautiful Crescent*.

Kathy Chappetta Spiess
Karen Chappetta
Editors

CHAPTER I
The Part the River Played

Before there could be a city, there had to be a place for a city, but for millions of years, there was no land where New Orleans stands today. The entire state of Louisiana was part of a huge body of water, an extension of the sea into the continent. The Mississippi River did not exist until one million years ago (a brief period in geologic terms), when it began to meander southward unobtrusively.

During the **Ice Age** 25,000 years ago, sheets of ice covered the North American continent but did not come within 400 miles of the site of New Orleans. The Ice Age wiped out a number of other drainage systems in the Midwest and rerouted drainage toward the Mississippi, enlarging the river considerably. Embedded in the ice were tons of debris, and during this period, there were violent windstorms that deposited silt in the Mississippi Basin. Then, when the ice melted, the water flowed rapidly, taking its debris with it, causing the Mississippi to extend its delta, filling in its southern end.

As the delta filled, the sea retreated, leaving Lake Pontchartrain behind, a child of the Gulf, separated from its parent about five thousand years ago. Between the lake and the river, a stretch of swampland emerged, which would become the geography of the city of New Orleans.

Of all the geologic factors that shaped the site of the city, the river played the leading role. Its serpentine course and erratic behavior in the last several thousand years determined the exact location and dimensions of the city, the arteries of transportation and communication, and even, in time, the patterns of colonization and styles of architecture. The colonists who would later settle on the crescent of marshland would be forced to develop a lifestyle that could be supported by their water-locked environment. It is the story of these people that will be told here.

The process of shaping and molding is not complete, even today.

The city is still sinking at a rate of approximately two inches per year (Navarro 2010). There are places in the delta where sugarcane fields, planted in the eighteenth century, are now under water. Yet, there would not have been a city at all, a site for a city, or a delta, except for the Ice Age and its aftermath.

The bedrock, or sand strata, that lies on the floor of the saucer beneath New Orleans is of pre-glacial material, dating back to the Pleistocene era of one million or so years ago. It consists of clay, silt, and silty sand. North of Lake Pontchartrain, this Pleistocene material is at the surface, forming a bluff paralleling the lakeshore. The Pleistocene material has eroded into low hills covered by beautiful pines, an area without "foundation" problems or flooding. This marvelous Pleistocene land (now the sites of Mandeville, Madisonville, and Covington) is the result of faults in the earth's crust, which have allowed the material to crop out. From the north shore of the lake, the material drops below the surface of the water, dipping gently southward, until it rests some seventy feet beneath the city of New Orleans. Because of the range of stability, no New Orleanian would think of erecting a building of any height or weight without first sinking pilings to gain solid footing on the bedrock.

There are no natural land surfaces (except for the levees) in the city that are higher than fifteen feet above sea level. Canal Street meets the river at an elevation of fourteen feet above sea level; Jackson Square, only six blocks downriver, is just ten feet above sea level. The Tulane University area is a mere four feet above sea level, while the intersection of Broad Street and Washington Avenue (originally part of the backswamp, now Mid-City) is two feet below sea level. All of these facts, part of the geologic picture of the city's relationship with the river, help us to understand many things about the life of the natives of the city.

The earliest known waterways through the city of New Orleans are two abandoned distributaries of the Mississippi: **Bayou Metairie** and its eastern sector, **Bayou Gentilly**. Between 600 BC and AD 1000, Bayou Metairie wandered away from the Mississippi about twenty miles above the French Quarter, near what is Kenner today, and strayed eastward toward the Gulf of Mexico, running more or less parallel to the river. The eastern portion of this distributary is shown on some old maps as **Bayou Sauvage**, on others as Bayou Gentilly. In time, the river abandoned these wanderers, leaving them to meander lazily through the marshes of the backswamp.

The course of these two connected waterways was, roughly, along what are today Metairie Road and City Park Avenue to Dumaine Street, across Bayou St. John, then left to Grand Route St. John, then right to Gentilly Boulevard, which becomes Old Gentilly Highway.

The Metairie and Gentilly bayous were not important to the early settlers as a water route, but became important because a levee of well-drained soil developed alongside them, which provided a flood-free land route into the city from the west by Metairie Road and from the east by Gentilly Road (Chef Menteur Highway). There is another land route into the city from the west, along the riverfront from Baton Rouge, called River Road. From the east, however, Gentilly "Ridge" is the main road, for it carries both a national highway (U.S. 90) and the main line of the Louisville and Nashville Railroad. During the Civil War, the federals used maps showing these highways as routes of entry into the city.

Over the centuries, the river built delta land by depositing material where it empties into the sea, forming sandbars, which in time became islands. The islands split the river into two or more distributary channels. This is how the Metairie and Gentilly bayous were formed. The same thing is happening today about twenty miles below **Venice, Louisiana,** where the river divides into three major distributaries: **Pass L'Outre, South Pass,** and **Southwest Pass.** Southwest Pass is the deepest and carries the largest volume of ship traffic.

Another method the river has of making delta land, which is more important to the development of a city, is by abandoning its lower course for hundreds of miles and lunging out to the sea by an altogether different route. The river does this regularly every several hundred years, leaving behind great gashes across its delta. The Mississippi as we know it today took up the diversion near New Orleans sometime between AD 1500 and 1600.

We are forced to wonder under what conditions a river jumps its banks. An understanding of how levees form might help to clarify. During a flood, the fast-moving waters of the river pick up heavy material and, spilling over its banks, deposit the material, systematically raising the banks (or natural levees) with the flood. Artificial levees, which are built on top of these natural levees, may be thirty feet high and faced with concrete. They are among the most prominent landforms in New Orleans. The natural levee may be only ten to fifteen feet above sea level but a mile or two wide, sloping downward from the river so gently that the decline would not be noticeable in a moving vehicle.

Natural levees end where they merge with the backswamp (lowland). Natural levees provide the only well-drained land in southeast Louisiana, which is one of the reasons why most settlements, urban or rural, were located on natural levees (of either the Mississippi or smaller streams). Another reason is that, in colonial times, the settlers had only the Mississippi for transportation. It was also the only place to build roads and buildings that were safe from floods.

So, for the first 200 years, the city of New Orleans developed along the natural levees of the Mississippi River and Bayous Metairie and Gentilly (Sauvage). The city came to an abrupt end when it reached the backswamp.

Prior to 1700, the Indians called Bayou Metairie **"Bayou Chapitoulas"** (or Tchoupitoulas), after an Indian tribe who lived near the stream's confluence with the Mississippi River. It was renamed Metairie (meaning farm) by the French settlers who established plantations there. Traces of the original bayou may still be found in Metairie Cemetery. Bayou Gentilly was first called Bayou Sauvage by the French because the French word *sauvage* meant savage, wild, or untamed and was used to describe the Indians. Bayou Sauvage therefore meant Bayou of the Indians or **Indian Bayou**. It was renamed Bayou Gentilly around 1718 to commemorate the Paris home of the **Dreux** brothers, early settlers along the waterway.

The upriver end of town is surrounded on three sides by the river, which sweeps a giant semicircle around that part of the city. The remainder of the upriver area is closed off by the lower, natural levees of the abandoned Metairie distributary. Thus, a "bowl" is created, which is, of course, below sea level. (This area is now **Mid-City.**) Pumps were invented in the early 1900s to drain the water from Mid-City and make it habitable, but in prehistoric times, when the "bowl" filled, it spilled over into the lowest place in the Metairie levees. Over the centuries, a channel formed there, small but immensely important to early New Orleans commerce. The channel was later called Bayou St. John, and it flowed northward into Lake Pontchartrain.

Long before the white man came to Louisiana, the Indians traveled from the Gulf of Mexico, through the **Mississippi Sound, Rigolets Pass, Lake Borgne,** and **Lake Pontchartrain** into **Bayou St. John,** which the **Choctaws** called **Bayouk Choupic** or Shupik (Bayou Mudfish). Five and a half miles after entering the bayou, they got out of their dugout canoes and carried them over a timeworn trail to the **Michisipy** (Great River). The Choctaws called Bayou St. John "Choupithatcha" or "Soupitcatcha," combination of the Choctaw *"supik"* (mudfish) and *"hacha"* (river).

This old Indian portage, which became a boundary of the city of New Orleans, can still be followed today. Beginning at Governor Nicholls and Decatur streets near the Mississippi River, one would follow Governor Nicholls through the French Quarter toward the lake. At North Claiborne, Governor Nicholls becomes Bayou Road, and the street angles northeast, crossing Esplanade Avenue at North Miro. A few blocks farther, Bayou Road intersects with Grand Route St. John. A sharp turn to the left and an additional three-quarters of a mile brings the traveler to the shores of Bayou St. John. The route of the portage, called Bayou Road in French times, has varied through the years.

The Mississippi River, beginning in **Lake Itasca, Minnesota,** and ending in the Gulf of Mexico, is 2,345 miles long. It runs as deep as 217 feet, and at the foot of Canal Street is 2,200 feet wide. It is the fourth longest river in the world after the Amazon, Nile, and Yangtze. It drains 40 percent of the forty-eight continental states and has a basin covering 1.25 million square miles, which includes parts of thirty-one states and two Canadian provinces.

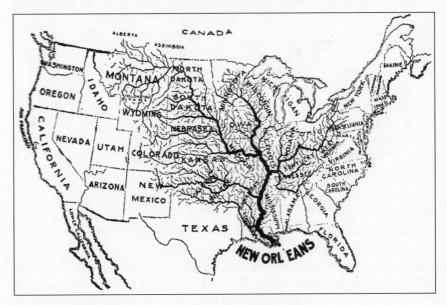

Map showing the drainage system of the Mississippi River.

With a river of such enormity, any big flood could break through the natural levee and spill over into the backswamp. Such a breakthrough is called a crevasse, a natural disaster feared by early settlers because it could pick up miles of farmland and wash it away completely. In addition, a crevasse made wide splits in the river's route, paralyzing transportation and communications. A crevasse at the Sauvé Plantation in 1849 caused an uncontrolled flood into Mid-City. The greatest danger of such a crevasse is that once the river jumps its banks, there might be no way of getting it back on its original course. The possibility existed that it might permanently change its course. The **Sauvé Crevasse** was brought under control, however, and the danger was averted.

There is geologic evidence that the Mississippi River has changed its course many times in the past 5,000 years, leaving old channels, each

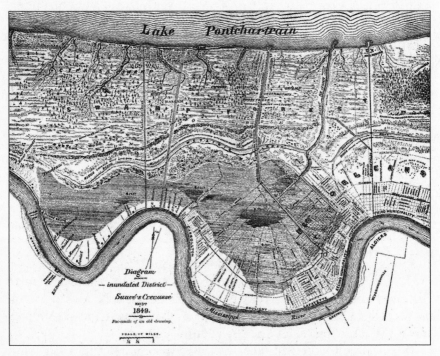

Map dated 1849 shows the areas of New Orleans flooded after the Sauvé Crevasse, May 3, 1849. The darkest areas were the worst. Mid-City was nine feet under water. Bayou St. John connects the Carondelet Canal (Old Basin Canal) to the Vieux Carré (First Municipality). The New Basin Canal connects the lake to the Second Municipality and City of Carrollton (a suburb). (U.S. Census 1887)

with its own delta. Bayou Teche now occupies the oldest visible course. A more recent ancestor of the Mississippi is **Bayou Lafourche,** which was apparently the last course it took before the one it now follows. Another earlier route is the St. Bernard Delta east of New Orleans.

The Mississippi River has run its present course since the sixteenth century. It was on the verge of jumping again when explorers appeared on the scene. If such a jump were to occur now below New Orleans, it would require a completely new system of navigation from the Gulf to the city. But if it were to occur above (upstream of) New Orleans, the result would be disastrous. The largest port in the United States would no longer be situated on a river but a stagnant stream.

New Orleanians can recite a litany of difficulties they live with involving the river:

- Most of the city is below sea level; the river flows ten to fifteen feet above sea level.
- The present Mid-City area, lying as it does in a bowl, used to flood constantly and was a breeding ground for yellow fever and malaria. The swamp teemed with snakes and alligators; when it was dry, it was the consistency of glue.
- The bedrock beneath the city, which is only compacted clay, is seventy feet below the surface in some places.
- The only avenues into the city when the white man came were the natural levees. During flood times, if crevasses occurred, the levees would be cut and transportation disrupted.
- Hurricanes frequently strike south Louisiana. Today, Louisiana's eroding coastal wetlands do not buffer the storm surges as they once did.

In view of all of this, one wonders why more than a million people (U.S. Census 2016) live and work in the greater New Orleans area. But more than that, one wonders why Jean Baptiste Le Moyne, Sieur de Bienville, chose such a site for his city. To Bienville, it was simple: it was the most logical and necessary spot for a city.

It was clear to Bienville that the river demanded that a city exist at its mouth, but in all of the 200 miles south of the site of **Baton Rouge,** it provided no place to put one. Naturally, the settlers wanted high ground, and the site of Baton Rouge met that requirement, but it was too far upriver to be convenient to ocean-bound ships.

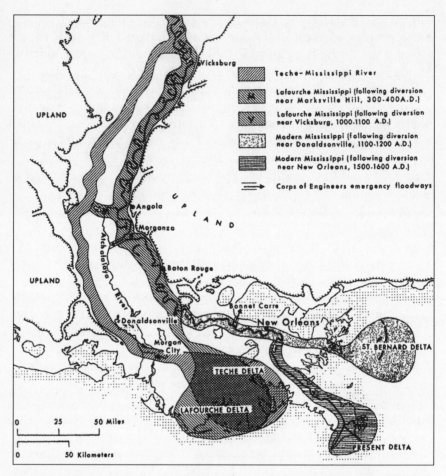

The Mississippi with its ancient deltas. In recent times, the river appeared to be threatening to jump its course again, either into Lake Pontchartrain at Bonnet Carré or into the Atchafalaya at Morganza. Either would have been disastrous to New Orleans. The Army Corps of Engineers built spillways at both locations to prevent flooding and keep the river in its present course. (H. N. Fisk, *Geological Investigation of the Atchafalaya Basin and the Problem of Mississippi River Diversion* [Vicksburg: Mississippi River Commission, 1952]. Modified by William D. Thornbury in *Regional Geomorphology of the United States* [New York: John Wiley, 1965], 61. Used with permission.)

The site of the old Indian portage from the Mississippi River to Bayou St. John could be reached not only by coming up the river from the Gulf but also by traveling westward from the Gulf Coast through the Mississippi Sound and Lake Borgne and into Lake Pontchartrain. This was the place where Bienville decreed that the city of New Orleans would be built.

The **Mississippi River Basin** is shaped like a funnel, and the city that was to be founded on Bienville's "Beautiful Crescent" of land in the bend of the river would control the tip of that funnel. It would be the gatekeeper to the richest river valley on earth. This was the destiny of New Orleans. Had there been nothing more than a sandbar in that bend of the river, Bienville would have urged his settlers to camp on it, fighting the elements until their own ingenuity provided the answers to their problems. This, of course, is what eventually happened, for the settlers did not leave. They endured with proprietary pride, and slowly, against the indomitable odds, the city grew and prospered.

Almost every river in the world provides a site for a city near its mouth where there is high ground on which to build and where the river is narrow enough for land traffic to cross it conveniently. But not the Mississippi. At the mouth of almost every river, there is an embayment, where the sea has entered the mouth of the river and flooded it, forming a bay at the point where the river narrows. But the Mississippi does not narrow at any point. At the foot of Canal Street, it is nearly a half of a mile wide. It runs uniformly wide for hundreds of miles. It does not provide any site for a city south of Baton Rouge. It does not form a bay, and it wildly jumps its riverbanks every five hundred to six hundred years, aloof and indifferent to the needs of man.

The river last jumped its riverbed in the sixteenth century to follow a diversion near New Orleans instead of near the city of Donaldsonville, to which it had diverted in the twelfth century. So, in 1541, the scene was set for the discovery of the river in its present location, and into this chapter of history sailed **Hernando De Soto**, a Spanish explorer, the first European to locate and describe the Mississippi River Valley.

De Soto's discovery of the Mississippi River, May 1541. (Courtesy Leonard V. Huber Collection)

CHAPTER II

Discovery and Exploration

The Indians spoke of a great river flowing through the continent and cutting it in two, and the white men jumped to the conclusion that it flowed east to west and could provide a western passage to China.

Hernando De Soto

Hernando De Soto was a young man who fought with the Spanish army during the conquest of Peru and made his fortune there. Because of that service, he was appointed governor of Cuba in 1538. Goaded by a desire to find still more gold, he set out in 1539 with 600 soldiers to explore Florida, which he heard was a "land of gold."

After landing in Tampa Bay in May 1539, De Soto took some of his men and moved north. The party he sent west discovered Pensacola Bay. After crossing mountains and fighting off Indians for two years, he sighted the Mississippi River in May 1541. The exact site of his discovery is in dispute. Some historians place it in Memphis, others in northern Mississippi. He described it as "wide, muddy, and full of logs" (New Orleans Regional Planning Commission 1969). He crossed the river into Arkansas but returned to Mississippi and, in 1542, died of fever. His men weighted down his body and buried it in the river.

Marquette and Joliet

More than a century after De Soto's death, the next chapter in the history of New Orleans unfolded. For 133 years, the lower Mississippi lay neglected by explorers. In 1673, a French-Canadian fur trader, Louis Joliet, and a Jesuit missionary priest, Fr. Jacques Marquette, came down the Mississippi River toward the Gulf of Mexico.

In that year, **Gov. Louis Frontenac** of Canada ordered Marquette and Joliet to take an expedition party in search of a route to the Pacific Ocean. With five other Frenchmen and some guides, they left Lake Michigan paddling canoes up the Fox River to the site of the present city of Portage, Wisconsin. They carried their canoes across the land to the Wisconsin River, which empties into the Mississippi. Going south on the Mississippi, they stopped for a peaceful meeting with the Illinois Indians, who gave them a *calumet*, a peace pipe. From there, they continued south as far as the Arkansas River, where they were surrounded by Indians with guns. It was the calumet that saved their lives.

Some of the Indians were friendly enough to tell them about some other white men, ten days farther south, who had given them the guns. Knowing this had to be a party of Spaniards, Marquette and Joliet decided that it would be dangerous to journey any farther. They ended their trip down the Mississippi and returned to Canada by way of the Illinois River, passing by the site of the present city of Chicago.

René-Robert Cavelier, Sieur de La Salle

The real story of Louisiana begins with its third episode: the expedition of René-Robert Cavelier, Sieur de La Salle down the Mississippi River in the year 1682. La Salle was born of a wealthy family in Rouen, France. He went to Canada in 1666 at the age of thirty-two to become a fur trader. To this end, he bought a piece of land eight miles from Montreal and established a trading post. He did much trading with the Indians, who taught him their language and customs and told him stories about a great river called the Ohio, which flowed south to the sea. La Salle believed this to be the much sought-after route to the Pacific Ocean. So, in 1669, he sold his land and set out to explore the Ohio River.

Five years later, in 1674, La Salle was called to the French court to receive honors on the recommendations of the governor of Canada. He used this opportunity to ask permission of Louis XIV to explore the rich Illinois country and wherever it would lead him. This was a privilege that required royal sanction at the time. The king granted

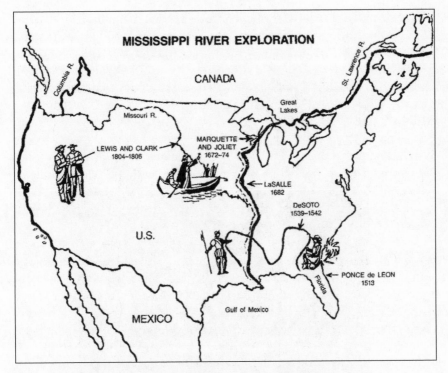

Mississippi River explorations. (Map by Joan B. Garvey)

permission since he believed that colonies in the New World would add immeasurably to the prestige of France as a world power. His treasury, however, was depleted from war with England. La Salle had to pay to have his own ship built.

On February 6, 1682, La Salle led an expedition of fifty-six people down the Mississippi River from the Illinois River to the Gulf of Mexico, where he arrived on April 9, 1682. On this date, he disembarked and erected a cross on the shore and a column inscribed with the name and coat of arms of the king. Then, he claimed all the land drained by the Mississippi River for France and named the region Louisiana, in honor of King Louis XIV.

La Salle then returned to France for supplies and settlers for a colony at the mouth of the river. In his company was an Italian adventurer named **Henri de Tonti** (or Tonty), who shared his dream of an empire stretching from Canada to the Gulf of Mexico. Tonti had long been his trusted companion and was to be the principal historian

LaSalle claims Louisiana for France, 1682. (Courtesy
Leonard V. Huber Collection)

on the expedition. It is not difficult to imagine their excitement as
they considered the possibility of developing a region larger than the
country of France and then controlling trade on the only highway
through this vast continent, since travel at the time was done almost
entirely by water. The court of France, still in financial difficulty,
agreed that the value of such a possession was inestimable.

La Salle left France on July 4, 1684, on his way to the Gulf of
Mexico with four ships, a force of marines, 100 soldiers, and 250
settlers including women and children, all ready to be the first to live
in Louisiana. Stopping in Santo Domingo to rest and refit their ships,
they moved on in November 1684 for the Gulf of Mexico.

Why La Salle didn't return to the Mississippi River by his original route is not recorded. Perhaps he thought the southern route shorter. Perhaps he simply wanted to explore it. Undoubtedly, he was so heady with his earlier success that he expected no problems in finding the river from the south. How could anyone miss a river of such size? But as anyone who has sought entry into the Mississippi from the Gulf knows, there are several mouths of the river and they look little different from the low grassy sandbars surrounding them; and all look exactly like the bayous, which lead inland from the Gulf and then fade away. It certainly doesn't look like the mouth of a great river coming from the Gulf of Mexico. Few maps charted these estuaries, for European explorers and settlers had not yet sailed that way, so the probability of error was great.

In addition, La Salle had never viewed the river from the south, so he had no points of reference. He became confused, lost his bearings, and made a few trial runs into the coast. Finally, the ships landed in **Matagorda Bay** on the Texas coast in February 1685.

The bay was situated at the mouth of a large river emptying into the Gulf of Mexico. La Salle knew by the curve of the coastline that he had missed the mouth of the Mississippi River. **Taneguy Le Gallois de Beaujeu,** his ship's captain, with whom he argued constantly, then left to return to France, leaving La Salle the brig *La Belle*. In this ship, La Salle hoped to continue his search.

La Salle built Fort St. Louis at Matagorda Bay, completing it in 1685. Then, his brig was wrecked in a storm, and he became determined to return to Canada by land to get help for his colony. Although he left Europe with four ships, he now had none. The Spanish captured one ship in the Gulf of Mexico; another had been lost when entering Matagorda Bay. Beaujeu had left with the third; and the last, *La Belle*, had been wrecked in a storm.

Some of the settlers agreed to stay in the fort, but La Salle continued on his incredible journey with his brother, his nephew, and a few companions, including a man named **Joutel,** who survived to relate the story. In 1687, the heroic La Salle was murdered by his own men and buried in alien soil. We can only surmise that the assassins were exhausted and despondent after their unsuccessful adventure. The many months had taken their toll. Both ships and lives had been lost. The men were unsure of their position, without supplies, and fearful for their lives. It is understandable that on a long, difficult journey, violence would erupt. The survivors of the march continued on to Canada, where they told the sad story of "La Salle's Folly." The Indians later destroyed the colony established in Texas.

But another part of the story has not yet been told. Tonti, La Salle's friend, had come down the Mississippi River from the Illinois country, planning to meet La Salle coming northward from the Gulf of Mexico at the camp of the Bayogoulas (between New Orleans and Baton Rouge). Tonti waited as long as possible for La Salle and his party, but when he could not wait any longer, he left a letter with an Indian chieftain. That letter would not be delivered until 1699, and not to La Salle, but to Bienville and Iberville, the next French explorers in our story.

CHAPTER III

The French Period

La Salle was gone, but France's desire for an empire was still strong. For ten years, France was in no position to attempt further colonization. She had been at war with England until 1697 and now looked to the New World for an empire. A favorable time had come for colonization plans to be presented at the court of France, and **Pierre Le Moyne, Sieur d'Iberville,** a young French-Canadian, had his plans ready at the right time.

Iberville's father, Charles Le Moyne, was a successful fur trader with a wealth of eleven sons. Two of his sons, Pierre Le Moyne, Sieur d'Iberville, and **Jean Baptiste Le Moyne, Sieur de Bienville,** could foresee that the fur-trading business would not provide for them all. So, they made other plans for their future. Iberville, the older of the two, had distinguished himself in the war against England. He presented his plans to found a colony near the mouth of the Mississippi River to the king, Louis XIV, who received them favorably. Iberville, however, needed more than just permission. He was not a wealthy man and had to seek a sponsor for this enterprise. He was fortunate to find **Louis de Phélypeaux,** Comte de Pontchartrain and secretary of state of the Maison du Roi, to fund his venture.

Iberville left France in October 1698, with two large frigates and two freight ships, a company of marines, and 200 settlers, including women and children, for his colony. In his company were his brother Bienville and **Fr. Anatase Douay,** a survivor of La Salle's expedition.

Iberville built forts at the mouth of the river to protect the settlement against British encroachments. In Santo Domingo, he was joined by the **Marquis de Chateaumorant,** in command of a war vessel, who presumably was to protect him in this venture. He sailed to Apalachicola Bay, Florida, and then followed the coast in search of the river. On January 29, 1699, he reached Pensacola, Florida, but the Spanish governor did not allow the Frenchmen to enter the harbor. They set sail again, and in February arrived at Mobile Bay, where the Indians told Iberville that the Mississippi was only a short distance to the west. Moving on, Iberville anchored before the Chandeleur Islands. He landed on Ship Island, which his men so named because it had a good harbor. He built some huts there and then went on with his brother to explore what are now Biloxi and Ocean Springs along the coast. From there, he and his men set out in small boats to look for the river.

Iberville found many other islands. One they called **Massacre Island,** because there were so many bones there (later renamed **Dauphin Island**). Another was christened **Horn Island** because a powder horn was left there. They also found **Cat Island,** so called because of the many raccoons, which they mistook for cats; and **Deer Island,** because deer were plentiful there.

On March 2, 1699, Iberville arrived at the mouth of the Mississippi River, where there was fresh water and a strong current. The following day, **Shrove Tuesday,** they began their journey up the river. Finding a bayou twelve miles upstream, they named it **Mardi Gras Bayou** in honor of the holiday, and thus was Mardi Gras introduced to the Louisiana Territory.

Father Douay said mass the following Sunday for Iberville's company at the village of the Bayogoula Indians, who informed them that a letter had been left by Tonti to La Salle in 1686. The letter was found in the possession of the Mongoulacha Indians. In addition to the letter, there was a prayer book, a list of names of La Salle's companions, and a coat of arms from La Salle's expedition. At last, Iberville knew he was on "La Salle's River."

At the bluff above the river, which Iberville considered a good spot for a settlement, he saw a red stick, the maypole used by the Indians for hanging up offerings of fish and game. Iberville called the place Baton Rouge.

The Indians asked him if he would like to return to Ship Island by a different route. Enthusiastically he agreed. However, Iberville had to know that the Indians were aware that he was on a serious mission to establish settlements for white colonists, which was to their detriment. Iberville showed tremendous courage in agreeing to the alternate route since he had no way of knowing if he would make it back to Ship Island alive. But curiosity is the essence of men like Iberville, and eagerly, he went with them.

From Baton Rouge, they took him south on the Mississippi River as far as **Pass Manchac** (which means "back door"), then by way of the bayou to the Amite River, and then through two lakes and a bay before returning him to his fleet at Ship Island. Iberville named the larger one Lake Pontchartrain, for his benefactor; the smaller one Maurepas, for Pontchartrain's son; and the bay St. Louis, for the patron saint of the king.

Sailing on to Biloxi Bay, Iberville established colonies at Ocean Springs and Biloxi in March 1699. Then, having sown the seed of his Louisiana colony, Iberville made a trip back to France, leaving command in the hands of **François-Marie Lemoyne, Sieur de Sauvole**, a brave and capable young French officer.

English Turn

In his brother's absence, Bienville often left the fort at Biloxi to explore the Mississippi. On September 15, 1699, returning from such an exploration with a small band of friends, he was surprised to encounter the English corvette, *Carolina Galley,* towering over him. The ship loaded with settlers and bent on colonization had dropped anchor some twenty-seven leagues (approximately seventy-five miles) from the mouth of the river. The British officer in charge asked Bienville for directions to the Mississippi River. Bienville told the officer that the Mississippi was much farther west, that he was in French territory heavily guarded by forts, and that he was in danger in those waters.

The British vessel weighed anchor and, turning around, sailed to the Gulf. The bluff had worked. To this day, the point in the river where the meeting took place is called English Turn. It is about ten miles below (downriver from) New Orleans. It was an unlucky day for the British that they chanced to meet Bienville in that place. Had they not, it might have been the English who headed up the river and founded a city at the site of New Orleans instead of the French. A century later, not far from English Turn, the Battle of New Orleans was fought, and once again, the British were turned back.

By 1700, Bienville's colonists built **Fort Boulaye** as a protection below English Turn. On Biloxi Bay, they built **Fort Maurepas,** one of the few forts in North America that was stoutly built, according to the European style. It has outlasted all of the others in the area. From 1699 to 1723, the capital of Louisiana remained on the Gulf Coast.

Settlers came from France and Canada, some disembarking at Ship Island, Cat Island, and Dauphin Island, where they were to remain until a more permanent settlement was established. The land was hard on newcomers. Sandy soil made farming difficult, and fresh water was in short supply. An account by Sauvole himself tells of the beauty of the white beaches on the Mississippi Sound, the magnolia and oak trees, and the infertility of the soil, explaining that the colonists relied on provisions sent from France.

It was not as difficult for the Canadian fur traders and trappers, who were used to an outdoor life, but those who came from France were often debtors and vagrants, unaccustomed to the wilderness and to farming. In France, if a citizen was out of work for three days, he was given a free trip to Louisiana. Women of the streets, thieves, smugglers, dealers in contraband, vagabonds, and even prisoners were sent to populate the colony. Some had been imprisoned for little or no reason, but they still preferred Louisiana to the Bastille. Passengers on those first ships to arrive were not as well regarded by their descendants in the way of those who revered their *Mayflower* ancestors.

Advice coming from France was not much help, either, since it was "to search for mines and pearl fisheries, to domesticate the buffalo for their wool, and to raise silkworms." Tormented by mosquitoes, suffering from the heat, and itching from the sandy soil, the settlers profited little from such advice.

Members of the French court didn't like the exotic names of the colonies: Biloxi, Natchez, and Massacre Island. They thought Mobile suggested instability. It is written that Bienville even considered changing the name to Immobile.

Iberville returned to the colony in 1700, accompanied by the Jesuit priest **Fr. Paul du Ru**, who was to found missions among the Indians on the Mississippi River. Iberville ordered a fort built in the Natchez country, which he would call Fort Rosalie (for the beautiful Duchess de Pontchartrain). He gave command of Fort Maurepas and the Ocean Springs settlement to Bienville, who stayed there until the death of Sauvole in 1701, when Bienville became commander of the Louisiana Territory at the age of twenty-two. The seat of government was changed from Biloxi to **Fort Louis de la Mobile,** which was established in 1702.

Iberville, the Father of Louisiana, died of yellow fever in 1706 in Havana, leaving Bienville the acting governor.

Very little help was forthcoming from France, and Bienville was often obliged to scatter his men among the Indians, who took good care of them. Penicaut, Bienville's young friend, who was a carpenter and Indian interpreter, took a few colonists and went to live with the **Acolapissa Indians** on the north shore of Lake Pontchartrain for a year. He leaves a description of dining on buffalo, bear, geese, ducks, fruits of the season, and dishes prepared with corn. At evening parties, his friend played violin and the French danced with each other, while the Indians tried to imitate the minuet. Penicaut dined with the chief on sumptuous meals and repaid the hospitality by giving the chief's daughter French lessons.

In 1705, the first commercial cargo came down the Mississippi, passing the site of the future city of New Orleans. A load of 15,000 bear and deer hides came from the Wabash River in the upper Mississippi through the lake passages: the Amite River; Pass Manchac; Lakes Maurepas, Pontchartrain, and Borgne; the Mississippi Sound; and the settlement at Ocean Springs before moving on to France.

In 1707, word reached France that the limited supplies on Dauphin Island, which had been sent from France to support the garrison, were being sold for six times their worth. **Martin d'Artaguette d'Iron** was sent from France as commissary general of Louisiana to investigate, and Bienville lost his position as commandant and acting governor. His replacement, **Nicholas Daneau,** Sieur de Muy, died en route, however, and Bienville was reinstated, but d'Artaguette stayed on to supervise the affairs of the colony.

In November 1708, the first concessions of land in what was later to be the city of New Orleans were made on the west bank of Bayou St. John. Bienville granted this tract to Louis Juchereau de St. Denis, a friend from Canada and an outstanding figure in Louisiana history. He was one of the first settlers in Louisiana, arriving with Iberville in 1699 at the age of twenty-three. He later founded the city of Natchitoches, the oldest city in Louisiana. The St. Denis Concession is shown on a map drawn by **Allou d'Hemecourt,** which can be found in the Louisiana State Museum Library.

Other concessions along the bayou were granted to **Antoine Rivard de La Vigne,** two and a half arpents; Nicholas "Alias Delon," two and a half arpents; and Baptiste Portier, three arpents; three others were granted the same day but were not recorded. "These concessions had narrow water frontages two and a half to three arpents each. They were long, narrow ribbons of land extending from Bayou St. John to Bayou Gentilly, granted by the French Colonial Government at Mobile" (Frieberg 1980).

The village of Bayou St. Jean, as the French called it, and the suburb of Gentilly, which was built up on the natural levees of the Metairie-Gentilly distributary, were the earliest habitations and plantations in the region. Bayou St. John, in its present form, came into being four hundred to six hundred years ago, when all flow activity in the Metairie and Gentilly distributaries ceased.

By the year 1712, the Louisiana colony as a whole had not prospered. The sites were not self-supporting and war between France and Spain made it difficult for France to maintain a colony so far away, scattered over such an immense territory and protected by five forts. Therefore, Louis XIV, in 1712, transferred control of Louisiana to a wealthy banker named Antoine Crozat for a period of fifteen years.

In 1713, Crozat replaced Bienville with **Antoine de La Mothe, Sieur de Cadillac,** the founder of Detroit, who was to be the governor of Louisiana. In his new position, Cadillac failed miserably. He lacked tact in dealing with the Indians, and the first Natchez War broke out in 1716.

The Natchez were a brilliant tribe of Indians. They worshipped the sun and kept a fire burning perpetually in their temple. The story of Noah's Ark was part of their culture. In 1716, they rose against the French, and Bienville was sent to fight them. With only a few men in his detachment, he put two of them to death and made terms with the others. In the same year, Bienville built Fort Rosalie on the site that had been selected by his brother years before.

In 1717, just five years after Crozat was granted his charter, he gave it up. Trade with the Spanish in Mexico had not materialized and trade with the Indians was not profitable. He declared that he spent four times his original investment and saw no profit.

Louisiana, then a colony of 700 people, transferred from Crozat to the Company of the West (called the Company of the Indies after 1719). The Company was to have authority in the colony for twenty-five years, enjoy a monopoly of trade, and name the governor and other officers and would, in turn, be obliged to send to Louisiana 6,000 white colonists and 3,000 blacks within ten years. The president of the

Company was the infamous John Law, private advisor to Philippe, the Duc d'Orléans.

John Law, Impresario of High Pressure

John Law was a Scotsman, a professional gambler, and a financial genius. He escaped Great Britain fifteen years earlier after killing a man in a duel and spent the intervening years traveling all over Europe, trying to develop his great plan.

Law was a well-known manipulator. It is therefore easy to understand that he sought and secured the good will and confidence of **Philippe of Orléans,** regent of France, after the death of Louis XIV. Like Law, Philippe was a gambler and womanizer, and the friendship of the two rogues was inevitable. In time, Law became the advisor to the regent and, with his aid and encouragement, started his campaign to populate the Louisiana colony in record time and make himself a fortune in the bargain.

His fraudulent scheme called for combining of the Bank of France and the Company of the West, an arrangement that he successfully managed. The Mississippi Bubble, a name later given to his plan, still incites the envy of high-pressure salesmen everywhere. The plan was to induce noblemen and rich businessmen to buy shares of stock in Louisiana land and purchase land for them and to entice (or force) the poor of Europe to become *engagés,* hired field hands, for the Company or the concessionaires. Shareholders would prosper, Law promised, when the gold, silver, diamonds, and pearls were found in the New World. With nothing but gaudy promises to back his "shares," Law found himself inundated by the demands of speculators. He could not print the shares fast enough.

In 1716, Law signed a contract with the government of France (with the blessing of Philippe), allowing him to establish a private bank, which would provide him with all the credit he needed. Then, in 1717, he replaced the governor at the age of thirty-seven.

A brilliant, ruthless sales campaign followed, unprecedented in Europe. Posters and handbills flooded France, Germany, and Switzerland, offering free land, provisions, and transportation to those who would volunteer to immigrate to the New World. They were told that the soil of Louisiana bore two crops a year without cultivation and that the Indians so adored the white man, they would not let him labor, but took the burden from him. In addition, immigrants were promised the imaginary goldmines and pearl fisheries, as well as a delightful climate where there was no disease or old age.

Many paupers who strayed into Paris or prisoners who would not volunteer were kidnapped and shipped under guard to fill the emptiness of Louisiana. Prostitutes and the inmates of jails and hospitals were all sent to populate the colony and to start the flow of wealth to the stockholders.

Alexander Franz, in his 1906 *Die Kolonisation des Mississippitales Bis Zum Ausgange Der Französischen Herrschaft: Eine Kolonialhistorische Studie* wrote:

> The company even kept a whole regiment of archers which cleaned Paris of its rabble and adventurers, and received for this a fixed salary and 100 livres a head. . . . Five thousand people are said to have disappeared from Paris in April, 1721, alone.
>
> Prisoners were set free in Paris in September, 1721 . . . under the condition that they would marry the prostitutes and go with them to Louisiana. The newly married couples were chained together and thus dragged to the port of embarkation.

Meanwhile, Bienville set his men to work clearing forests and erecting sheds and barracks at the site of the Indian portage, the site he selected for the settlement on his first visit to Louisiana with Iberville in 1699. The portage was roughly where Esplanade Avenue is today. It is a trail from the river to Bayou St. John (Bienville named the bayou in honor of his patron saint). The trail led through cypress swamps teeming with snakes and alligators near a fortified Indian village called Tchoutchouma. The spot where the river comes closest to the lake, this *"beautiful crescent"* in the river, would be the site of his new trading post.

He wanted the spot for two reasons. First, it was the halfway point by water between Natchez (Fort Rosalie) and Mobile (Fort Louis de la Mobile). Second, it was a spot "safe from hurricanes and tidal waves," according to an early account of the city.

Bienville had to argue for the site with **Pierre Le Blond de La Tour,** the royal engineer; with **Adrien de Pauger,** assistant engineer; and with John Law, president of the Company. They all thought it was absurd to select a site in the middle of a swamp, but Bienville persevered, and the *"beautiful crescent"* became the city of La Nouvelle Orléans.

In June 1718, Bienville wrote in his diary:

> We are working at Nouvelle Orleans with as much zeal as the shortage of men will permit. I myself conveyed over the spot to select the place where it will be the best to locate the settlement. . . . I am grieved to see so few people engaged in a task which requires at least a hundred times the number. All the ground of the site, except the borders, which are drowned by floods, are very good and everything will grow there. (Kendall 1922)

John Law ordered a garrison, a director's building, and lodging for the director's staff to be built to establish the beginnings of trade.

Some inhabitants of the city in 1718 were Bienville, his Intendant (the head of civil affairs), surveyors (the Lassus brothers from Mobile), carpenters, troops, and a few concessionaires. There was La Tour, the royal engineer; Pauger, second engineer; Ignace Broutin, who built the Ursuline Convent; doctors; priests; and soldiers. French soldiers usually had a secondary trade. Some were wigmakers, rope makers, weavers, gardeners, shoemakers, laborers, brewers, locksmiths, bakers, papermakers, or cabinetmakers.

In June 1718, the first wave of European immigrants began to arrive in response to John Law's campaign at the same time that Bienville was supervising the work in New Orleans. Three hundred settlers came in three ships, accompanied by 500 soldiers and convicts, joining a colony where only 700 already lived, thus doubling in one day the population of New Orleans (Deiler 1909).

They were held, for lack of a better place, on Dauphin Island. They were crowded, unsheltered, hungry, and wretched. Many starved and died, but there was no place else to go until Governor Bienville came for them with his few boats and his few men to move them around the countryside. Some he sent to Natchez, some to the valley of the Yazoo River, and some to New Orleans, where they were crowded into tents and rough sheds.

John Law's career ended with his flight from Paris, bankrupt and a fugitive, on December 10, 1720. He fled to the Belgian frontier in a coach lent to him by Madame Brié with escorts provided to him by the Duc d'Orléans.

The German Law People

During the years of the John Law promotion, 10,000 Germans left their homelands to come to Louisiana. Fr. **Pierre-François Xavier de Charlevoix,** the Jesuit priest who came from Canada to Louisiana in 1721, wrote about passing by the "mournful wretches" who settled on John Law's grant on the Arkansas River. These Germans were originally from the Rhine region, which had been devastated in the Thirty Years' War between France and Germany (1618-48). After the war, Louis XIV seized Alsace and Lorraine. Both Germans and French in the area suffered the consequences of war: pestilence, famine, and religious persecution. There is little wonder that the glorious picture painted of the New World enticed them to immigrate.

Only a small percentage of the German Law people ever reached Louisiana. Of the 10,000 immigrants, only 6,000 actually left Europe. They lay crowded in French ports for months, awaiting the departure of vessels. They starved, fell ill with disease, and died in the ports. Many survivors died on the "pest ships" from lack of food and water or diseases contracted when the ships stopped in Santo Domingo. Only 2,000 reached the New World. They disembarked in Biloxi and on Dauphin Island and still more perished.

One significant group of Germans was led by **Karl Freidrich d'Arensbourg.** They arrived in Biloxi in June 1721, where they met the survivors of some of the "pest ships." D'Arensbourg organized the survivors, and they settled on the banks of the Mississippi, about twenty-five miles upriver of New Orleans.

Meanwhile, an earlier group of Germans who settled on the Arkansas River in 1720 had been too ill and too busy providing shelter to produce a crop by 1721. No financial help came from bankrupt John Law. So, in January 1722, they abandoned their concession and descended upon New Orleans, where they demanded passage back to Europe. Bienville tried to induce them to remain. They were given rich lands near the **"d'Arensbourg Germans"** in the area that is today called the German Coast (the parishes of St. Charles and St. John the Baptist).

Hanno Deiler tells us that these "Arkansas Germans," on their descent to New Orleans, must have met their fellow countrymen, the d'Arensbourg Germans, who had just settled there. This was undoubtedly a determining factor in their decision to accept Bienville's

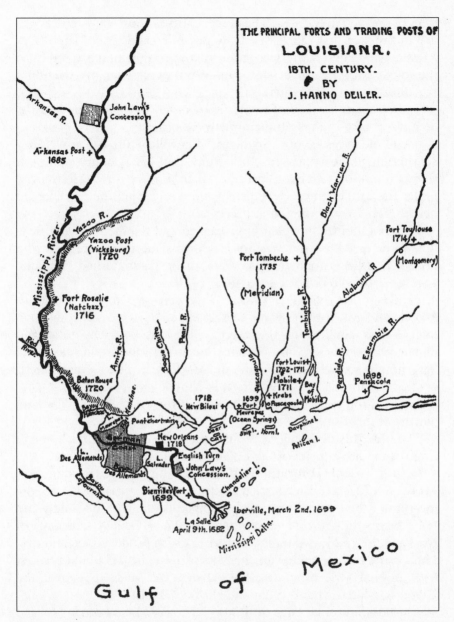

Map from The Settlement of the German Coast by Louisiana and the Creoles of German Descent, *by J. Hanno Deiler, 1909.*

offer of the land in the area. The descendants of those early settlers still live in the area first called "La Côte des Allemands," and later "Des Allemands." These early German settlers brought much stability to the colony with their successful farming and were better able to endure the climate than the French.

There was a shortage of unmarried women in the colony and the men were forced to take Indian squaws as brides.

"Send me wives for my Canadians," Bienville wrote to Paris. "They are running in the woods after Indian girls." In 1721, eighty-eight girls from a house of correction in Paris, *La Salpêtrière*, arrived in the city under the care of three Gray Sisters and a mid-wife; they nicknamed her *La Sans Regret* (the No Regret).

Within a month, nineteen girls married and ten died, leaving fifty-nine to be cared for, this was not an easy task, as they were girls who "could not be restrained." They are to be distinguished from the Casket Girls, who did not arrive until 1728.

Les filles à la cassette or Casket Girls were said to have come to Mobile and Biloxi to be wives to the settlers. They were from good middle-class families, and they were skilled in housewifely duties and excellent of character. The Ursuline nuns claim there is no historical basis for the story that they came to New Orleans. However, there is evidence of the Casket Girls' arrival in Mobile (Kazek 2015).

Some of the concessionaires that came to work their own land are worthy of mention.

The **Marquis de Mezières** from Amiens, France, built his home in 1720 at the present site of the Le Petit Salon on St. Peter Street.

Claude-Joseph Dubreuil de Villars and his family arrived in New Biloxi in 1721. He later settled in the Tchoupitoulas area, near the location of the original Ochsner Hospital. There, with his family and ten servants, he grew rice and indigo. By 1724, he had an avenue of trees and, by 1725, two indigo factories, which produced ink and dye. He became the contractor for the Mississippi Valley. He built the first levee in New Orleans and a canal between the Mississippi River and Bayou Barataria (what is today the Harvey Canal).

Antoine-Simon Le Page du Pratz (1695-1775) was born in Holland and came to Dauphin Island in 1718, after having served with the French army in Germany. In his three-volume work, *Histoire de la Louisiane*, he tells of settling a plantation on Bayou St. John, then moving on to the Natchez country, where he spent eight years. He wrote of their lives and customs, leaving the most accurate account we have of these original inhabitants of Louisiana. After sixteen years in America, during which time he served as manager of the Company of the Indies and manager of the King's Farm, which dealt in slave trade at Algiers Point, he returned to France, where his books were published in 1758. They were, and still are, a treasure trove of early Louisiana history.

Antoine Philippe de Marigny de Mandeville (1722-79), Chevalier de St. Louis, born at Fort Louis de la Mobile, was the stepson of Ignace Broutin, the royal engineer. He built a beautiful summer home in 1788 in Mandeville, a town north of Lake Pontchartrain, which bears his name. His grandson was Bernard de Marigny, a colorful Creole of New Orleans (King 1921).

Other names of early settlers were **Villère, de La Ronde,** and **Delery.**

It is interesting to note that most settlers were less than five feet three inches tall. The average height was five feet. The average age was twenty-one years old. There were few people over fifty, and few in their teens.

Before the hurricane of 1721, the city is described by Fr. Pierre de Charlevoix in one of the first hundred letters written from New Orleans. He wrote that there were a "hundred barracks," placed in no particular order, a wooden storehouse, and two or three houses "which would be no ornament to a village of France . . . " (Frasier 2003). He also wrote that he felt the city would be the "future capital of a fine and vast country" (Rightor 1900).

The city of which he spoke consisted of 470 people living on three streets, which had been laid out by Pauger. The hurricane of 1721 devastated the town and destroyed all the buildings.

In April 1722, the first complete plan for the city of New Orleans was signed by Pierre Le Blond de La Tour, who dispatched Adrien de Pauger to supervise the construction of the city. The area on which La Tour planned to build was scattered with wooden houses built by immigrants from Illinois. Pauger cleared a strip of land on the river wide enough and deep enough to put the plan into execution. The hurricane of 1721 had taken care of most of the original buildings, which were not in keeping with the engineer's plans, and would have had to be removed in any case.

Then with the help of some *piquers,* he traced on the ground the streets and quarters which were to form the new town, and notified all who wished building sites to present their petitions to the Council. To each settler who appeared, they gave a plot of 10 fathoms front by 20 deep, and as each square was 50 fathoms front, it gave 12 plots in each, the two middle ones being 10 front by 25 deep. It was ordained that those who obtained these plots would be bound to enclose them with palisades, and leave all around a strip of at least three feet wide, at the foot of which a ditch was to be dug, to serve as a drain for the river water in time of inundation. (French 1853)

The streets were laid out in a grid pattern, and they were straight, not conforming to the curve of the river. The exact site of the Vieux Carré today is the place Bienville chose in 1718, and the spot where the St. Louis Cathedral is today was the location of the St. Louis Parish Church. The wooden church was blown down in 1723, but in 1724, construction of a brick church began on the same spot.

From left to right, vertically, the city's streets were Canal, Iberville, Bienville, Conti, St. Louis, Toulouse, St. Peter, Orleans, St. Ann, du Maine, Clermont (changed to St. Philip), Rue Arsenal (changed to Ursulines), Hospital (changed to Governor Nicholls), Barracks, and Esplanade. The original city ended at Iberville Street. (Our present **Vieux Carré Commission** has no jurisdiction past Iberville.) The

The first parish church of St. Louis, designed by Pauger, dedicated on Christmas Eve, 1717, on the site of the present St. Louis Cathedral. Drawings reconstituted from plans in French National Archives. (Courtesy Leonard V. Huber Collection)

streets Conti, Toulouse, and du Maine (Dumaine) are the names of King Louis XIV's illegitimate sons.

Horizontally from top to bottom, the streets were Rampart, Bourgogne (changed to Burgundy), Vendome (changed to Dauphine), Bourbon (family of the king), Royal, Condé (an extension of Chartres, later changed to Chartres), and Rue de la Levée (changed to Decatur).

Map of the Vieux Carré

The **Place d'Armes** fronts the church, jail, and priest's house (now the Cathedral, flanked by the **Cabildo** and the **Presbytère**). Barracks were on either side of the square, moved by a later governor to a location beyond the Ursuline Convent on Barracks Street.

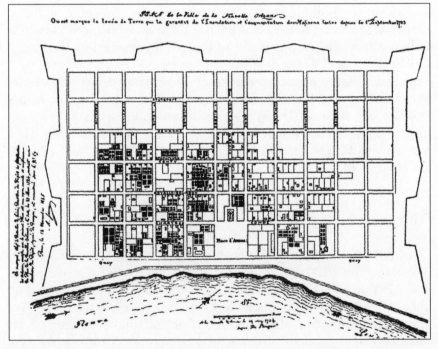

Map by Adrien de Pauger, May 26, 1724. Pauger laid out the original city in 1721. This shows the additional houses constructed after the overflow of September 1, 1723, the shaded houses being the first erected.

New Orleans was a city bounded on three sides by swamps and on the fourth by the river. A levee was built on the river side, and drainage ditches were dug to allow the water from the river to drain around the city to "Back of Town."

A description of eighteenth-century New Orleans, from *History of Regional Growth:*

> At high tide, the river flows through the streets. The subsoil is swampy. New Orleans becomes famous for its tombs. Buried coffins must have holes so that they do not float to the surface when the land is flooded. Dikes have to be built along the river. . . .
>
> Those living in the city dedicated to the Duke of Orleans feel as if they were living on an island in the middle of a mud puddle." (New Orleans Regional Planning Commission 1969)

Alongside the river were high banks covered with great cypress forests, occasionally broken by the home of a concessionaire or an Indian village. Buildings were constructed of thick wood with sloped roofs like Norman houses in Canada. Galleries were later added for cool comfort and the protection of the exterior against decay.

The French in Louisiana, gregarious by nature and possessing a remarkable ability to adapt, settled in groups instead of seeking solitude, as much for social ability as for safety. They were predominantly traders, not farmers. Unlike the American frontiersmen, they built large, comfortable, substantial houses of hewn timber or brick. They were survivors, and they were here to stay. Their attitude is reflected in the types of homes they built.

The Code Noir of 1724

In 1719, the Company of the West brought an influx of slaves into Louisiana. By 1724, there were so many slaves and free people of color in the colony that the French government enacted a set of laws called the Code Noir, or Black Code, whose purpose it was to protect the slaves and the free blacks and to define and limit their activities. It governed the treatment of slaves by their masters. Slave owners were ordered to have their slaves baptized Catholic. They were not to work their slaves on Sundays or holidays, except for marketing.

The Code was not as cruel as it is often made to appear. It provided more lenient treatment of slaves than could be found almost anywhere else in the South. It was the basis of Louisiana slave laws until the late 1820s, when the state adopted parts of the much more severe slave codes of the southeastern states (Taylor 1984).

New Orleans, the Capital of Louisiana

Bienville tried as early as 1719 to have the Louisiana seat of government moved to New Orleans, but the Superior Council argued that it should be transferred from Mobile back to Biloxi. The Council won. Biloxi, however, had just burned down and was abandoned. In 1722, three commissioners arrived in the colony, charged with the administration of the Company's affairs after John Law's failure. In 1723, the commissioners allowed Bienville to make New Orleans the capital of Louisiana.

The Ursuline Nuns Arrive

Bienville laid the groundwork for the Ursuline nuns to come to the Louisiana Territory, although he was "between terms" and not in the colony when they finally arrived. A school for boys was started by a Capuchin monk, Father Cecil, on St. Ann Street across from the Presbytère (where the Place d'Armes Hotel stands today). Bienville tried to get the **Soeurs Grises** (Gray Sisters) from his native Canada to come to New Orleans to teach the girls, but he failed. He consulted **Fr. Nicholas Ignace de Beaubois,** Superior of the Jesuits in Louisiana at the time, who advised him to try to procure the services of the Ursuline nuns. Bienville did so, and twelve nuns arrived on August 7, 1727. Their Superior was **Mother Marie Tranchepain,** and among them was the talented **Marie-Madeleine Hachard,** to whom we owe a charming description of the journey and the city in 1727. Their first convent was built in 1734.

In February 1724, Bienville was ordered to return to France to render an account of his conduct. Disagreements between Bienville and his Superior Council had always existed, and the officers were successful in having him recalled. During his second administration, he took Pensacola in 1719 (though it was returned to Spain in 1723),

The Old Ursuline Convent (Photo by Kathy Chappetta Spiess)

undertook a war against the Natchez and defeated them, and began negotiations for the coming of the Ursuline nuns. Nevertheless, he was replaced by **Gov. Etienne de Périer,** who arrived in 1725.

The Natchez Massacre

During de Périer's administration, a great war with the Indians took place. In 1729, the Natchez were ordered by the commandant of Fort Rosalie, a vile little man named the **Sieur Etienne de Chépart,** to abandon one of their finest villages, the White Apple, in order that he might establish a plantation there. The Natchez Indians decided that they would never have peace until they destroyed the French at Fort Rosalie. On November 28, 1729, they surprised the fort, killing 200 men and taking women, children, and slaves as prisoners.

The Choctaw allied themselves with the French, killing many of the Natchez and recovering some of the prisoners. Then the Choctaw dispersed.

The Natchez entrenched themselves and resisted for some time. Finally, they escaped to a mound in the Black River, leaving their prisoners behind. On November 15, 1730, de Périer left with 650 soldiers and 350 Indian warriors for the Black River. He brought back 427 prisoners, whom he sent to Santo Domingo and sold as slaves. The rest of the tribe was adopted by the Chickasaw, and the Natchez name was lost forever.

When the children orphaned in the Indian War arrived in New Orleans, the Ursuline nuns began their orphanage. They put bars on the windows of their convent (which remain today) in fear of a similar Indian attack in New Orleans.

The war with the Indians was very costly and in 1731, the Company of the Indies gave Louisiana back to France. In April 1732, Louisiana once again became a royal province. The population by this time numbered 5,000 whites and 2,000 blacks in the entire territory. France removed the duty on goods coming from France to Louisiana in order to stimulate trade.

In 1732, Bienville returned for his third term as governor. This administration was a disaster because of war with the Indians. Bienville was forced to make war on the Chickasaw, and hostilities did not end until April 1740. In 1743, Bienville asked to be relieved of his command and returned to France. He was sixty-two years old and had spent approximately forty-four years in Louisiana.

Pierre de Rigaud, Marquis de Vaudreuil-Cavagnal

Bienville's successor was Pierre de Rigaud, Marquis de Vaudreuil-Cavagnal, called the Grand Marquis. While it is true that he brought culture, elegant manners, and elaborate entertainment to the colony, such pleasures were available only to the wealthy. His administration was filled with nepotism, misuse of army provisions for personal profit, trade monopolies, and general negligence of duty. His wife, the Marquise de Vaudreuil, looked quite elegant driving her "imported from Paris" four-horse carriage around New Orleans, but once inside the governor's palace, she engaged in selling drugs, and the governor shared the profits.

A good picture of the times is painted in the report of the ceremony honoring Vaudreuil's appointment as governor of Canada. **Louis Billouart, Chevalier de Kerlérec,** was host at a dinner for 200 guests followed by a remarkable show of fireworks. To ignite the display, two doves were released by Madame Kerlérec and Marquise de Vaudreuil.

The doves carried lit tapers in their beaks to set the extravaganza ablaze.

Therefore, a more accurate account of Vaudreuil's term would be ten years of political corruption and Indian wars. He kept up the enmity between the Chickasaw and the Choctaw, and civil war broke out among the former. Receiving reinforcements from France, Vaudreuil undertook an expedition against the Chickasaw in 1752, which accomplished little except for the devastation of their country.

Vaudreuil was, however, the first governor to establish a real levee system in New Orleans, which offered some relief and protection from floods. He also suggested *colombage* as a method of construction. This method employed a heavy framework of squared timber filled in with either brick, *briquette entre poteaux,* or a mud-and-moss mixture, *bousillage.* You can still see evidence of *bousillage* construction in some French Quarter buildings. He suggested that buildings be placed three feet off the ground, and that they be built no higher than two stories and constructed with galleries.

At the time of Vaudreuil's administration, the Jesuits settled on the plantation Bienville abandoned when he returned to France. It ran from Canal Street to Felicity Street and included the site of the present Jesuit Church (Immaculate Conception) on Baronne Street. It was in that area in 1751 that they planted sugarcane sent to them by the Jesuits in Cuba.

In 1753, Vaudreuil left to become the governor of Canada. He was replaced as governor of Louisiana by Chevalier de Kerlérec. Kerlérec was nicknamed Chef Menteur (Chief Liar) by the Indians. This was the name originally given to the stream that meandered beside the present-day highway of the same name through the Rigolets to the lake and on to the Gulf. It was the "Chief Liar" among streams because its current flowed deceptively in either direction with the tide. The Indians seemed to understand Kerlérec very well.

Governor Kerlérec had violent disputes with his commissioner, Vincent de Rochemore, who accused him of being a dictator and of robbing the treasury. Kerlérec, in turn, accused Rochemore of theft and neglect of his duties. These conflicts, together with a *laissez-faire* attitude toward the colony, made economic progress impossible. The unsuccessful wars of Louis XV limited the help that could be given to Louisiana, and the poor financial policy of the colony caused instability in the currency. In 1761, Kerlérec was recalled to France and thrown into the Bastille, but his friends managed to secure his release.

The French and Indian Wars had been going on in North America since 1689. The last of these wars involved a conflict between French and British possessions in the New World. In this war, Col. George Washington fought against the French in the Ohio Valley. Louisiana was almost a forgotten territory. No new colonists came and few ships or supplies arrived.

The Acadians

For half a century, French Acadians lived side by side with the British in Acadia (now called Nova Scotia). At the end of **Queen Anne's War** in 1713, Acadia was formally ceded to the British. Now, the British feared that if Acadia were invaded, the French Acadians would fight against them. Therefore, the governor demanded that the French Acadians swear allegiance to the British crown and give up their Catholic religion. They refused and were exiled. Many of the Acadians were excellent farmers and they found new homes in Louisiana during the period of Spanish domination.

After France lost most of her northern holdings to Britain in Queen Anne's War, the Louisiana colonists feared that there would soon be a change of domination for them as well. When the French and Indian War began later, the king of France, Louis XV, preempted a British takeover of Louisiana by giving it to his cousin, King Charles III of Spain, in the Treaty of Fontainebleau.

Treaty of Fontainebleau

This was the second time that Louis XV tried to give Louisiana to Spain. In 1761, he offered it to Spain in exchange for a loan and on the condition that Spain enter the war against England. Spain refused. In 1762, England declared war on Spain and was targeting Spain's colonies. France wanted peace with England, but this was impossible as long as England and Spain were at war. Once again, Louis XV offered Louisiana to his cousin Charles III, but this time not on the grounds of *entering* the war but *ending* it. When England took Havana and invaded Florida, Charles accepted the offer. The act of ceding

Louisiana to Spain was finalized in the secret Treaty of Fontainebleau, November 13, 1762.

Louis XV truly believed that he was giving Spain something of little value. France had owned Louisiana since 1699 and received no profit from it. In fact, France spent huge sums of money on the territory. The king considered this loss one that would bring him little sorrow.

On February 10, 1763, the **Treaty of Paris** was signed, ending the French and Indian War. In this treaty, Louis XV ceded to England all of Canada, except for two small islands, and everything east of the Mississippi (except the Isle of Orleans, which had already secretly been given to Spain). Britain returned Cuba to Spain in exchange for Florida and eastern Louisiana. (After 1763, the British settled in Florida and the portion of Louisiana east of the Mississippi. This included the territory from Baton Rouge eastward through the Florida Parishes to the Perdido River north of Lake Pontchartrain. Great Britain divided these colonies into East and West Florida.)

The fact that New Orleans had been ceded to Spain remained unknown to the people of New Orleans for almost two years. In truth, they were not too interested. During Kerlérec's loose administration, they did pretty much what they wanted. They traded with the Americans, English, and Spanish, whoever suited their purposes. They weren't interested in being governed by anyone. France was negligent in its control of the colony and, while the people of New Orleans had no great desire for independence, they did have a great desire for noninterference.

As we leave this period of French colonialism, we find Louisiana an area with great style and little substance, relatively speaking, still in need of farmers for food supplies and products for export. The people still depended on trade for most of their other needs. The colonists of New Orleans were traders, not farmers. They preferred bargaining for their food to growing it.

The historian Joe Gray Taylor titled this period "a study in failure" (Taylor 1976). This seems a trifle harsh. John Law, on the other hand, touted Louisiana as "a little Paris." A Paris it was not, but it was not too different from other infant colonies. One remarkable characteristic of the French in Louisiana was the staying power of their language, their customs, and their culture. Their influence on New Orleans remains strong even though many other ethnic groups have settled there in large numbers since.

The feeling, the flair, and the style of the city always were and still are French. The love of balls, celebrations, and holidays is a large part of its lifestyle. It was this lack of restraint that shocked the Spanish and surprised Americans coming into the city in the years to follow. The loose keeping of the Sabbath and the easy interpretation of religion that the French Catholics allowed amazed these newcomers, who jokingly remarked that it was caused by the humidity.

The colony had not been fortunate in its governing officers, however. Taylor tells us, "Probably the origin of chronic corruption in Louisiana government can be traced back to the French attitude that political office was a form of property from which the holder should profit."

All of these harsh words were directed against French colonialism because the French royalty approached Louisiana as a moneymaker. It was never that, and so, in one way, it must be admitted that it was a failure. But a city was established, trade began, and New Orleans was a living, breathing, seductive lady, to whom much had happened. Now, the lady was to become Spanish, or so the treaty said.

CHAPTER IV
The Spanish Period

Although the city remained tenaciously French throughout the period of Spanish domination, Spain's influence in New Orleans is still felt today. Spanish colonial Louisiana became part of the existing Spanish colonial administrative structure, in which the governor of New Orleans reported to the governor general in Havana, Cuba, who in turn reported to the viceroy of New Spain in Mexico.

New Orleans was strategically positioned within the transportation and communications systems of the Gulf of Mexico's half-moon that linked Cuba, Puerto Rico, Santo Domingo, and Mexico's Gulf Coast and Yucatan with the rest of Central America. During the antebellum period and after, the port of New Orleans was a nexus of trade in goods and slaves, smuggling and piracy, capital ventures, immigration and emigration, troop movements, filibustering adventurers, and travel between the eastern United States and southern tips of North America.

The first Spanish-language newspaper in the United States, *El Misisipi*, was founded in New Orleans in 1808. Prior to the Civil War, at least twenty-three periodicals in Spanish were published in the city. New York, the nearest contender of Spanish-speaking populations, had only thirteen newspapers. The major French-language newspapers, *L'Abeille* and *L'Avenir du peuple*, both printed Spanish-language sections throughout the 1830s.

Nineteenth-century expatriates and émigrés from around the Caribbean and Spanish America found New Orleans the least alienating city in the nation—besides the substantial population of Spanish speakers, most of their educated classes knew French and could get by without speaking a word of English. New Orleans's dominance of the banana industry brought in massive waves of Hondurans in the 1940s, followed by Cubans in the 1960s and other groups up through the present (Gruesz 2002).

When the French colonials came to Louisiana, men brought their wives and families, and so their heritage remained intact. The Spanish settlers arrived in smaller numbers. Men often came alone and married Creole girls native to Louisiana. The language spoken in most of their homes was, therefore, French, as were the customs and traditions. The Spanish were assimilated into the already-established French way of life and made little change in the people they controlled. They were, perhaps, more sober in their Catholicism than the pleasure-loving French Creoles, but in time, the French even managed to convert the Spanish to a more lethargic religious life.

The word "Creole" derives from the Spanish *criollo,* "a child born in the colonies," according to John Churchill Chase in *Frenchmen, Desire, Good Children* (Chase 1960). Therefore, native-born Orleanians of Spanish and French descent were designated Creoles, even if their parents were strictly European.

Only one group of Spanish settlers arrived en masse to stay. They were the **Canary Islanders** or **Isleños,** who settled in **St. Bernard Parish** in 1778. Colonists migrated to Louisiana from Spanish Florida and settled in the parish called New Iberia (New Spain).

The indelible impression left by the Spanish from their forty-year rule (1762-1800) is the Spanish style of architecture with which the Vieux Carré is stamped. Even this was the outcome of accident, not purposeful design, as we shall see.

As to the beginning of Spanish rule, it is well to say that at the outset, the change in administration was not made without a struggle. The transfer of Louisiana from France to Spain was legalized in the Treaty of Fontainebleau on November 23, 1762, but the treaty was kept secret to all but the Spanish. The king of France continued to act as sovereign over Louisiana.

In 1763, because of problems with the hierarchy of the Church, the **Jesuits** were expelled from the province of Louisiana and the entire French Empire. The Jesuit Order was disbanded throughout the world. The property of the Jesuits in New Orleans was confiscated, including land that had once been part of Bienville's plantation. Pope Pius VII reinstated the Jesuits in 1801, and in 1837, they began the first Catholic college for boys, **St. Charles College** in Grand Coteau, Louisiana. By 1847, they established the second college in New Orleans, the College of the Immaculate Conception. The confiscation of their property in 1763 was questioned by former Jesuit student

Thomas J. Semmes, because the French ordered the confiscation when, by treaty, Louisiana had already been ceded to Spain. Semmes was right, but the Jesuits wisely dropped the suit since it would have involved most of downtown New Orleans.

On April 21, 1764, Louis XV sent a letter to **Jean-Jacques Blaise d'Abbadie,** governor of Louisiana, informing him and the colonists of the formal transfer of Louisiana to Spain. Both governments seem to have been responsible for the delay in transferring the colony. The Spaniards felt that they needed a larger contingent of troops to take possession of Louisiana. The French Minister of State, the **Duke of Choiseul**, suggested that the French soldiers in Louisiana enlist in the Spanish army. Spain agreed, and the obstacle seemed to be overcome.

When the colonists heard, in October 1764, of the concession to Spain, they were despondent. They had had a great affection for France in spite of the infamous Louis XV. But more than that, they had enjoyed the *laissez-faire* type of government and the freedom of trade they had been allowed. Many colonists left West Florida when it was ceded to England in 1763 and came to New Orleans hoping to remain Frenchmen. A meeting of the Superior Council was held for prominent colonists to discuss the event. At the meeting, the attorney-general, **Nicolas Chauvin de Lafrenière,** suggested that a representative be sent to Louis XV to ask him to revoke the act of concession. Jean Milhet, a wealthy merchant, was sent on this mission.

In Paris, Milhet visited Bienville, then eighty-four years old. Together, they called on the Duke of Choiseul, who refused to let them see the king and expressed his sympathy. He told them that the concession was a *fait accompli*. Milhet did not to return to New Orleans until 1767 to report the news. For a while, the citizens of New Orleans began to hope that the Spanish king would not take possession of the colony. He had not appeared anxious to do so. More than three years had passed since the Treaty of Fontainebleau, and no Spanish official had yet appeared on the scene.

Don Antonio de Ulloa

On July 10, 1765, however, Don Antonio de Ulloa wrote to the Superior Council of New Orleans from Havana to inform them that he had been appointed governor of Louisiana by Charles III of Spain.

He arrived in New Orleans on March 5, 1766. He was greeted by the French Commandant and the acting governor, **Charles Philippe Aubry,** who succeeded d'Abbadie upon his death in February 1765.

Ulloa did not assume authority in a public way. He had with him only two companies of infantry (a total of ninety men), since he had anticipated many enlistments among the French soldiers in Louisiana, but the French troops were unwilling to enlist in the Spanish army.

This remained one of the problems that plagued Ulloa throughout his stay in the colony. Another important obstacle to good relations with the colonists was the decision of the Spanish court to enforce typical Spanish mercantile restrictions on trade in Louisiana. Two such decrees (in 1766 and 1768) prohibited trade with any country except Spain and its colonies. The colonists had been free of such restrictions and were unwilling to submit to these hardships. A third conflict arose when Ulloa offered to exchange French currency for Spanish at 75 percent of its value, a ratio established by Louis XV. The colonists were furious but powerless.

Ulloa never had sufficient funds to operate the government of the colony. The allotment was set at 150,000 pesos annually for Louisiana from the treasury of New Spain. Repeatedly, Ulloa wrote letters, pleading for additional funds, as he was unable to pay salaries of those employed by the Spanish government, but funds were not forthcoming.

Trouble between Ulloa and the Superior Council arose almost as soon as he arrived in Louisiana. Acting on Aubry's advice, Ulloa refused to present his credentials to the Superior Council, even when they demanded to see them. The document of transfer, turning over the government of the colony to Ulloa, was signed by Governor Aubry only, and not in the capital city of New Orleans, but at the fort of La Balize at the mouth of the river. No member of the Superior Council was present.

All this was done in La Balize, because Aubry warned Ulloa that the transfer could never be made in New Orleans without a large contingent of troops. Spanish control of the colony would not be recognized, in any case, until the Spanish flag flew over the Place d'Armes in New Orleans, but the status of the colony was never in doubt after 1764. The colonists recognized Ulloa as their governor, even if they did so half-heartedly. The use of Spanish currency was proof enough that the colony was a Spanish possession. Nevertheless, the colonists were prepared to oppose Ulloa and the Spanish government in every way possible.

Actually, Ulloa was a man of merit, a former naval officer and a distinguished scientist. Until 1764, he had been in Peru as governor of Huancavelica, where he undoubtedly met the Peruvian Marchioness d'Abrado, whom he married by proxy. The historian Gayarré describes Ulloa as a man "of medium stature, with stooped shoulders and pale cheeks . . . tactless, highly sensitive to criticism . . . retiring and unsociable" (Gayarré 1885). It is no wonder the Creole colonists considered him haughty and "strange." Even today, it seems strange that he waited in the fort at La Balize for seven months for his Peruvian bride without once coming to the city of New Orleans. In truth, it was through Aubry that Ulloa governed Louisiana during his entire stay in the province.

In 1767, Milhet returned from France with the story of his failure. This news, in addition to the hostility aggravated by the trade restrictions, brought about an event known in history as the Revolution of 1768. It began with the signing of a petition by 560 influential colonists, asking the Superior Council to order Ulloa to present to that body his credentials, proving legitimacy of the Spanish regime he headed or face banishment as a disturber of the peace. Ulloa refused. He considered himself the legal governor and therefore not subject to the demands of the Council. An impasse had been reached.

After this, armed bands of colonists from the outskirts of the city, including Acadians and Germans, led by Joseph Villere, arrived in New Orleans. Fearing for Ulloa's safety, Aubry convinced the governor to take refuge on board the Spanish frigate *El Volante,* anchored in the New Orleans harbor, while Aubry tried to calm the rebels. On November 1, 1768, Ulloa set sail for Havana. Legend has it that his ship was set adrift by drunken patriots returning from a wedding party. The Spaniard was thus expelled from the colony, and the revolution appeared to have succeeded.

The colonists continued in their opposition. They had the Superior Council draw up a document entitled Representation to Louis XV, which was carried to France by Ensign Bienville de Noyan, a nephew of Governor Bienville, and other delegates, but the king refused to see them. It was becoming clear that Louis XV had disowned his subjects in Louisiana. The colonists in New Orleans, now numbering only 3,190 including slaves, could no longer resist the power of the king of Spain.

General O'Reilly

At this time, **Don Alejandro O'Reilly** an Irish soldier of fortune and exile from religious persecution in his native country, now in the service of the king of Spain, was appointed governor and captain general of the province of Louisiana. He is known today as the Father of Spanish Louisiana.

O'Reilly had an extraordinary military background. Because of his outstanding service in the Seven Years' War and later in the reoccupation of Havana in 1763, he was recalled to Madrid. With his excellent record, he was appointed lieutenant general on July 15, 1767. Such zeal as he exhibited in the service of King Charles III did not go unnoticed. The king believed

Gen. Alejandro O'Reilly, sent to take over Louisiana for Spain, 1769. (Courtesy Leonard V. Huber Collection)

him the right man to suppress the rebellion in Louisiana and establish proper colonial administration.

King Charles sent O'Reilly with a *cedula,* appointing him commander of the expedition to bring Louisiana to order, "to take possession of it in my Royal Name . . . and punish according to the law, the instigators and accomplices of the uprising which occurred in New Orleans . . . I give you . . . such power and jurisdiction as shall be necessary" (Texada 1970).

O'Reilly arrived at La Balize on July 20, 1769, on a frigate accompanied by twenty other ships and 2,056 soldiers, forty-six cannons of various sizes, mortars, a large supply of arms and ammunition, medical provisions, and food. He sent his aide-de-camp, **Lt. Col. Dominique Francisco Bouligny,** with a letter to Charles Aubry, notifying the French of his arrival, informing Aubry of his royal commission to take possession of the colony, and asking his cooperation. Bouligny was greeted in New Orleans by a large crowd, including three Spanish officers who had been detained by the colonists as security for debts owed them by the Spanish government. He proceeded to Aubry's home to deliver the letter. Aubry now promised his cooperation and assembled the colonists in the Place d'Armes to inform them of O'Reilly's arrival.

Three representatives were sent to greet O'Reilly. They promised submission and explained that their rebellion had been brought about by the "severe nature of Don Antonio and the subversion of privileges, which had been assured in the act of cession" (Texada 1970). Then they asked for time sufficient for those who wished to immigrate to do so.

O'Reilly replied that he wanted to become well informed about the events that occurred before he acted. The men dined with him and then returned to New Orleans, full of admiration for O'Reilly.

During the night of August 16, 1769, the Spanish convoy moved quietly into the city of New Orleans, and the colonists were awakened on August 17 by cannon shot from the flotilla. When they arrived at the river, they found the Spanish fleet at anchor.

On August 18, O'Reilly took formal possession of the colony in the Place d'Armes. He walked to the center of the square and presented Aubry with the letter from the king. Aubry placed the keys of the city at O'Reilly's feet. Spanish flags were run up in all parts of the city, and artillery was fired. Then all retired to the Cathedral to say a *Te Deum* in thanksgiving.

Following the ceremony, O'Reilly consulted privately with Aubry, demanding that he prepare a complete account of the events surrounding the rebellion. The French governor, obeying the orders of his new sovereign, wrote a complete report. Because of this information, O'Reilly arrested **Nicolas Chauvin de Lafrenière, Denis-Nicolas Foucault, Bienville de Noyan, Pierre Hardy de Boisblanc,** members of the Superior Council, and **Braud,** the printer. Each of these men was summoned separately to his home. Later, **Pierre Marquis,** an officer of the troops; **Julien Jerome Doucet,** a lawyer; **Joseph Petit** and **Mazant,** planters; **Jean and Joseph Milhet;** and **Pierre Caresse** and **Pierre Poupet,** merchants, were also arrested.

According to historian Charles Gayarré, **Joseph Villere**, who had led the Germans to join the rebels, was on his plantation on the

German Coast when he received a letter from Aubry saying that he had nothing to fear from O'Reilly and that he could come to New Orleans in perfect safety. Villere descended the river to New Orleans and found himself arrested. Outraged, he struck the Spanish officer, who pierced him with a bayonet. He lingered and later died in prison, awaiting trial (Gayarré 1851).

> The trial of those indicted as leaders of the rebellion began in late August 1769 and did not terminate until October 24. It was conducted according to the standard Spanish judicial procedures. The Spanish Court set out to prove that there had been a conspiracy to oust Ulloa, and that treason and sedition had been committed. The defendants and other witnesses were interrogated separately, as there was no trial by jury under Spanish Law, nor a trial held in public court. (Texada 1970)

Their sentences were pronounced by O'Reilly on October 24, 1769, and on the following day, October 25, five rebels—Lafrenière, Noyan, Caresse, Marquis, and Joseph Milhet—were shot to death by Spanish soldiers, there being no hangman in the colony. Petit was imprisoned for life; Mazant and Doucet were sentenced to imprisonment for ten years and de Boisblanc, Jean Milhet, and Poupet to imprisonment for six years, all in the Castle Morror in Havana. Braud, the printer of the petition, was discharged. Shocked into submission, the rest of the colonists gave up the fight. The French Creoles never forgave O'Reilly for his act. Henceforth, he was to be known as **"Bloody O'Reilly,"** and as such, he has taken his place in the history of Louisiana.

The question of whether O'Reilly was cruel or justified in his treatment of the rebels continues to be a matter of dispute among historians. François Barbé-Marbois said, "The Court of Madrid secretly disapproved of these acts of outrage." Historian Judge François-Xavier Martin said, "Posterity . . . will doom this act to public execration. No necessity demanded, no policy justified it."

On the other hand, if it was treason, it was considered a most grievous crime by all nations and punishable by death.

Historian Henry Edward Chambers puts the blame for the execution of the rebels on the shoulders of Governor Aubry. O'Reilly, he says, came to the colony with orders from the king to suppress rebellion and punish leaders. "[He] . . . was compelled . . . to make an example of the leaders . . . lest other Spanish colonials follow the Louisiana example." Aubry, he feels, kept Ulloa and the colonial leaders from coming to terms. "He inserted a wedge of mutual antagonism," which thus caused rebellion.

O'Reilly began his administration by abolishing the Superior Council and substituting a Cabildo, composed of six *regidors* (councilmen) and *alcaldes* (mayors), an attorney-general, and a clerk, all presided over by the governor. The laws of Spain, the *Siete Partidas* (Seven Parts), were substituted for those of France.

Under the Cabildo Governing Council of Louisiana, O'Reilly abolished Indian slavery. He permitted many French officials to stay in office and helped farmers by establishing land titles. Under O'Reilly's Ordinance of 1770, a system of homesteading land was established, allowing an owner a parcel of land six to eight arpents fronting on a river or bayou and forty arpents in depth if he occupied the land and enclosed it within three years. The front of the land was to be cleared.

During his governance, roads and levees were built. The only religion tolerated in the colony was Catholicism, which worked no hardship on the Creole Catholic population. Medicine was divided into three disciplines during his term: medicine proper, surgery, and pharmacy. An Ursuline nun was the first pharmacist in Louisiana.

Don Luis de Unzaga

As we can see, O'Reilly's administration was not without merit. He left Louisiana in 1770, turning over the reins of government to **Don Luis de Unzaga y Amezaga,** a successful, well-liked man whose rule was mild and paternal, as was that of every other governor during the next three decades of Spanish domination. Unzaga married a Creole native of Louisiana. As governor, he did whatever was needed to make the colony successful. Expediency was the byword of the Spanish domination. Unzaga winked at smuggling and allowed the British traders to do business with the Spanish settlers along the Mississippi, because the colony needed what they supplied.

One of the most well remembered Spanish immigrants to come to New Orleans during this period was **Don Andrès Almonester y Roxas,** who came from Andalusia, Spain, in 1769, at the age of forty-four. A widower whose wife and child died in Spain, he was appointed Royal Notary for the king of Spain. At his first meeting with the Cabildo Council, he was also appointed clerk and notary to

Governor Unzaga and his Intendant and Royal Notary for Louisiana. Almonester was to become a real-estate genius, New Orleans's greatest benefactor, and the father of the celebrated Baroness de Pontalba.

Don Bernardo de Galvez

In 1777, Don Bernardo de Galvez took over the duties as governor. Galvez was only thirty-one years old, a member of an influential family, and another Spanish governor to marry a Creole girl from Louisiana, **Felicie de St. Maxent d'Estrehan.** He proved himself to be extraordinarily heroic and admirable. He allowed great freedom to the colonists in their commerce and gave help openly to the American Revolutionists. Spain declared war on England on May 8, 1779, and on July 8, Charles III authorized his Louisiana subjects to take part in the war.

With a small fleet and an army of 1,430 men, Galvez led successful attacks against the British outposts at Baton Rouge and Natchez, capturing Fort Manchac along the way. In 1780, he conquered Mobile and then undertook a lengthy attack against Pensacola. The English commander capitulated on May 9, 1781, an act by which the province of West Florida was acquired by Spain. By eliminating the British presence from these forts, Galvez's Louisiana Regiment and militias effectively ended the attacks launched against American troops from the Mississippi and Gulf of Mexico. As a consequence, the descendants of Galvez's troops are entitled to become members of the Daughters of the American Revolution and the Sons of the American Revolution organizations.

The second Treaty of Paris was signed in Paris, September 1783, acknowledging the independence of the United States, with a southern boundary line of thirty-one degrees latitude. The description was important, since it became the dividing line between the United States and the Spanish colonies. Both Floridas thus passed to Spanish control.

In 1785, Galvez was made captain-general of Cuba, Louisiana, and the two Floridas. The same year, he succeeded his father as viceroy of Mexico. Galvez died in Mexico on November 30, 1786, at the age of thirty-eight. He remains one of the most romantic figures in colonial Louisiana history. A statue of Galvez stands at the foot of

Canal Street between the ferry terminal and the World Trade Center, and St. Bernard Parish is named in honor of St. Bernard, Galvez's patron saint.

Don Esteban Rodríguez Miró y Sabater succeeded Galvez in 1785. He, too, married a native Creole girl, **Marie Celeste Elenore de McCarty.** It was during Miró's time that 5,000 French-Acadian exiles began arriving in Louisiana. During the French and Indian War, they had refused to swear allegiance to England and had therefore been exiled. They were shipped to different points along the Atlantic coast and to the far-flung ports of England and France. At one port in France, 375 families arrived (a total of 1,574 people).

Since the Spanish needed farmers to provide food for the colonists in Louisiana, bowing once again to expediency, they transported the Acadians on Spanish ships from the ports of France to make their homes in Louisiana. The Acadians settled in the Bayou Lafourche-Bayou Teche area, where they would become substantial farmers and permanent inhabitants of the region. The Spanish gave the newcomers land grants, livestock, and grain to begin their new lives in southwest Louisiana. To Louisiana, they brought warmth and gaiety, love of home and family, and a love of the land. Like the Germans, they provided food for the tables of the colonists. But unlike the immigrants who eventually amalgamated, they kept to themselves in the bayou country, working their land and establishing their homes. They spoke almost exclusively to one another, using the seventeenth-century French of their forefathers. Few of them spoke anything but French until the First World War.

The Disastrous Fires

In 1788, during Miró's administration, the first of two terrible fires in New Orleans occurred. On Good Friday, March 21, 1788, **Don Vincente Jose Nunez,** the military treasurer, was in his private chapel in his residence on Chartres Street near St. Louis. It was a very windy day, and a candle fell from the altar, setting the chapel on fire. Flames spread and engulfed the entire city. Residences and business places burned to the ground. The fire spread around the Plaza and ignited the town hall, the arsenal, the parish church, and the quarters of the Capuchins, all of which disappeared into smoke.

Prisoners were released from jail just in time to escape the flames. In the morning, tents covered the Plaza and the levee, and only chimneys remained of the 856 buildings that had been lost. Nearly half the town was in ashes.

Six years later, in 1794, children playing on Royal Street accidentally set fire to a hay store. Within three hours, 212 stores and houses had burned down. The new buildings that had been built at the bottom of the Plaza survived, but only two stores were left standing and, once again, the levee and the Plaza became camping grounds for the city's inhabitants.

From this time on, buildings were erected with sturdier material. Tile roofs came into general use. Homes now displayed Spanish-American features, and the beauty of the town, as well as its safety, was improved. The new buildings stood shoulder to shoulder with party walls, each a different color of stucco over brick. The overall effect was Caribbean, from where much of the architecture was borrowed.

An ordinance had been passed that buildings of more than one story be made of brick. Walls were designed with lovely arcades, and patios came alive with the plangent sounds of fountains. There were prominent doors and windows and heavy iron bolts and gratings, all of which adorned sturdy structures. As a finishing touch, magnificent wrought-iron lacework decorated the balconies of the two- and three-story dwellings. The French called the inner yards "courtyards," for they were the heart, *le coeur,* of the household. The Spanish called them *patios,* a word that sounded like horses' hoofs on cobblestones.

Charles III of Spain died in 1788 and was succeeded by Charles IV, a weak and ineffectual ruler. Soon after, **Fr. Antonio de Sedella** (known as **Père Antoine** to the French) was sent to Louisiana as a representative of the dreaded Inquisition to introduce this tribunal to New Orleans. Governor Miró had the Commissary of the Inquisition arrested at night, put on board a ship, and taken back to Spain. In his official dispatch to the Spanish government, Miró commented: "When I read the communication of the Capuchin, I shuddered. . . . The mere name of the Inquisition uttered in New Orleans would not only be sufficient to check immigration . . . but would also be capable of driving away those who have recently come" (Gayarré 1885).

Father Antonio (Père Antoine) returned in 1795 and spent the rest of his life in New Orleans, where he assumed the role of pastor. Although he was a thorn in the side of the hierarchy, he was much loved by his parishioners. He died in 1829 at the age of eighty-one, mourned by Protestants and Catholics alike.

In 1789, the foundation of the new St. Louis Cathedral was laid, with funds donated by Don Andrès Almonester. The Cathedral, built at a cost of 100,000 pesos, was designed by the French architect **Gilberto Guillemard.** The central tower was constructed in 1819 by Benjamin Henry Latrobe to house the clock. The bell in the Cathedral is inscribed to commemorate the Battle of New Orleans in 1815. In 1825, **Francisco Zapari**, an Italian, decorated the interior of the Cathedral (Gayarré 1903).

Labor on this and other philanthropic projects sponsored by Don Almonester was completed by his slaves, who were masons, carpenters, blacksmiths, and brick makers. Much of the raw material, such as lime and timber, came from his own forests.

Also, in 1786, due to the generosity of Almonester, a new Charity Hospital was rebuilt after it was destroyed by a hurricane and named in honor of the Spanish king. Almonester endowed it with property, rents, and slaves and drew up a list of hospital regulations, which were very advanced for his day:

> The doctors must have studied at the colleges of Cadiz, Madrid or Barcelona. . . . Special attention was to be given to the "poor in real distress." . . . Incurable or infectious patients were not to be admitted. . . . All patients were to be supplied with a wooden bed, a table, bed clothing and garments for hospital wear. Almonester prepared a complete list of menus, which included a ration of meat.
>
> Treatment of disease . . . was designed to rid the body of corruption . . . and depended largely upon bleeding, sweating, blistering, purging, and vomiting. (Edwin Adams Davis 1971)

Physicians seemed to believe that the more loathsome the remedy, the quicker the cure. "Such remedies as crabs' eyes, dried toads and urine were prescribed along with mercury, arsenic, antimony, camphor, opium, ammonia, alum, quinine, calomel, ipecac, hemlock, much wine and brandy, rhubarb, licorice and myrrh" (Edwin Adams Davis 1971).

The cost of bleeding a patient was fifty cents; purging, one dollar; dressing a wound, fifty cents; and liquid medicine, twenty-five cents to one dollar.

The disease of leprosy reached serious proportions in the early

1780s. On Miró's recommendation, a leper hospital was built on Metairie Ridge behind New Orleans in 1875, to which Almonester contributed generously. The wild, primitive area soon came to be known as *La Terre des Lepreux* (Lepers' Land). By the end of the Spanish period, the disease had almost completely disappeared.

Baron de Carondelet

Francisco Luis Hector, Baron de Carondelet, known in Louisiana history as the City-Builder, began his administration in 1791. The civic improvements made during his term were many. A lighting system was created for New Orleans and a night police force was established, which was, necessarily, bilingual. To meet these expenses, a tax of $1.12½ was laid on every chimney. Consequently, the same chimney was used on all floors of a three-story house, thus stamping the Quarter, having been rebuilt after two fires, with a homogeneous architectural appearance.

Carondelet built the Carondelet Canal (later called the Old Basin Canal), with the turning basin behind the present site of the Municipal Auditorium, which connected New Orleans with Bayou St. John, and thereby with Lake Pontchartrain, facilitating trade with the Gulf Coast cities that had been founded around the same time as New Orleans.

To guard the city against attack, Carondelet built forts, redoubts, batteries, and deep ditches around it. He made treaties with the Indians in the area, established a policy of free trade, and began the first newspaper in Louisiana, *Moniteur de la Louisiane.*

The year 1795 saw the beginning of the granulation of sugar by Etienne de Boré, whose plantation was approximately six miles above New Orleans at the site of the present Audubon Park. Sugarcane had been introduced in 1751 by the Jesuits. From it, syrup was made and a liquor called *taffia*. Granulation now opened up a tremendous market for sugar.

In 1797, Carondelet left the city, having governed with outstanding ability. His successor, **Brig. Gen. Manuel Luis Gayoso de Lemos,** died of yellow fever in 1799. He is the only Spanish governor to be buried in New Orleans.

The Spanish governors after Gayoso were **Marques de Casa Calvo,** who served as acting governor from 1799 to 1801, and **Don Juan**

Manuel de Salcedo, who served from 1801 to 1803, even though the Treaty of San Ildefonso had been signed in 1800, giving Louisiana back to France.

The Treaty of San Ildefonso: Louisiana Retroceded to France

Napoleon Bonaparte, after his glorious campaigns of 1796 and 1797, returned to France in 1799. He gathered an army, crossed the Alps into Italy, and, in June 1800, defeated the Austrian army. Peace with Austria followed, and it seemed certain that peace with England would come soon.

Napoleon now wished to revive France's empire, chiefly Louisiana, which had been ceded to Spain by Louis XV in 1762. On October 1, 1800, by the Treaty of San Ildefonso, Charles IV, king of Spain, retroceded Louisiana to France. Historians are not clear why Charles agreed, but it was a demand made by a powerful ruler with recent conquests to his credit, which could not easily be denied. This treaty, too, was kept secret, as peace had not yet been declared between France and England.

In October 1801, preliminaries of peace were signed between England and France, and the retrocession of Louisiana to France became known in the United States. The news caused great excitement in the colony. When the Peace of Amiens was signed between England and France in March 1802, Napoleon prepared for the occupation and government of Louisiana.

In the last decade of Spanish rule, there were forts on the four corners of the city and behind the Cathedral. Later, in the 1800s, they were demolished, but at this time, there were mounted guns in each fort, a moat (either natural or manmade), and barracks for 100 men. When the forts were in use, the gates were closed at nine o'clock each night. The back gates led to the suburbs, which were almost as big as the city (composed of two hundred to three hundred houses). The Bayou Gate led to Gentilly, Metairie, and Grand Bayou. Metairie was comprised of "moi-toi" (you and me) partnerships between owner and farmer.

The streets of the Vieux Carré were wide and straight, thanks to Pauger. Houses were made of wood until the two fires, then of brick.

In neighborhoods such as Faubourg Marigny, Treme, and Faubourg St. John, there were generally beautiful houses belonging to people from all over the world. The Creoles dominated society and business, but within the next decade, the Americans would begin to control more trade and commerce than the Creoles. In the 1790s, there were oceangoing vessels in the river, as well as coastal schooners, barges, and pirogues (the cypress dugout canoe adapted from the Indians).

The Right of Deposit

The right of deposit, the right to place goods on the docks in New Orleans awaiting shipment to Europe and South America, was vital to American merchants. Spain and the Americans had been on the verge of war ever since the Treaty of Paris in 1783, when Great Britain gave the Americans the right to free navigation on the Mississippi, a right that Spain did not consider theirs to give, since the mouth of the Mississippi was in Spanish Louisiana. Hostilities grew worse, and in 1784, trade was ordered to cease between Spain and the Americans. Governor Miró, however, disregarded the orders, knowing that his colonists needed what the Americans had to sell. In this matter, he was in constant conflict with his Intendant, Juan Morales.

The Treaty of San Lorenzo

In 1795, Spain and America signed the Treaty of San Lorenzo, in which Spain granted Americans the right of free navigation on the Mississippi River and the right of deposit at New Orleans for three years. Although the right of deposit expired in 1798, the privilege continued until 1802, when Morales ordered it stopped.

Flatboatsmen and Keelboatsmen

After the American Revolution, many of the goods coming into New Orleans and subject to the right of deposit were carried in on the keelboats and flatboats of the New Americans. The men were called "Kaintocks" by the Creoles, and they were a dirty, noisy bunch of rogues and scalawags. For more than four decades, keelboatsmen were on the river bringing flour, coffee, soap, textiles, and shoes to the people of New Orleans.

They traveled in canoes, rafts, ferryboats, and scows, all manpowered or pulled by mules on the riverbanks. They came from Kentucky, Tennessee, Mississippi, and Ohio, areas whose population was increasing rapidly. They were strong, practical, and tough. They were well suited to the job as physical strength was needed to push, pull, and maneuver the loaded ships to their destination. Flatboats were propelled with two great oars. Keelboats were moved by one long oar in the center of the boat. Crewmen also used poles to push the boat along, which was steered by a giant rudder. These men often sold their boats with the goods and then traveled back upriver on horseback, following the old Indian trail, the Natchez Trace.

Their flatboats were then broken up and the gunwales, the long fore- and aft-planes, were sold for paving streets and *banquettes* (sidewalks) and for house construction. The rest of the timber was sold for firewood.

Keelboatsmen had appetites to match the roughness of their trade. Upon reaching port, they sold their cargo and they were ready for whiskey, women, and gambling. Dens of vice, such as those on Tchoupitoulas Street near the river, on Gallatin Street, and in the "swamp" on Girod Street at the river's edge, supplied their needs. Fistfights were inevitable. The Creoles deplored these men. They considered all Americans to be like the "Kaintocks" in the beginning, and thus the battle lines were drawn between the Creoles and the Americans.

Insurrection in Saint Domingue

Until now, we have used the name Santo Domingo to refer to the island of Hispaniola, discovered by Columbus in 1492 and claimed for Spain, who called their colony Santo Domingo. In the 1600s, French colonists settled the western part of the island, which Spain gave to France in 1697 through the Treaty of Ryswick. The French called their colony Saint Domingue. It was a sugar-growing colony where a bloody insurrection occurred in 1791.

The successful slave uprising was led by Toussaint L'Ouverture against the white plantation owners, whom they outnumbered ten to one. After a voodoo ceremony of crazed dancing and the drinking of animal blood, a half-million black slaves revolted against 50,000 whites and an equal number of privileged mulattoes. Plantations were destroyed, and 2,000 white islanders were killed.

By 1804, shiploads of whites and free people of color from the island poured into New Orleans. Many of these *gens de couleur libres* were artisans, craftsmen, and sculptors, who would add to the talent and literacy of the city's population and help to build the beautiful monuments, tombstones, and iron balconies that still grace its streets. The quadroon women were to become the beautiful concubines of song and story, so desired by the Creole men of the city.

Social Improvements

Living standards were high for those who could afford them. There were handsome houses, lavish furnishings, and elegant clothes. The most important piece of furniture in the Creole household was the armoire. Next in importance was the iron or brass bed. In fact, part of the volunteer firemen's equipment was a large key worn on the belt to unlock the bed, so that it could be removed in case of fire. The armoire was made to come apart so that it could be taken out of the house in pieces by one man.

During this period, there were some attempts at fire prevention already in place. Each house was required to have at least one good leather bucket and a ladder long enough to reach the top of the house. The first fire insurance was a donation of money to a volunteer fire group, in exchange for a fire mark, which the donor displayed prominently. In case of a general fire, the most common fires in those days, the volunteer firemen would concentrate their efforts on the houses displaying the fire mark of their group.

One example of the high living of the day was said to have occurred in 1798, when Gayoso had three visitors from the court of France: **Louis Philippe, Duc d'Orléans,** future king of France; **Duc de Montpensier;** and the **Comte de Beaujolais,** all brothers and all great-great-grandsons of the namesakes of New Orleans, Philippe, Duc d'Orléans. Entertaining these guests was **Pierre Philippe de Marigny de Mandeville,** who arranged lavish dinners for them. A story is told that special gold tableware was used, which was thrown into the river after one such elaborate meal, indicating that no one else was worthy of using it. **Bernard de Marigny** placed both his home and his purse at their feet, and they accepted both. The historian Grace King tells us that later on, Marigny, in financial straits, appealed to the court of France for the return of some of his money.

The value of exports grew tremendously in Louisiana during the Spanish rule. In 1767, these consisted of indigo, deerskins, lumber, naval stores, rice, peas, beans, and tallow, valued at $250,000 annually. By 1770, the yearly total had risen to $600,000 and, by 1802, had multiplied several times.

In 1790, wrought iron was brought from Spain. It required no painting to protect it against the elements. The date is significant because it was midway between the two great fires, the last of which caused the whole town to be rebuilt. Wrought-iron decoration was an outstanding feature for both its protective and visual attributes.

By the end of the Spanish period, Louisiana was more self-sufficient in foodstuffs. Natives had been encouraged to cultivate indigo, tobacco, flax, hemp, and cotton as commercial crops. (Perique tobacco, for example, was grown only in St. James Parish.) Louisiana was exporting 125,000 pounds of tobacco annually. Indigo production increased for a time but later declined because of a bug that infested it. Handling it over a period of five years had proved fatal to slaves.

The population had increased six-fold in Louisiana during the Spanish period. Settlers trickled down from the North until the end of the American Revolution, after which the trickle became a torrent. This flood of people lasted until the end of the 1700s, when the population had reached the 50,000 mark in Louisiana. Many people came from West Florida (acquired by the British in 1763), because they did not want to be under British rule. The Acadians began arriving in the 1750s and continued to come throughout the Spanish period.

It was during the Spanish period that Almonester rebuilt the St. Louis Cathedral and the Cabildo and built the first floor of the Presbytère as a domicile for the clergy. He contributed to a retreat for lepers and rebuilt Charity Hospital when it was blown down by a hurricane in 1779. In 1789, he gave the Ursuline nuns a chapel for their convent.

The Spanish settlers in New Orleans are to be thanked for three decades of stable government, for the city's first fire and police protection, for the Old Basin Canal, and for the first attempts made at establishing public schools in 1771. They are also to be thanked for a reconstructed Vieux Carré with its Spanish-American architecture, which is a monument to the period of Spanish domination.

The Spanish were also responsible for roofing the Indian Market. This was known as the **French Market** but was actually supplied by German farmers, Yugoslav oystermen, and, later on, Italian vendors, who sold their harvest to residents of the city, the personification of New Orleans gumbo.

CHAPTER V

On Becoming American: 1803-15

On April 30, 1803, when **Thomas Jefferson** was America's third president, the territory of Louisiana was purchased from **Napoleon Bonaparte**, consul of France, by the United States, for the sum of $15 million. This event took place before any ceremony had officially made Louisiana French again. It wasn't until November 30, 1803, that the Spanish flag was lowered and the French flag raised in the Place d'Armes, although the transfer of Louisiana from Spain to France had taken place three years earlier, and another transfer had since been arranged. On that same day, **Pierre Clément de Laussat,** colonial prefect of France, was given the keys to the city and put in possession of the province for France. Although Laussat's actions were purely symbolic (coming after the sale of Louisiana to the United States), he nonetheless abolished the Spanish Cabildo, appointed the Frenchman **Etienne de Boré** mayor, appointed two adjuncts, and created the first city council of New Orleans, which consisted of ten members.

Just twenty days later, on December 20, 1803, the same ceremony was repeated in the Place d'Armes. This time, however, the French flag was lowered and the flag of the United States took its place. **William Charles Cole Claiborne, Gen. James Wilkinson** (acting for the president of the United States), and **Pierre de Laussat** (representing France) signed the papers making the Louisiana Territory part of America. Claiborne was to be in charge of civil affairs and Wilkinson in control of the army.

In one year, New Orleans had been under three flags: first Spanish, then French, and finally American.

Circumstances leading up to and surrounding the purchase are interesting and complex. To begin with, Napoleon, having recently lost the island of Saint Domingue in the Caribbean, felt that his dream of a French empire in America had ended. He feared that it would be impossible to protect Louisiana financially or militarily if he went back to war with England, and if he couldn't protect Louisiana against the British, he preferred America to have it. Also, badly in need of money for his European wars, he was receptive to entreaties by Edward Livingston, U.S. minister to France, who urged him to sell the Isle of Orleans and West Florida to the United States. Napoleon, through his negotiator, **François Barbé-Marbois,** offered to sell all of Louisiana for $15 million.

President Jefferson, without consulting Congress, agreed to the purchase, although there was a total of only $10 million in the U.S. treasury at the time. This act came close to causing the president's impeachment.

Further reasons for Napoleon's sale of Louisiana to the United States are given in his own words: "This accession of territory strengthens forever the power of the United States, and I have just given England a maritime rival that will sooner or later humble her pride" (Lossing 1881). The irony of the situation is that the United States had to make loans from British and Dutch banks in order to finance the purchase.

The Louisiana Territory included 827,987 square miles, which would later be divided to form thirteen other states, or parts of states, in the nation. The territory extended from Canada to the Gulf of Mexico and from the Mississippi River to the Rocky Mountains. Boundaries were in dispute, so it is impossible to give an exact size and value to the purchase, but nonetheless, it was the greatest real-estate buy of its time.

Throughout the territory, colonists settled the areas along the rivers and bayous: the Mississippi, Red, Atchafalaya, and Ouachita rivers and Bayou Teche and Bayou Lafourche. There were, at the time of the purchase, approximately fifty thousand people living in the territory (excluding Indians), most of who lived in what is now the state of Louisiana.

In 1804, the territorial government declared all land grants after 1800 null and void and confiscated all property given the colonists by a Spanish or French king. On March 26, 1804, Congress divided the land that had been included in the Louisiana Purchase into the Louisiana Territory and the Territory of Orleans. The Territory of Orleans consisted of the present state of Louisiana minus the Florida Parishes (later annexed) and an area near the Sabine River. The Louisiana Territory included the rest of the purchase.

In 1803, New Orleans was a city of a population just under ten thousand with a majority of whites. The population was composed of Creoles, Acadians, refugees from Santo Domingo, immigrants from the German Coast who spoke perfect French, Castilian soldiers, Indians, black slaves, and free people of color, as well as ex-galley slaves and adventurers. Overall, it was a great place to live.

Four of the five forts by this time had fallen into disrepair. Only Fort Ferdinand remained. The city had four or five general stores, three Scottish banks, a German business firm, and eight or ten commission houses opened during the Spanish period by Americans. The largest percentage of the population consisted of French and Spanish Creoles.

New Orleans was a trade center, dealing in the products of the countryside: rice, indigo, sugar, tobacco, and cotton. These were the cash crops grown for sale. Agricultural products were scarce, and vegetables were, as yet, hard to obtain and expensive.

Education in New Orleans in 1803 was poor. Few citizens could read and write. The Ursulines taught fewer than two hundred students, including boarders. There were no colleges, bookstores, or libraries. Men worked as apprentices to learn their trades.

The city was devoutly Roman Catholic, but remarkably liberal in its acceptance of the many brothels, saloons, and gambling halls. Also accepted—or ignored—was the custom of *plaçage,* in which white men took quadroon girls into more or less permanent concubinage and set them up in a house in the French Quarter or adjoining the Quarter on Rampart Street. In *Fabulous New Orleans,* Lyle Saxon wrote, "There seems to be a certain insidious chemical in the atmosphere which tends to destroy Puritanism" (Saxon 1928).

Into this diverse community now came the Americans. They were certainly not all flatboatsmen, as many of the French had formerly believed. There were East Coast businessmen, Southern planters and farmers, and Yankee clerks as well, very few of whom knew a word of French. New Orleans was American now—a part of their country—and they had a right to settle in the Crescent City.

William C. C. Claiborne

President Jefferson appointed William C. C. Claiborne as governor of the Territory of Orleans (after both the Marquis de Lafayette and James Monroe had declined). Claiborne was twenty-eight years old when he arrived in New Orleans, a Virginian Protestant who did not speak French. He kept a French and Spanish interpreter at hand and, wisely, did not dispose of the French mayor, Etienne de Boré. Understandably, de Boré did not enjoy his role and he resigned six months later.

For two years (1803-5), Claiborne acted almost as a dictator in the territory. He set about learning French and translating the laws into English and re-codifying them. In 1804, he lost his twenty-one-year-old wife, his daughter, his secretary, and many friends in an epidemic of yellow fever. Five years later, his second wife, also twenty-one at the time, perished of the same disease. He wrote to President Madison about the filth, garbage, and refuse thrown into the river, which he could see from his bedroom window.

Claiborne's opinion of the people he found in New Orleans is expressed in the letters he wrote to James Madison in 1804, when Madison was still secretary of state:

[January 10, 1804:] The more I become acquainted with the inhabitants of this Province, the more I am convinced of their unfitness for a representative government . . . I have discovered with regret that a strong partiality for the French government still exists . . . in some circles a sentiment is cherished that at the close of the War between England and France, the great Buonaparte will again raise his standard in this country.

[January 24, 1804:] The period allowed by the Treaty for the withdrawing of the French and Spanish forces from the ceded Territory expires this day, and still little or no preparation is made for an Embarkation. The Spanish Officers have conducted themselves with great propriety . . . I cannot speak equally favourable of the French forces . . . some of these are mischievous, riotous, disorderly characters . . . added to this [is] the ignorance and credulity of the mass of people . . . I would think it wise policy in Congress to appropriate one hundred thousand dollars annually for the encouragement of Education in Louisiana.

[January 30, 1804:] On my arrival in New Orleans, I found the people very Solicituous to maintain their Public Ball establishment, and to convince them that the American Government felt no disposition to break in upon their amusements. Gen. Wilkinson and myself occasionally attended these assemblies . . . I fear you will suppose that

I am wanting in respect in calling your attention to the Balls of New Orleans, but I do assure you, Sir, that they occupy much of the public mind. . . . (Claiborne, n.d.)

Joseph Dubreuil, one of the wealthiest planters in Louisiana, wrote, "It is not unknown here, after reading over Northern public papers, that the ceded territory has been described to Congress as some sort of 'Tower of Babel,' suffering from a confusion of tongues, and Louisianans as men stupefied by despotism or ignorance, and therefore unable to elevate themselves for a long time to the heights of a free constitution."

Dubreuil and others like him considered Claiborne wholly incompetent and entirely dependent on the English-speaking people for this information. He considered the governor a stranger in New Orleans—a stranger as far as the soil was concerned, its local interests, its customs, its habits, and even the language of the inhabitants, and therefore without the most absolutely necessary knowledge to govern.

The city government, created by charter in 1805, provided for a mayor, treasurer, recorder, and a city council of fourteen aldermen. The mayor was to preside over the council and head the police force and fire department, both of which were largely voluntary. The new government did its best to clean up New Orleans. It outlawed cockfights and forbade the dumping of human waste into the river. It reorganized the police force, inspected ships for disease, added streetlights, and repaired roads and bridges. It purchased more firefighting equipment and enacted a building code. In the first decade of the American Era, however, five epidemics of yellow fever raged.

The years 1803-5 constituted a **period of conversion.** The people of New Orleans had been firmly French or Spanish. By the time of the Louisiana Purchase, they had become American, but they needed time to adjust, to let go of their European ways, and to learn what it meant to be a part of a democracy.

It was a **period of confusion.** Most New Orleanians spoke only French; their governor spoke only English. Communication was difficult, and many of the impressions Claiborne first expressed were due to a lack of understanding. Because of the language difference, there had to be an English court and a French court, an English police force and a French police force, and interpreters everywhere.

It was a **period of legal confusion and conflict.** The American government wished to impose British Common Law upon its new territory, the law that was practiced in England and throughout the rest of America. According to Common Law, once a precedent had been established, any similar case was decided on the basis of that precedent. New Orleanians fought tenaciously to retain their Civil Law, in which the courts interpreted the law and were not bound by previous decisions.

The fight for Civil Law was not just an emotional demand. The welfare of the citizens depended upon it. Their property rights, the rights of illegitimate children, the rights of the free people of color, and forced heirship—all of these were protected under the Civil Code existing then in Louisiana; under Common Law, they would have had to be re-determined.

Slaves in New Orleans could work for hire. Urbanization had made them less deferential to whites and more defiant of the French Code Noir, which had continued to govern them during the Spanish period. And yet, the Code Noir gave more rights to slaves than they enjoyed anywhere else. Slave owners could be brought to court by other slave owners if they mistreated their slaves. Masters were forced to abide by the Code Noir.

About one-third of the blacks in New Orleans in 1805 were **free people of color** (f. p. c.), who enjoyed a legal and economic status unparalleled among black people in the American slave states at the time. They had full freedom to enter into business contracts and to own and transfer property, and they had full rights in civil and criminal litigation against blacks and whites alike. If Louisiana would have lost its Civil Code and been forced to accept Common Law, all blacks would have thereafter been treated alike. Rights and privileges would have disappeared, and a revolt like that of the Saint Domingue uprising would not have been difficult to imagine.

In Louisiana, unlike the rest of America, illegitimate children also had legal rights. Bastards could be legitimized by marriage and could inherit as if born during marriage. This directly opposed British legal thinking, which was best expressed by William Blackstone as "for he can inherit nothing, being looked upon as the son of nobody" (Blackstone 1769).

The people of Louisiana fought to keep their Civil Law and in the end were permitted to do so. Louisiana's Civil Code of 1808 and the Code of Practices of 1824 were based on Roman rather than English law. The Napoleonic Code of 1804 provided the framework, but other elements contributed to its development.

Culture shock was another experience felt by both natives and new American immigrants. Most Americans had had few business dealings with free people of color, for one thing. Americans were also not prepared for the French Creoles, who were poorly educated and provincial but haughty and proud of their heritage. The Creoles considered themselves a breed apart and far more cultured with their theater and their opera than the Americans with whom they were now doing business. They were different and cultured in areas they considered important. By American standards, they were culturally backwards, but the Creoles were not interested in using American standards or being measured by them.

The Creoles, like the colony itself, were not moneymakers to any great extent. Creoles such as **Bernard de Marigny** could have learned much from entrepreneurs such as the American **Samuel J. Peters** and the English actor **James H. Caldwell,** who, in 1828, offered to buy and develop the Marigny Plantation and build hotels, theaters, and gasworks. The offer was declined. That they had the knowhow to carry out such projects was later proved, not in Faubourg Marigny but Faubourg Ste. Marie on the upriver side of Canal Street.

When the Americans began arriving in large numbers, they settled in Faubourg St. Mary, as *they* called it. They lived along the natural levee, crowding into sugar plantations that had existed for decades. In the first ten years after the Louisiana Purchase, enmity between Creoles in the Vieux Carré and Americans in Faubourg St. Mary came alive.

Canal Street: Never a Canal

Canal Street was laid out at 171 feet wide, 50 feet of which were allotted for a canal. It is shown in the planning stage on some old maps, but it never materialized. The canal was designed to tie the river with the Carondelet Canal (the Old Basin Canal), which ran to Bayou St. John and then to Lake Pontchartrain. Industrialists envisioned a river-to-lake waterway. They hoped that the lake would become important commercially, but on the New Orleans side, it never did. There was a drainage ditch down Canal Street for a time, but that was as close as it ever came to being a canal.

Canal Street, the widest street in the United States, became a kind of boundary line between the feuding Creoles in the Old Town and the Americans in Faubourg St. Mary. The wide median down the center was called the "neutral ground," a sign of a truce that existed, however fragilely, between the hostile residents of the two communities. In time, all medians in New Orleans came to be called neutral grounds.

In the early territorial period, fear of war with Spain was another disturbing element. After the Louisiana Purchase, the Spanish soldiers were still in New Orleans, as we have seen in Claiborne's letters to Madison. They were also in the Spanish cities around New Orleans: Baton Rouge, Covington and Mandeville north of Lake Pontchartrain, and Mobile and Pensacola to the east. The United States must have realized that they could not continue to hold on to New Orleans if they did not have control of West Florida. A main concern was whether or not West Florida was included in the Louisiana Purchase. At one point, the United States insisted that it was indeed included. (West Florida consisted of the parishes of St. Helena, East and West Feliciana, East Baton Rouge, Tangipahoa, Livingston, Washington, and St. Tammany.) This area was inhabited by many Americans and English who had migrated down from the thirteen colonies when West Florida was not included in the Louisiana Purchase, and to make sure of this, they delayed acknowledging the transfer.

In 1810, the people living in the West Florida parishes revolted against Spain, taking over Fort San Carlos in Baton Rouge in a minor skirmish and declaring their independence from Spain. They established the **West Florida Republic.** The flag of the new republic was blue with a white star, and its president had the unlikely name of **Fulwar Skipwith.** Within six weeks, he asked to have his republic united with the Territory of Orleans. Evidently, he was too late, because Claiborne had already received orders from President Madison to take possession of West Florida. He did, and West Florida was annexed to the Territory. Spain and Great Britain protested the annexation, but it was all in vain.

Louisiana Becomes a State

When Claiborne was appointed governor in 1803, he was to govern the Territory of Orleans, which was later to become part of the state of

Louisiana. From the beginning, the people of the Territory of Orleans wanted statehood. They wanted the benefits of American citizenship and pressured Congress for help in this effort.

In 1810, the Territory of Orleans had a population of 76,500. A population of 60,000 was required for statehood. In January 1811, **Julien Poydras,** the territory's delegate to Congress, proposed statehood for Louisiana. The next month, Congress authorized the territory to draw up a constitution. Delegates drew up the constitution, and on April 8, 1812, Congress ratified it. It did not include the West Florida parishes, which had been annexed to the territory in 1810, but were added to the state by an amendment on April 14, 1812.

The Territory of Orleans became the state of Louisiana on April 30, 1812, and the eighteenth star on the flag. A gubernatorial election was held, and Claiborne, who had endeared himself to the people of Louisiana, won easily over Creole **Noel Destrehan.** His efforts to overcome his personal losses and to win the respect of the haughty Creoles had been rewarded.

Claiborne's opinion of the people had also changed. By 1812, he was quick to say that the natives of Louisiana had a natural ability; they might not have had much schooling, but they were very right, intense people who knew how to do things and what they were about.

Several major events in the history of the city occurred during this period. Shortly after Louisiana had been retroceded to France, the Ursuline nuns became terrified that since France was now under the Emperor Napoleon, the French government might not honor the Catholic Church. So great was their fear that some of the nuns left New Orleans and went to Cuba. Those who stayed, knowing New Orleans was now to become American, wrote to Thomas Jefferson, asking if they were going to be allowed to practice the Catholic religion. Jefferson wrote them a beautiful letter, allaying their fears, enumerating the many services the Ursulines had rendered in the past, and stating his wish that they would continue to serve the territory in the future. Reassured, the nuns remained.

The Legislative Council attempted to divide the territory into areas called counties. Municipal districts were called counties in the rest of the United States, and it seemed logical to call them that in Louisiana. From the beginning, however, boundaries of church parishes had been used to mark off municipal divisions in Louisiana. (Boundaries of the original parishes in New Orleans are not known.)

In 1805, the year the city of New Orleans was incorporated, counties were established in the territory. For a few years, counties and parishes existed side by side, and the courts labored under the confusion that resulted. In 1807, parishes were legalized by the territorial government but not incorporated into the State Constitution until 1845, after which counties were forever abolished in Louisiana.

The Aaron Burr Conspiracy

Aaron Burr, born in 1765 and elected vice president in 1801, ended his political career when he killed Alexander Hamilton in a duel in 1804. While vice president, Burr had become a candidate in the gubernatorial election in New York in 1804 and was defeated due to Hamilton's efforts. He challenged Hamilton to a duel and killed him. The coroner declared that Burr willfully murdered Hamilton. Burr fled and began recruiting an army, allegedly conspiring with **Gen. James Wilkinson** to wrest Louisiana and other Western states from the United States or a part of Mexico from Spain in order to set up his own country.

In the summer of 1805, Burr met in New Orleans with **Edward Livingston, Daniel Clark,** and a group of adventurers who wanted to invade Mexico. In 1806, rumors flew about Burr's developing army. Many believed that the Spanish in West Florida were working with Burr.

Claiborne accused Daniel Clark, then a United States congressman, of complicity with Burr. Clark challenged Claiborne to a duel and succeeded in wounding Claiborne.

Burr was tried for treason in 1807 and acquitted. He went to Europe, still attempting to get support for his Mexican scheme. He returned to the United States under an assumed name in 1812 and practiced law in New York until his death.

The Code Duello

The two duels just mentioned in the Burr story make it clear how widespread the practice of dueling was at the beginning of the nineteenth century. Duels could result from any accusation or breach of etiquette, real or imagined, serious or slight. Rules for fighting were spelled out in the Code Duello. Creoles in New Orleans never fought

The Famous New Orleans Duelling Ground.

Rules governing "affairs of honor" were spelled out in the Code Duello.
Gentlemen fought many duels beneath the Dueling Oaks in today's City Park.
(Courtesy Leonard V. Huber Collection)

The Dueling Oaks in City Park provided the favorite setting for affairs of
honor. Bernard de Marigny is said to have fought nineteen duels under these
magnificent trees. Unfortunately, only one of the oaks still stands, the other being
lost in a hurricane in 1949. (Photo by Kathy Chappetta Spiess)

with fists, as the Kaintocks did, but with weapons, and they were trained by weapons masters whose academies were established on Exchange Alley. The duel was called an affair of honor. It sometimes resulted in death, but more often, the offended party's honor was satisfied by merely wounding his opponent. Under the "Dueling Oaks" at the Allard Plantation, now City Park, or in Père Antoine's garden, behind the Cathedral, thousands of duels were fought using everything from swords and rapiers to rifles and shotguns.

The Introduction of Steamboats

The advent of the steamboat had a lasting effect upon the lives of the people who lived along the Mississippi. Of particular interest was the maiden voyage of the steamer *New Orleans,* the first steamboat on the Western territorial waters. It was built in 1811 in Pittsburgh, Pennsylvania, by **Nicholas Roosevelt,** pioneer in steam navigation, former associate of Robert Fulton, and great-great-uncle of the future president **Theodore Roosevelt.** Nicholas Roosevelt was on board for the maiden voyage, which was eventful, to say the least. The boat, 116 feet long and 20 feet wide, left Pittsburgh in September 1811 and did not arrive in New Orleans until January 1812. Anything calamitous or extraordinary that could happen did.

A baby was born to Mrs. Nicholas Roosevelt (daughter of architect Benjamin Latrobe) in Cincinnati during a month's layover, while the passengers waited for the water to rise. The earthquake of 1811 occurred, frightening the Indians and causing them to attack the steamboat. (The Indians thought the smoke-burping ship had caused the earthquake.) In the midst of all this, the ship caught fire. And when the ship landed in New Orleans in January 1812, the captain wooed and married Mrs. Roosevelt's maid.

Until this time, there were mostly flatboats and keelboats on the river. There were few boats coming up from the mouth of the river. With the invention of the steamboat, keelboatsmen who sold their boats with their merchandise in New Orleans could travel back upriver by steamboat if they could afford it or have their merchandise shipped by steamer. At last, travel up and down the river in the same vessel was possible.

The Embargo Act of 1807

In 1807, England and France were at war. Although the United States was a neutral power, both warring nations repeatedly seized its ships. President Jefferson's appeals were ignored. Therefore, Congress passed the Embargo Act of 1807, prohibiting the shipment of American goods to either England or France.

Port cities such as New Orleans, suffered greatly because of the Embargo Act. Imports and exports dropped to one-third of their former volume. Businesses closed. Smuggling resulted. By 1812, the injustices of the British in impressing American seamen, blockading American ports, and encouraging Indian attacks on settlers moving westward led to American involvement in the European war. In addition, war hawks in Congress were convinced that victory over the British would win Canada and Spanish Florida for the United States. New England states were opposed to the nation's entry in a war for which it was ill prepared. Nevertheless, within days of Louisiana becoming a state, the United States declared war against England.

The Battle of New Orleans

Early in the war, the British enjoyed far more successes than the Americans. The British continued to blockade American ports. They defeated the Americans at Dearborn and Detroit and captured and burned Washington, D.C. In spite of Oliver Perry's victory in the Battle of Lake Erie, most Americans began to realize the state of unpreparedness of the new nation and abandoned hopes of owning Canada.

Meanwhile, in Louisiana, Governor Claiborne prepared for a defensive war. Early in 1814, Gen. Andrew Jackson was assigned to march south to calm the Creek Indians, who had been encouraged by the British to massacre white settlers on the Alabama River.

Word reached New Orleans in the spring of 1814 that the British would attack the Gulf Coast and New Orleans. In September 1814, the British ship *Sophia* sailed into Grand Terre, the stronghold of the privateer-smuggler Jean Lafitte. Lafitte was offered the rank of captain in the British military and other monetary rewards if he would fight with the British against the Americans. Lafitte refused and informed Claiborne of the offer.

Stories are confused at this point. Some historians claim that Claiborne believed the buccaneer and interceded with federal authorities on his behalf. Others say that it was Claiborne, with the Committee of Defense, who sent a force of United States soldiers to bombard Grand Terre and capture Lafitte. Whatever the case, most of the buildings of Lafitte's compound and many of his ships were destroyed. Lafitte and his brother, Pierre, disappeared into the swamps.

Andrew Jackson (Courtesy Library of Congress)

Jean Lafitte

Lafitte had been preying on Spanish shipping and other vessels in the Gulf since 1806, under a letter of marque from Latin American countries, which somehow legalized his piracy. His base was at **Barataria** in the swamps to the south of New Orleans.

A constitutional prohibition against the importation of slaves in 1808 played right into Lafitte's hands. At Barataria, he held slave auctions once a week, at which he sold hundreds of slaves who were smuggled into the city. Cutting New Orleans merchants in on his profits from all merchandise made them reticent to prosecute him. At his peak, he had a mansion, a fleet of barges, and 1,000 men at Grand Terre.

Hundreds of tales of Lafitte; his brother, Pierre; Dominique You, a former gunner for Napoleon Bonaparte; and Renato Beluche, a future rear admiral in Gran Colombia's navy and now buried in Venezuela's Pantheon of the Heroes of Independence, have been fictionalized beyond recognition, but no one doubts that the pirate was one of the most colorful characters in New Orleans history (Grummond 1983).

Lafitte's Blacksmith Shop, at 941 Bourbon, was purportedly used by the Lafitte brothers as headquarters for their smuggling operation. Built between 1722 and 1732, it is of briquette entre poteaux *construction.* (Photo by Kathy Chappetta Spiess)

From his blacksmith shop on Bourbon Street, Lafitte plotted his illegal seizures and the sale of contraband.

As early as 1813, Claiborne had issued a proclamation offering a $500 reward for Jean Lafitte's capture. The brazen pirate then issued his own proclamation offering $1,500 for the capture of Governor Claiborne. **Pierre Lafitte** was imprisoned, but Jean organized a jailbreak to free his brother. Somewhere along the line, Jean Lafitte turned patriot. It was at this point that he passed the information on to Claiborne that the British had approached him.

General Jackson was incensed that Lafitte's stronghold had been bombarded by the Americans. He was afraid that now, the pirate would turn against the United States.

In September 1814, General Jackson defeated the British in Mobile, and in October, he turned them back in Pensacola. He received letters from Claiborne explaining his poor defenses, the prevalence of spies, and other problems.

When Jackson received word in November 1814 that British troops were gathering in Jamaica for an invasion of Louisiana, he left for New

Orleans on November 22, just days ahead of the British, arriving in the city on December 2. He began setting up his defenses at once. Batteries and earthworks were erected at the Rigolets Pass, Chef Menteur Road, and the other two forts below the city, one on each side of the river, thus protecting the approaches to the city by water. He then ordered his troops to stand by in Mobile, Natchez, and Baton Rouge in case the British attacked by land.

He recruited every man who could bear arms. He accepted the help of military units comprised of free people of color, who were to distinguish themselves in battle. Then, he invited Lafitte and his pirates to join him in fighting the British, promising full pardons in return for service. Lafitte and his pirates arrived with flint, muskets, and other arms and ammunition.

On December 22, British forces began moving across Lake Borgne to Bayou Bienvenu and set up camp on the Villere Plantation. On the night of December 23, Jackson made a surprise attack on the weary British army. It was a brilliant strategy, and the Villere Plantation was captured.

In the last week of December, the British brought in fresh troops and supplies. Jackson had recruited every available man and put them to work building a line across Chalmette between the river and the swamp, marked off by a wall of cotton bales. Everyone came to help: Choctaw Indians, pirates, free blacks, and Creoles. By the time the British under **Gen. Sir Edward Pakenham** had regrouped, Jackson's line was finished. With a reinforcement of 2,000 Kentuckians, Jackson had about 6,000 men, 3,000 of whom were at Chalmette.

Pakenham's first advance on December 28 was met with heavy American artillery fire and stopped. Then, early on the morning of January 8, 1815, when the fog lifted, the Americans, crouched behind their cotton bales, could see neat lines of brightly clad British soldiers advancing in their direction with drummers, bagpipes, weapons, and ladders to scale the earthworks.

Jackson gave the order to fire, and his Kentuckians with their long rifles fired, reloaded, and fired again. The British line crumbled; Pakenham reassembled his men and charged again, but for the second time, the British troops were mowed down, and Pakenham himself was killed. His major general, John Keane, took up the leadership of the British and drove them back into battle. Once again, they were decimated, as was General Keane. The British broke and ran.

The Battle of New Orleans, engraved by H. B. Hall, 1861 (Courtesy Library of Congress)

Chalmette battlefield, site of the Battle of New Orleans (Photo by Kathy Chappetta Spiess)

When the battle ended, 2,000 British had been killed, and the American army lost 7 men. It was an unexpected and staggering victory. Shallow graves were dug for the British dead, and their wounded were treated in New Orleans hospitals and homes. On January 27, the British left New Orleans, never to return as enemies.

The Battle of New Orleans was unique in American history. It brought together people of many ethnic backgrounds of every social stratum to fight for a common cause, the defeat of the British: Acadians from the bayous, Germans from the German Coast, slaves and free blacks, Creoles, Kentuckians, Tennesseans, and buccaneers from Barataria all manned guns under the oaks at Chalmette. It was there that they amalgamated to become the American Army in New Orleans and proved themselves a force to be reckoned with.

Andrew Jackson, hero of the Battle of New Orleans, later became president of the United States and led the nation into a new era called the Jacksonian democracy.

The British troops then fought against Napoleon, defeating him at Waterloo. Governor Claiborne died two years later at the age of forty-two. Lafitte then moved his privateering operations to Galveston Island from 1816 to 1820. In 1822, Lafitte learned that Simon Bolivar was commissioning private armed vessels into the Colombian state service, though no longer granting letters of marque. On August 19, he was assigned the forty-ton schooner *General Santander*. On February 4, 1823, Jean Lafitte engaged Spanish ships off the coast of Honduras. He was wounded in battle and is believed to have died around February 5, at the age of forty-one. He was buried at sea, although historians continue to speculate about his life and death— and his treasure (William C. Davis 2005).

When news reached New Orleans that Napoleon had escaped from the island of Elba, where he had been exiled, **Mayor Nicholas Girod** offered sanctuary to the deposed ruler. Napoleon, however, regrouped his army, was defeated again, and this time was exiled to St. Helena. Once more, it was announced that Napoleon would be made welcome in the city. The Napoleon House, on Chartres and St. Louis streets, was supposed to have been prepared for his stay while he recruited and planned his next move. The Baratarians, including **Dominique You**, his former gunner, were to rescue him in a ship purchased by a group of wealthy New Orleanians, but just days before their departure, Napoleon died.

We often read that the Battle of New Orleans was the battle that was fought after the war was over, since the **Treaty of Ghent**, Belgium, was signed on December 24, 1814. A delay in communications prevented Pakenham from receiving the news, and so his army attacked at Chalmette. The treaty, however, specified that the fighting was to continue until the treaty had been ratified and exchanged, and it was not ratified until a month after the Battle of New Orleans. Jackson declared that he would remain in New Orleans, that martial law would continue, and that the militia would be kept on the alert until official word came from Washington. On March 13, 1815, word reached New Orleans. Jackson then returned home to Nashville and the British troops left the area.

The Battle of New Orleans broke America away from Europe and denied Britain's hopes for colonial possessions in the New World. The Battle of New Orleans ended an era in the city's history. Survival was no longer the city's main objective—she had survived. No longer a tool of strategy or a pawn of empires, New Orleans was a valued port city in a growing country, willing and able to contribute to the growth and strength of the United States of America.

CHAPTER VI
Progress in a Period of Peace: 1820-60

From 1810 until the Civil War, New Orleans was the largest city west of the Appalachians. Its population tripled in the first seven years as an American city (1803-10). Over the course of the next fifty years, the Crescent City enjoyed a period of growth, expansion, prosperity, and change. New Orleans became a boomtown in a period of peace, reaching for the fulfillment of its destiny.

Favorable circumstances came together between 1820 and 1860 to make the city grow and prosper. The invention of the cotton gin in 1793 and the granulation of sugar in 1795 made these two products inexpensive and available to all. Their production increased a hundredfold, creating a plantation aristocracy in the South. By 1860, 2 million bales of cotton were crossing New Orleans' wharves annually.

The coming of the steamboat presaged a whole new era of transportation and trade. The river became a highway for steamboats laden with cotton, timber, sugar, and other cash crops on their way to Europe and South America and with manufactured goods on their way back.

People of all nationalities and backgrounds crowded the levees and markets, enjoying the new availability of flour, meat, lard, grain, agricultural products, game, and seafood of all kinds. Ships arrived with building materials, lumber, pipes, and lead. The wharves were lined for miles with steamers, schooners, and flatboats.

Steamboats

For a brief time, the inventor of the steamboat, Robert Fulton, and his partner, Robert Livingston (the American negotiator of the Louisiana Purchase), enjoyed a complete monopoly of steamboat commerce on the waters of the West, a privilege they had wrested from the territorial government. In 1814, however, the monopoly was put to the test. Capt. Henry Shreve arrived in New Orleans with his own steamer, the *Enterprise,* and the ship was seized by court order. Gen. Andrew Jackson was in New Orleans at the same time, preparing to defend the city against the British. He sent Captain Shreve and the *Enterprise* upriver for supplies, thereby temporarily averting a showdown. Later, in April 1817, by court order, the Livingston-Fulton monopoly was ended forever.

The Steamboat Era

The Golden Age of steamboating on the Mississippi lasted only fifty years, from 1820 to 1870. Nevertheless, in those years, steamboats won a unique and revered place in American folklore. Authors, poets, and songwriters have made them the settings of their works—and with good reason. They were as ornate as wedding cakes. They rivaled the finest hotels of the times, boasting bars, barbershops, orchestras, lounges, restaurants with gasoliers and the finest china, carpeting, and even their own newspapers. The tall, stately vessels gleamed white in the sun, churning through the muddy Mississippi with their twin paddlewheelers and their double smokestacks. Rooms on steamboats were called staterooms because they were named for states that existed in the period.

The captain ruled his boat like a king, the pilot knew every snag and shoal in the ever-changing river, and the engineer was able to keep the engines churning in spite of all kinds of difficulties. When the steamboat whistle sounded, townspeople rushed to the riverbanks to watch as goods and passengers embarked and disembarked.

Some steamers were of prodigious size. The *Henry Frank* deposited its cargo of 9,226 bales of cotton at the New Orleans levee on April 2, 1881. Hundreds of draymen readied their teams and their floats, or drays, to haul away the flood of merchandise brought downriver on the steamers. Levees were lively with peddlers, female vendors, beggars, and machine pitchmen. According to J. Dallas in the *Levee— Third Municipality in 1854,* "the busy hum of labor, voices of every tongue . . . boxes and bundles, pork and bananas, mules and beautiful women, Yankees and ruffians, Indians and Dutchmen, Negroes and molasses, all huddled together in Babel-like confusion, presenting a picture of life and abundance nowhere else to be seen in the world."

Keelboats, flatboats, and steamboats carried merchandise to New Orleans for decades following the American Revolution. (Courtesy Leonard V. Huber Collection)

The list of riverboat passengers included businessmen, vacationers, and the inevitable gamblers, who made or lost a fortune at the felt card tables of the salons.

Sidewheelers gave way to sternwheelers, which were sturdier, simpler, and more economical to operate, even if they were less beautiful. Steamers that served regular routes were called packets.

During the Civil War, steamboats were replaced by gunboats, and after a brief resurgence following the war, the faster, more functional railroads almost entirely replaced them.

Showboats were floating theaters, offering shows appropriate for the whole family. They presented songs, dances, and dramatic scenes. The first showboats were keelboats and flatboats that drifted downriver with troupes of players. Every showboat had a calliope that called river dwellers to the docks, where actors gave a sample of the treats in store for those who had the price of admission.

Eugene Robinson's Floating Palace of the 1890s consisted of a museum, a menagerie, an aquarium, and an opera. Actors often dropped a line to fish between performances, and more than once, a player missed his cue while landing a catfish.

The showboat operator usually sent an advance man to announce the ship's coming. Although the movie *Showboat* depicted a self-propelled vehicle, showboats were usually towed into ports.

Banking

The growing business activity in the port city caused an increase in the number of banking houses, insurance companies, commission houses, and cotton and sugar factories. As early as 1811, the Bank of New Orleans and the Louisiana Planters Bank were established. By 1827, there were five banks in the city, including a branch of the United States Bank. They were financed by banking institutions in England and the Northeast.

Faubourg Ste. Marie

After two disastrous fires in the Vieux Carré, **Don Beltram (Bertrand) Gravier** decided to subdivide his plantation, which was upriver of Canal Street, and sell it for residential lots. Gravier named the suburb **Faubourg Ste. Marie**, after his wife's patron saint, and it was the first suburb in New Orleans (today's Central Business District). Since Americans populated this suburb, it also became known as the American Sector.

The Americans had come to New Orleans for one reason: to make money. They were enterprising and determined to succeed. They circumvented morality and avoided the penalties of the law, focusing their energies on becoming rich. The Creoles, who enjoyed the leisure of aristocracy and were lethargic by both heredity and environment, scorned their American competitors on the "uptown" side of Canal Street.

Faubourg Marigny

On the downriver, or downtown, side of the Vieux Carré, the plantation of the millionaire playboy **Bernard de Marigny** was subdivided in the early nineteenth century and began developing into a suburb in the 1820s and 1830s.

Bernard de Marigny was the son of **Pierre Philippe de Marigny,** who had accumulated a fortune in the service of Spain and was the grandson of Antoine Philippe de Marigny. He was called in his obituary the "last of the Creole Aristocracy, one who knows how to dispose of a great fortune with contemptuous indifference" (Stanforth 1992). In 1803, when he was fifteen years old, he inherited $7 million but squandered much of it away gambling, entertaining, and enjoying life. He was a raconteur and an incessant gambler, who brought the game of *Hazards* to the city, naming it *le crapaud*, meaning toad or frog, because of the position the players assumed while playing it.

He subdivided his beautiful plantation into what is now Faubourg Marigny. He even named one of the streets "Craps" because of his passion for the game. Later, however, the street name was changed to Burgundy to relieve a source of embarrassment in the delivery of mail to the four churches on the street. Bernard de Marigny died at the age of eighty-three in a two-room apartment with only one servant.

French Creole Plantation Culture

The stories of two other colorful Americans of French descent are classic examples of the extravagant, wealthy characters who were part of the Creole plantation culture.

Gabriel Valcour Aime lived from 1798 to 1867. In the 1830s, he rebuilt a plantation in St. James Parish that was left to him by his father and dated back to the 1790s. Aime was a scientist, planter, financier and philanthropist with an income of well over $100,000 annually. He could serve a ten-course meal with everything ranging from fish to coffee, wine, and cigars, all from his own plantation. He led the way in scientific experimentation with sugarcane cultivation. He also operated a private steamboat from New Orleans for the use of his guests. He became a recluse after his son's death from yellow fever, and he died of pneumonia in 1867.

His estate, which was of Louisiana classic design, was set in the heart of a 9,000-acre plantation. Facing it from a distance, one could see a series of lagoons with stone bridges, gardens where peacocks preened, and a wooded area with rabbits, deer, and kangaroos. The first floor of his home was set out in a diamond design of black and white marble. The second floor was made of stone. There were three great stairways of marble and secret stairways inside the walls. His mansion was called Petit Versailles, an appropriate title for the property of a gentleman referred to as the Louis XIV of New Orleans. The home burned down in the 1920s.

Charles J. Durand was a Creole whose displays of opulence, as well as his life itself, bordered on the fictitious. Yet, they are as often related and as akin to the outlandish deeds of Marigny and Aime as to make us willing to suspend our disbelief.

Arriving in St. Martinville from France in 1820, already an enormously wealthy man, Durand became the owner of thousands of acres of plantation land, which was to be even more valuable later on when it was planted with sugarcane. He built a magnificent home on the **Bayou Teche** with an *allée* of pine and oak trees that extended from the bayou to his mansion, which he called Pine Alley.

After the death of his first wife, who had borne him twelve children, he became inconsolable. He visited her grave each day, swore never to marry again, and even had an iron statue of himself, kneeling, placed before her tomb. Within a year, however, Durand had remarried and, by his second wife, he fathered another dozen children.

In 1850, as the story goes, two of his daughters were to be married on the same day. He imported from China many huge spiders, which he set loose along the *allée* of trees a few days before the wedding so that they had enough time to spin cloudlike webs across the canopy of the natural arcade, which Durand then had sprinkled with gold and silver dust by a number of young slaves with bellows. The 2,000 guests arrived, their gilt-decorated carriages rolling on Persian rugs spread beneath the cathedral-like nave of sparkling webs that floated above them in the breeze.

During the Civil War, Pine Alley was devastated. The slaves ran away, and the Union army stripped the mansion and ruined the crops. The family scattered, and the house began to deteriorate. Some years ago, it was completely demolished. Of the three-mile alley of trees, only a mile remains, leading back from Louisiana Highway 86. Beneath a cathedral-like nave, the effect enhanced by the narrowness of the alley and the height of the trees, the road leads to nothing.

Lafayette's Visit

In 1825, the **Marquis de Lafayette** visited New Orleans, an event that would long be remembered in the city. The legislature appropriated $15,000 to furnish an apartment in the Cabildo for the use of the Revolutionary War hero. He arrived on the steamboat *Natchez* from Mobile. The militia passed in review before him and he was fêted in Caldwell's **American Theater** and the **Théâtre d'Orléans.**

Creoles versus Americans

Between 1825 and 1830, the number of merchants doing business in the city grew from 60 to 272. The number of taverns increased more than 70 percent, a good sign of the prosperity and ebullient spirits of the times. The most impressive gains were made in the **Faubourg St. Mary.**

Within a few years after the Americans began to settle in the area, the value of property equaled that of the Vieux Carré. The Vieux Carré was the retailing center of the city, but importers, exporters, and brokers proliferated in the American Sector.

Competition between Creoles and Americans manifested itself in many ways. The Creoles objected to the use of English as the official language in the city and also in the courts, which they thought showed favoritism to the Americans in their decisions. The Americans, on the other hand, complained that all civic improvements were being made in the Vieux Carré and none in the suburbs.

Each sector had its own public square: the Place d'Armes (later Jackson Square) in the Vieux Carré and Lafayette Square in the American Sector. Each had its opulent residential avenue: Esplanade in the Vieux Carré and St. Charles Avenue in the American Sector. Between 1830 and 1850, magnificent structures rose to change the skyline of the city. In the American Sector, they included the St. Charles Hotel, two blocks above Canal Street; City Hall (now Gallier Hall) on St. Charles Avenue; the University of Louisiana on Common Street; St. Patrick's Church on Camp Street; and the new Custom House at the foot of Canal Street. All dynamically changed the visual features of the area. In the Vieux Carré, the opulence was matched by the St. Louis Hotel on St. Louis Street; the United States Mint at Esplanade Avenue and the river; the Pontalba Buildings flanking the Place d'Armes; and the St. Louis Cathedral, rebuilt in 1850.

Canal Street in 1850, from Chambers' History of Louisiana, *1925* (Courtesy Leonard V. Huber Collection)

The Medical College of Louisiana on Common Street, established in 1834, became part of the University of Louisiana in 1847, when a law school was added. Closed during the Civil War, it later received occasional state appropriations until 1883, when it was the recipient of a huge bequest from Paul Tulane. In 1884, it became Tulane University of Louisiana. In 1984, it moved to St. Charles Avenue. (Courtesy UNO Library)

Nineteenth-Century Architects

The Irish architect **James Gallier, Sr.,** was responsible for many of the magnificent edifices mentioned above, many of which are still revered today. He designed the **St. Charles Hotel** to outdo any other hotel in the world in terms of size and extravagance. It was completed in 1837 at a cost of $600,000. With its white dome, cupola, and flagstaff aloft at 203 feet, it was a commanding landmark, visible for miles upriver and down. Under its rotunda, slave auctions were held regularly.

The **Second Municipality Hall,** later City Hall and today Gallier Hall, was also designed by Gallier in 1845. This building was the seat of government in 1852. Its Ionic portico and Greek details can be matched only by temple-type buildings and churches in the Northeast.

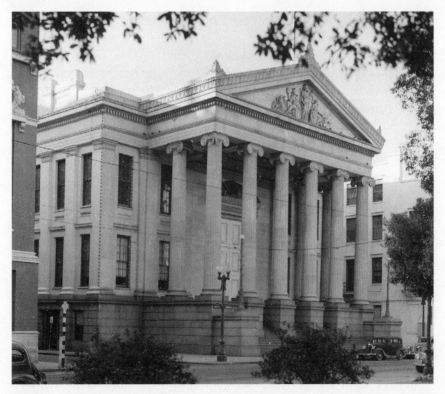

The Second Municipality Building (later City Hall, today Gallier Hall) was built on Lafayette Square, also by Gallier in 1845 (Courtesy Library of Congress)

The **Custom House** with its colossal columns, an **Alexander Thompson Wood** design, is said to have the finest Greek Revival interior in America. Work was begun in 1848, but it was not completed until 1881.

St. Patrick's Church at 724 Camp Street was built by the architect **James H. Dakin** for $115,000. It was built on the site of the small wooden church, which it replaced in 1838. The church far surpassed every attempt at Gothic architecture on this side of the Atlantic.

The Dakin brothers, James Gallier, Sr., and **Henry Howard** were primarily responsible for the spread of the Greek Revival style of architecture in America. New Orleans Greek Revival architecture is comparable in quality to that found anywhere in the United States (Christovich and Toledano 1972).

The Beginnings of Theater in New Orleans

The first theater in New Orleans was started in 1792 by two brothers from Paris, **Jean-Louis Henry** and **Louis-Alexandre Henry.** Their theater was the only one in New Orleans for fifteen years (Le Gardeur 1963). Louis, a carpenter, built the theater near what is now 732 St. Peter Street and acted in the cast for several years. Jean supplied the capital for the venture and became the business manager. According to New Orleans archives, notarial acts were signed in June 1791, transferring a piece of property measuring 64 feet by 128 feet from Louis McCarty to Louis Henry. Henry then sold half the lot, retaining a piece 32 feet by 128 feet on which he built the theater.

The state government issued some interesting regulations for conduct in the theater: "The performance shall never be interrupted by shouting, whistling, or in any other manner that might tend to force an actor to be silent. . . . It is further forbidden to force the actors to repeat their lines. . . . No one shall stand during the performance, nor put on his hat" (Le Gardeur 1963).

In 1793, a certain **Madame Dursoier** was directing the troupe; she had engaged quadroon actresses and was acting in the cast herself. A possibility exists that they all could have been refugees from the riots in Port-au-Prince, Saint Domingue, in 1791 (Le Gardeur 1963). Also in the theater in New Orleans at that time was **Denis-Richard Dechanet Desessarts** (godfather of Jean Henry's son), another actor formerly connected with the Saint Domingue theater.

On May 22, 1796, the one-act comic opera *Silvain* was performed. It was the first recorded operatic performance in the city.

The theater was closed late in 1803 because of insufficient revenues. When it opened in 1804 under the American regime, the cast was made up largely of refugees from Saint Domingue. The continuous history of drama and opera in New Orleans dates from that year.

Louis-Blaise Tabary has long been credited with beginning the theater in New Orleans. This he did not do, according to historian René J. Le Gardeur, Jr., who has made an extensive study of records of the period. Tabary's name first appears in city records in 1806, when he published a prospectus for a new theater to be built on Orleans Street between Royal and Bourbon streets. Governor Claiborne laid the first brick in October 1806, but Tabary had to abandon the project for lack of funds, and it was later taken over by others. This was the **Théâtre d'Orléans,** the first of two by the same name on the same site. Tabary was, however, a pioneer in this effort, and he gave twenty-six years of service to the development of theater in New Orleans, an accomplishment that, in and of itself, is worthy of notice. The second Théâtre d'Orléans opened in 1819 with a performance of *Jean de Paris.*

The old French Opera House, built on the corner of Bourbon and Toulouse in 1859, burned down in 1919. (Courtesy Library of Congress)

For eighteen years, beginning in 1819, **John Davis,** who operated the Théâtre d'Orléans, staged ballets, concerts, operas, and plays in that theater. Davis gave up his control of the opera in 1837.

Meanwhile, in 1835, in the American Sector, **James Caldwell** built the **St. Charles Theater** on St. Charles Avenue near Poydras Street.

Charles Boudousquié was the impresario of the **French Opera House,** which was built in 1859. He brought a troupe that included **Julie Calvé** to the city during that period. The French Opera House, on the corner of Bourbon and Toulouse streets, built by James Gallier, burned to the ground in 1919.

Municipal Developments

By the 1830s, one could ride **"in omnibus"** with a dozen other passengers for one bit (half of a quarter). Such a vehicle ran along Tchoupitoulas Street from New Orleans to Lafayette City, a distance of three miles. The driver, perched high in front, blew a bugle as the signal to start. Passengers could sit inside the carriage or on top.

Banquettes (sidewalks) were made of flatboat gunwales in the 1830s. By the 1850s, some were composed of broad slabs of slate. Streets were of mud or dust, kept in fair condition by chain gangs of convicts.

Sanitary conditions in New Orleans were deplorable until the Civil War. Women vendors in open markets cleaning fowl or fish dropped the entrails onto the earthen floor, where the waste was trodden underfoot. In areas such as Connaught Yard, a collection of boardinghouses on Girod and Julia streets at the river, refuse of every description and "night filth" were thrown daily into the streets from upstairs windows with a prayer that the rain would wash them away. Such areas were extremely prone to disease.

James Caldwell introduced street lighting in the American Sector in the form of gas lanterns suspended on ropes or chains and hung diagonally across intersections from poles. His imported English gas-making machine, which he had used to light his American Theater on Camp Street in 1824, enabled him to begin a gas company that provided street and household lighting to the city.

Railroads and Canals

In 1831, the Pontchartrain Railroad, the first railroad west of the Alleghenies, began running from the lower end of the French Market along Elysian Fields Avenue, all the way from the river to the lake. Businessmen in Faubourg Marigny hoped to develop a port on the lake, but this never materialized. The railroad connected the city with Milneburg, a small community on the south shore of the lake. The train, affectionately called Smoky Mary, chugged and snorted along at the great rate of ten miles per hour, scattering cinders and dust and transporting picnickers to a wharf at the lake's edge. There, several two-room camps, which could be rented by the day, had been built out over the lake on stilts. This route was part of the Louisville and Nashville Railroad.

In 1835, the **New Orleans and Carrollton Railroad** connected the town of Carrollton to New Orleans. It operates today as the St. Charles Streetcar, the oldest continuously operating car line in America.

The New Basin Canal

Perhaps the greatest engineering feat accomplished in the Faubourg St. Mary and certainly the one that would do most for its economy, was the building of the New Basin Canal, which opened for traffic in 1838. Two New Orleans entrepreneurs, **Maunsel White** and **Beverly Chew,** are credited with organizing the New Orleans Canal and Banking Company, which was chartered by the Louisiana legislature in 1831 (when the capital of Louisiana was in Donaldsonville). The company was to build a canal six miles long, sixty feet wide, and six feet deep, at a point "above Gravier Street" to Lake Pontchartrain. There was to be a turning basin at the city's end, allowing ships to return to the lake, bow first.

As the American Sector grew, so did the need for the canal. In 1828, there was not a paving stone in the Faubourg St. Mary. The site of the future St. Charles Hotel was a pool of stagnant water. There was not a wharf in the suburb. Drayage fees from the wharves on the riverfront in the Vieux Carré and from the Carondelet Canal (the Old Basin Canal) were enormous. The Carondelet Canal gave the Creoles access to Bayou St. John and thus to Lake Pontchartrain. It allowed them to control trade with the coastal cities of Biloxi, Mobile, and Pensacola and with cities north of Lake Pontchartrain: Mandeville, Madisonville and Covington.

The population of Faubourg St. Mary continued to expand upriver and farther away from the old canal. It became increasingly difficult for the Americans to use that waterway. A new canal in the American Sector would allow them direct access to Lake Pontchartrain and competition in the Gulf Coast trade.

Work was begun in 1832. The canal took six years to build. It cost $1,119,000, exclusive of the land. It took the lives of 8,000 workers, who died of yellow fever and cholera digging in the mosquito-infested swamps. It was a project of relatively greater difficulty than that of the Panama Canal given the differences in technology and equipment. Altogether, it was an awe-inspiring accomplishment.

There were no dredges in those days, so the digging had to be done with hand shovels. Workers shoveled mud into wheelbarrows, which were rolled up inclined planks to the banks of the canal. The most primitive pumps were constantly in use to keep the ditch free of water. Because dynamite would not be invented until 1867, the ancient roots of the giant, water-soaked cypresses had to be hacked through with hand-axes. Pilings for the wharves were forced into the soil by tons of stone loaded onto their tops.

Laborers, mostly Irish and German immigrants, earned $20 per month plus room, board, and whiskey money, which amounted to an additional $6.25 a month. They worked through the heat and humidity of six interminable New Orleans summers in the swamps of Metairie Ridge.

When the canal was opened in 1838, there was a turning basin, which was located where the Greyhound Bus Station and the Union Passenger Terminal are today. The landing was two blocks wide on Circus Avenue (now Rampart Street) between Julia Street and Triton Walk (now Howard Avenue).

From the beginning, the New Basin Canal flourished. Howard Avenue in the 1850s stretched from the turning basin of the new canal to the river and was lined with business houses of traders, speculators, agents, and merchants dealing in manufactured goods from everywhere in the United States. Merchants ran back and forth between the river and the basin as ships arrived and departed. Itinerant merchants joined their ranks, staying

The New Basin Canal, circa 1929, had its turning basin at South Rampart Street between Howard Avenue and Julia Street. It ran from South Rampart to the lake, 1838-1961. (Courtesy Leonard V. Huber Collection)

at the Washington Hall or Piney Woods Hotel, rushing out to buy and sell "on the levee," where fortunes were made and lost.

Not only businessmen benefited from the New Basin Canal. Pleasure seekers took the ride on mule-drawn barges from the city to the New Lake End, where there was little more than Dan Hickok's Hotel at the site of the present-day Southern Yacht Club. The flag-bedecked boats consisted of a cabin and a covered upper deck. Bands were hired to entertain the passengers. Tolls were collected from pedestrians on Old Shell Road and from boats on the water: 6½ cents for a man on horseback, 12½ cents for a bicycle rider, and 37½ cents per ton of freight on the waterway.

In 1946, a century later, the order came in to fill in the canal to make way for the Pontchartrain Expressway. The work was completed in 1961. A wide, green expanse still exists on the route of the canal between Veterans Highway and Robert E. Lee Boulevard, the only reminder that a canal once ran there.

The Three Municipalities

In anticipation of the New Basin Canal's completion, businessmen of Faubourg St. Mary requested a charter in 1836 for an independent city, such as had been granted in 1832 to the city of Lafayette. Alternatives were discussed, but the differences between the Creoles and the Americans had only sharpened into hostility in the past several years. In 1836, the municipal government of the city of New Orleans ceased to exist. The city split into three autonomous municipalities, each with its own recorder, who was the chief executive in his own municipality, and its own council. Each handled its own affairs, improvements, and taxes. Once a year, the general council, composed of aldermen from the three municipalities, met with the mayor in the Cabildo, to deal with matters having to do with the city as a whole (parish prison, old debts, license revenues, etc.).

The Vieux Carré was the First Municipality, Faubourg St. Mary was the Second, and Faubourg Marigny was the Third. Faubourg Marigny was less affluent than the other two. There was also less rivalry between Faubourg Marigny and the Vieux Carré, because many of the residents of Faubourg Marigny were displaced Creoles.

By 1852, it was clear that such an arrangement was both inefficient and expensive. All jobs and efforts had to be duplicated. Tension among the communities had relaxed somewhat, so the municipalities reunited by a charter of the legislature. Faubourg St. Mary became the First District of the City of New Orleans; the Vieux Carré, the Second District; and Faubourg Marigny, the Third. Under the same charter, the city of Lafayette was annexed and became the Fourth District.

The new government was bicameral, with two chambers: one of aldermen, elected by the districts, the other of assistant aldermen, elected by the wards. This system continued until 1870, though suspended in 1862, when Union forces took control of the city. The American Sector, with its steamboat traffic on the New Basin Canal and its thriving commercial enterprises, had sufficient influence in 1852 to have the seat of government moved from the Cabildo in the Vieux Carré to the Second Municipality Hall on St. Charles Avenue (thereafter called City Hall, now called Gallier Hall).

Irish and German Immigrants

The two largest groups of immigrants to settle in New Orleans in the two decades before the Civil War were the Irish and the Germans.

Before 1820, the Irish are hard to trace in population figures, since ports in the New World lumped British, Irish, and Scottish immigrants all together. From 1846 to 1856, because of the famines in Ireland, one-third of the immigrants entering America were Irish. By 1860, there were 25,000 Irish living in New Orleans.

The Irish vied with the blacks for jobs digging ditches, collecting refuse, or stevedoring on the riverfront. As a group, they were viewed with disdain, not only because of the work they did but also because they were rowdy, boisterous, clannish, hot tempered, hard drinking, and always eager for a fight. Their intemperate dispositions had been honed on the razor edge of hunger.

Besides the Irish colonies already mentioned on Tchoupitoulas, Julia, and Girod streets near the riverfront, many of the Irish settled in an area now referred to as the **Irish Channel,** which is in the lower Garden District. The New Orleans Historic District Landmarks Commission defines the boundaries of the Irish Channel as Magazine Street, Delachaise Street, Tchoupitoulas Street, and Jackson Avenue (Historic District Landmarks Commission 2011).

Actually, the Irish Channel was originally only one street—Adele Street—that ran two blocks from St. Thomas Street to Tchoupitoulas Street and lay between Josephine Street and St. Andrew Street.

One version of how it got its name is from the story of the Irish seamen coming up the river, who would see the light outside **Mike Noud's Ocean Home** saloon on Adele Street and cry out, "There's the Irish Channel!" Another version is that Adele Street often flooded after a rain. In reality, it was probably called the Irish Channel because so many Irish lived there.

In 1850, an Irishman could earn five dollars per day as a "screwman" on the riverfront, "screwing," or packing, cotton into the ship's hold. Their reputation as fighters often made the difference in obtaining these coveted jobs. Many claimed to be Irish even if they weren't, so as to be thought handy with their fists.

The Irish lived simply in small cottages. Often, when Creoles abandoned their big homes on the riverfront to build finer mansions on St. Charles Avenue, the Irish moved into these riverfront homes. In time, they became known as the "lace-curtain" Irish.

Irish families were large, and their food was coarse but wholesome: corned beef and cabbage, Irish stew, potato pancakes, and red beans and rice. The neighborhood itself was respectable, but the riverfront saloons gave it a bad reputation: Mike Noud's Ocean Home, the

Bull's Head Tavern, and the Isle of Man. Today, Parasol's Bar on Constance Street represents that green channel and entices Irishmen to celebrate their heritage.

One field in which the Irish excelled was fighting. The first official prizefight in New Orleans was between **James Burke** (alias Deaf) and **Sam O'Rourke** on May 6, 1836. Burke operated a club, the Boxiana, in which he taught the art of self-defense. **John L. Sullivan** trained at Carrollton Gardens. New Orleans was host to a fight between Sullivan and Jim Corbett in 1892 in the Olympic Club on Royal Street; Corbett won. They fought with gloves, because bare-knuckled boxing had been outlawed. In 1889, in Richburg, Mississippi, Sullivan fought an illegal fight of seventy-five rounds with Jack Kilrain. Most of the fans had come from New Orleans. The referee was **John Fitzpatrick,** who later became mayor of New Orleans.

Sir Henry Morton Stanley (1841-1904), the reporter who discovered explorer David Livingstone in Africa on November 10, 1871, had a home on the site of the orange groves of the Jesuit Plantation on Orange Street. Born in Denbigh, Wales, and christened John Rowlands, he was orphaned early. At the age of seventeen, he sailed to New Orleans, where he was adopted by Henry Morton Stanley, who gave him his name.

The statue of **Margaret Gaffney Haughery** (1813-82) honors the second woman in the U.S. to have a statue erected in her honor. The statue can be found in a triangular park bounded by Camp, Prytania, and Clio streets. It is the seated image of a woman sculpted in Carrara marble. The woman, in a calico dress and shawl, looks down on a child leaning against her. It bears the simple inscription, *Margaret.* After the death of her husband and child, Margaret Haughery devoted herself to doing good works and helping orphaned children. She established a dairy and bakery, both of which brought in unexpected profits. She gave most of her earnings to the poor. She signed her name with an *X,* never having learned to read or write, and at her death, she left $30,000 to charity. With this bequest, **St. Theresa's Orphanage** on Camp Street was begun.

In the 1840s, the largest number of Germans arrived in New Orleans. By 1860, there were almost twenty thousand Germans living in the city. The first German immigrants came to Louisiana in the colonial days in response to John Law's circulars. We have seen that they settled in what was to be known as the German Coast, which ran

Statue of Margaret Haughery—Friend of Orphans, sitting on an old chair and dressed in her familiar calico gown with her shawl over her shoulders (Photo by Kathy Chappetta Spiess)

from what is now Norco to Reserve, partly in St. John the Baptist Parish and partly in St. Charles Parish, on both sides of the Mississippi River. These Germans knew how to make use of the lushness of the land and farmed it successfully.

Many Germans spread into neighboring parishes: St. James, Assumption, Ascension, and Iberville. They spread into Donaldsonville and settled on Bayou Lafourche, marrying into Acadian families. Over time, great cultural changes occurred among these descendants of the early Germans. They spoke French fluently and were often confused about their ancestry, trying to trace their origin as Cajuns and discovering their German background. Over the generations, the name Foltz became Folse; Herbert became Hebert.

One of the reasons for this shift is believed to be that after the Thirty Years' War, the Germans who inhabited the Palatinate of southwest Germany lived in such abject poverty for the next fifty years that it is unlikely there were any schools. Many of the German immigrants to the New World probably could not write their names. Some may not even have pronounced them correctly but according to the dialect of the area. French and Spanish immigration officials wrote names as they heard them. Thus, Chaigne became Schoen. A German named Zweig might point to a limb of a tree to tell the meaning of this name and a French official might write Labranche, christening Zweig forevermore with a new French name.

In 1848, many waves of German immigrants came to America to escape political turmoil and revolution in Germany. Many were professionals and well educated. Many were redemptioners, immigrants who worked off their passage as metalworkers, draymen, brewmasters, carpenters, and bricklayers.

Germans were the largest group of foreign-speaking people in New Orleans from 1848 to 1900. They lived in Carrollton, Lafayette City, the Ninth Ward, and Mechanicsville (Gretna).

Because of the large German population, beer making became an important industry. One beer garden located on Bayou St. John named Tivoli was described as having "a large yard shaded by trees . . . little rustic tables and benches . . . beer men . . . with beer jugs . . . an orchestra . . . five cents is paid by each male partner for the privilege of a waltz . . . the 'frauen' pay nothing, heaven bless them!" (Merrill 2005, 170).

Between 1850 and 1855, 126,000 Germans came through the port of the city. Most of them did not stay in New Orleans but moved on to towns where land was cheaper and there was no annual threat of yellow fever. Competition with slave labor was discouraging to newcomers. Slaves in New Orleans were often leased by their owners. With jobs hard to find, many Germans moved on to Texas, Arkansas, Central America, and other places south and west.

From 1876 to 1880, **Fritz Jahncke** constructed the first paved streets of the city. Canal Street and others had previously been paved with Belgian block, cobblestones, or flatboat wood. He also brought about the formation of the Sewerage and Water Board and developed the New Basin Canal, bringing in sand and shells from Lake Pontchartrain.

Other famous Germans to come to New Orleans were
- **Philip Werlein** in 1853, who published Dan Emmet's composition "Dixie";
- **Peter Laurence Fabacher** in 1891, a brewer;
- **Jacob Schoen,** a mortician; and
- **Ashton Frey,** a butcher in the French Market.

All of these men served on the board of the Jackson Brewery, which thrived in the city from 1891 until the 1970s.

The Land of "Dixie"

Mention of the song "Dixie" should not be dismissed without a word about the derivation of the word. It was originally a nickname for New Orleans, a variation of the word *dix,* what people called the ten-dollar bill printed in the 1800s for use in New Orleans. One side of the bill indicated the denomination in English: ten; the other side, in French: *dix* (pronounced "deess" by the French but "dix" by the Americans). Since New Orleans was the only place the dix was used, it was New Orleans that was referred to as "Dixie."

"Dixie" was not the only music tied to New Orleans at this time. **Louis Moreau Gottschalk** (1829-69), a Creole of German and French descent, was considered the leading pianist-composer of his day. He gave concerts throughout the world. *The Dying Poet* and *The Lost Hope* are probably his most famous works. He also wrote "La Bamboula" from memories of the music and dancing of the slaves in Congo Square.

The Yugoslavs

The Yugoslavs of Orleans and Plaquemines parishes have prospered as a result of their cultivation of the Louisiana oyster. They came from Yugoslavia to New Orleans, San Francisco, and New York in the middle of the nineteenth century, seeking freedom from oppression and better economic conditions. They lived near the French Market for a time. Later they found in the Plaquemines area brackish water with the right mixture of fresh and salt water to produce good oysters. Over time, they developed techniques to improve the quality of the oysters. For more than one hundred years, they have been oystermen on the aquatic boundaries of our state: the Atchafalaya River, the Sabine River, and the Pearl River. They settled in Plaquemines Parish toward the mouth of the river and cultivated the Louisiana oyster in Bayou Cook, Bayou Chutte, and Grand Bayou.

Slavery

Blacks were a large part of the population of the city. They came first with Bienville as slaves for his colony to join forces with the Indians, the earliest slaves in New Orleans.

Slaves came to New Orleans and Louisiana from West Africa, Haiti, Belize, Virginia, and South Carolina. They arrived at Algiers Point, across the river from New Orleans.

Algiers Point, on the west bank of the river, had been granted to the city-founder, Bienville, in 1719, when a slave corral was housed on the Point, and African slaves were sold from it to the colonists. The Point was also the site of the French colony's slaughterhouse and was sometimes called **Slaughterhouse Point** during the colonial period. Powder Street in Algiers Point is evidence that colonists also held their powder magazines there. It was probably named for the original Algiers, from which pirates terrorized the Mediterranean Sea. A ferry route between Algiers and New Orleans was established in 1827, and Algiers began to develop; by 1870, it was named the Fifth District of New Orleans.

The slaves in New Orleans and their white masters exchanged cultural modes of expression and began a process of amalgamation early in the city's history, although this process was delayed in other parts of the South. The paternalistic French and Spanish rulers encouraged African culture among their slaves, allowing West African dancing, music, cooking, and architecture to survive without interference. In addition, New Orleans slaves, living in such close proximity to their white masters in a city of limited size surrounded by water, experienced a greater knowledge of the whites than the plantation slave did, and in the city, the two cultures overlapped.

In New Orleans, slavery was viewed with a unique attitude. A slave was bought for his brawn, which enabled him to work, but he was also appreciated for his cuisine, his humor, and his many cultural aptitudes.

The term "black" does not accurately describe the African Americans of our state or city, in the beginning or today. After the Haitian insurrection in 1791, incoming free people of color (*gens de couleur*) ranged in their racial mix. A number of terms developed to distinguish heritage, including mulattoes (half-black), quadroons (one-quarter black), and octoroons (one-eighth black). The term "café au lait" was used to describe people with a lighter skin tone, meaning coffee with cream or black with white.

A slave coming to New Orleans did not necessarily remain a slave. Occasionally, he was manumitted by his master to enter free society as an indentured servant. On rare occasions, he could work off his slavery as a redemptioner.

In New Orleans, both black people and white people owned slaves. Slaves were called "blacks"; free persons of color were called "colored." Africans, who appeared to the white citizens as brutes upon arrival in the city, could become transformed into dutiful Christians and skilled laborers.

Slaves were identified as Africans and Creoles. The former had been born in Africa and transported to America. The latter were children of Africans who had been born in Louisiana. In addition, if a slave was from Louisiana, he was referred to as a Creole slave, meaning simply a native of Louisiana. (Sometimes the term was confused and thought to refer strictly to a black person, but that is not accurate.)

In the city, there were many free blacks with slaves of their own. Between 1804 and 1809, many free persons of color came to Louisiana from their homeland in Saint Domingue to escape hostile action by the island's ex-slaves following the bloody slave insurrection of 1791. This more than doubled Louisiana's free black population.

"The slaves of New Orleans were perhaps the most sophisticated group of bondsmen since the days of ancient Rome" (Taylor 1984). Many were tradesmen who were working off their slavery and could foresee a free future for themselves and their families. In order to earn money, slaves could rent themselves out for hire on Sundays, as dictated by the *Code Noir*. The "Slave for a Day" rental service was generally frequented by country patrons who did not wish to bring their slaves with them to the city.

The invention of the cotton gin in 1793 by **Eli Whitney** fastened slavery onto the South. An institution that would have died out because of its cost, which was insupportable, now became a feasible investment. The free labor of slaves, together with a machine that could clean cotton as fast as fifty men working by hand, was to make cotton king of the South and create a Southern aristocracy of planters.

By 1860, approximately 25,000 blacks lived in New Orleans. Of these, 11,000 were slaves, owned by whites or free blacks. Some were awaiting sale on the auction blocks at the Cabildo, the St. Charles or St. Louis hotels, or Maspero's Exchange on Chartres Street. To make them appear more attractive, slave dealers sometimes dressed the men in top hats and evening clothes and the women in long dresses and *tignons*.

Slaves brought into Eastern ports, such as those in Virginia, South Carolina, and Georgia, were frequently sold down the river in New Orleans. The expression had ominous overtones. Many discovered on arrival, however, that for a slave, it was a better place to live than most other Southern cities. They enjoyed a mixture of people, excitement, and places of amusement (such as Place Congo, or Congo Square, where they danced on Sunday afternoons). They liked shopping for their masters in the colorful markets and shops. They enjoyed the looseness of the reins that held them in captivity and the hope that they could buy or earn their freedom.

John McDonogh

A Scotsman born in Baltimore, John McDonogh was one of the city's outstanding philanthropists. He was a founder of the American Colonization Society, which assisted 300 slaves in New Orleans in obtaining their freedom. Freedom could be purchased, worked for, or simply granted. In some cases, the state legislature granted freedom to slaves for some particular service.

John McDonogh owned a plantation in Algiers. He bought slaves, but unlike other slave-owners, he did not sell them. Instead, he educated them in a craft and then freed them. He helped many freed slaves leave Louisiana. Almost two decades before the Civil War, he helped eighty of his liberated slaves make their departure for Africa. He saw to it that they had money, clothes, household goods, and farm tools to establish themselves there as free men. Others worked for him as free men on his sugar plantation under the supervision of other blacks. He treated them all like human beings, and for this, he was called a radical. When he died in 1850, his estate was valued at $2 million. He left $700,000 to the cities of New Orleans and Baltimore for schools for the poor.

Free Men of Color

From the time of the Spanish period, free men of color enjoyed both economic and educational advantages in New Orleans. They had full freedom to conduct business and enter into contracts. Free blacks even had their own schools. They added substantially to the literate sector of Louisiana. By 1803, there were 1,355 free men of color out of a population of 10,000. Some of the men were tailors, mechanics, carpenters, or owners of small businesses. Some opened schools or performed in theaters. They were sober, law-abiding, and industrious. In 1860, the holdings of free men of color in New Orleans were between $13 million and $15 million. There were, at this time, 114,000 free persons of color in a population of 168,000 in New Orleans.

Free women of color were among the most beautiful women in New Orleans. Some of them lived as concubines with white men. In 1792, an ordinance was passed forcing them to become more recognizable as women of color by wearing a headdress known as a *tignon*. It became a mark of distinction rather than the branding it was intended to be. Surviving portraits of free women of color picture them in black dresses with white lace shawls and tignons.

Concubinage between black women and white men, a custom called *plaçage* (from the French verb *placer*, meaning to put or place), was a common practice in the late seventeenth and early eighteenth centuries. It was an understanding whereby a white man, usually a French colonist, and a mulatto woman, the *placée,* lived together more or less permanently. Arrangements were made between the mother of the eligible black woman and the white man to set up the daughter in a house. Sometimes this arrangement included slaves, carriages, and all the accoutrements of the wealthy. She would be the young man's mistress, usually until the gentleman married, at which time the house and all of its contents belonged to the mulattress for life. Any offspring were the responsibility of the man: boys were sent to Paris to be educated, and girls were sent to the Ursuline convent for their schooling. Faubourg Marigny and the French Quarter including Rampart Street were the sites for these houses.

According to some historians, the **Orleans Ballroom** (as well as other locations in the French Quarter) regularly held the famous Quadroon Balls, which were frequented by gentlemen seeking such arrangements. All was handled discreetly, with care taken to protect both parties as to laws and obligations.

Many of the progeny of these relationships moved on to live in Mexico, Haiti, or Paris, passing as whites. From these alliances came many remarkable people:

Norbert Rillieux, a free man of color born in 1806, son of a wealthy French engineer and a slave. While a student in Paris (1830-32), he discovered the multiple evaporation process of making sugar.

Eugene Warburg, the eldest son of Daniel Warburg, a German Jew, and Marie Rosa, a slave of Santiago, Cuba (whom Daniel Warburg freed), was a noted sculptor. His most famous work is the 1855 bust of the U.S. minister of France, John Young Mason.

Julien Hudson, a free man of color, was a portrait painter before the Civil War.

Henriette Delille (1813-62), a beautiful free woman of color, was the founder of the order of the Sisters of the Holy Family. The nuns lived at the site of the former Quadroon Balls in a building donated to the order by a free man of color, **Thomas Lafon.** (Today, at that same location is the Bourbon-Orleans Hotel.) Lafon is the only free man of color of whom a bust was made because of his generosity to his fellow men.

James Durham was sold as a slave to a New Orleans physician who taught him medicine and set him free in 1788 to become a physician for both blacks and whites.

Voodoo

Voodoo was a dominant force among the black population of New Orleans in the second half of the nineteenth century. It came to the colony from West Africa when the first Africans were brought over as slaves. The practice spread and intensified when black immigrants from Haiti arrived at the beginning of the nineteenth century. These Haitians, whose ancestors were also from Africa, believed strongly in voodoo and practiced it as a religion. They were allowed much freedom of personal expression by paternalistic rulers and lethargic owners.

The Haitians, when living in Saint Domingue, believed in voodoo gods and zombies (soulless human corpses taken from the grave and transformed by the voodoos into living creatures). In New Orleans, the voodoos had to make changes in their rituals to appeal to the needs and beliefs of the local populace.

Marie Laveau

Marie Laveau, the most famous of all New Orleans voodooiennes, lived in the same cottage at 1020 St. Ann Street for fifty years, conducting rituals in her yard in which she danced with a snake, which she called Zombi. After her sensuous exhibition, her performers (young men and women) danced practically in the nude, consumed large quantities of rum taffia, drank blood from the broken necks of roosters, swooned, trembled, and indulged in sexual intimacies.

Once a year, on St. John's Eve, June 23, a more elaborate version of the same ceremony took place near the old Spanish Fort at the point where Bayou St. John flowed into Lake Pontchartrain. It was a mixture of Christianity and barbarity, and most citizens considered it a blasphemy, but it attracted hundreds of viewers, including members of the police and the press.

Marie Laveau's fame spread as a fortuneteller, mind reader, and dispenser of love charms and satanic potions, and she was sought out by rich and poor, blacks and whites, for advice on personal matters and local and national political concerns.

Laveau was a free mulatto born in New Orleans in 1794. Many

In a voodoo ceremony in New Orleans, slaves dance the Bamboula, which inspired the song by the famous New Orleans composer, Louis Moreau Gottschalk. Illustration by E. W. Kemble (1861-1933).

accounts indicate that her father had been a wealthy white planter and her mother a mulatto with a strain of Indian blood. She was married to **Jacques Paris** in 1819 by Père Antoine. Both she and Jacques were recorded as free persons of color. Her life is shrouded in mystery. Although she earned great sums of money, she never lived as a woman of means. Her husband died three years after their marriage.

Marie Laveau began the practice of voodoo around 1826, changing the cult to a profitable business, selling charms, favors, and prophecies but retaining the showmanship necessary to keep the faith of her followers. To the hedonistic exhibitions, she added statues of saints, incense, and holy water for the benefit of the Catholics in her flock.

She later formed a liaison with **Christophe Glapion,** a union that produced fifteen children. Glapion stayed behind the scenes, possibly acting as her bookkeeper. She is said to have died at the age of eighty-seven.

Laveau's tomb is said to be in St. Louis Cemetery No. 1 and, indeed, there is a tomb with the inscription "Veuve [widow] Paris." However, it is also said that the voodoo queen is buried in her second husband's family tomb, the Glapions. Still others say that Laveau is buried in another tomb, along with her daughter, Marie Laveau II.

Voodoo charms can be found at the Voodoo Museum at 724

Dumaine Street. Love powders, boss-fixing powders, money-drawing incense, and come-to-me powders can be purchased there, as well as effigies, lotions, and charms. The museum is purported to be the only one of its kind in the country.

Jews in New Orleans

Although the **Black Code** of 1724 (the **Code Noir**) governed the treatment of slaves, its first article decreed that Jews be expelled from the Louisiana colony. It was a strange article not only because it appeared in the Black Code but also because there was no evidence that Jews were even in the colony.

In 1758, there is recorded an argument between Governor Kerlérec and his **Intendant, Vincent de Rochemore,** concerning the admittance of a ship, the *Texel,* whose captain was a Jew named Diaz. Rochemore declared that it was illegal for the ship to dock. Kerlérec wanted the goods on board. Kerlérec prevailed, and a Jew entered the colony.

In 1801, a remarkable Jewish gentleman arrived in the colony: **Judah Touro** (1775-1854). His business was wholesale consignment; he was an ice importer. By 1838, he was the owner and operator of two icehouses. A man generous to the community throughout his lifetime, he remained a bachelor and lived with two other bachelors at 35 Conde Street, an extension of Chartres Street. Some of his fellow boarders were **Jean Baptiste Olivier,** chaplain of the Ursulines, and **Alexander Milne,** who started the community on the lakefront and left funds with which the Milne Boys Home was built.

Judah Touro's total estate at the time of his death was $928,774. His beneficiaries were in Boston, Newport, and New Orleans and included Christians and Jews alike. In his lifetime, he purchased many slaves for the purpose of freeing them. He gave liberally to numerous charities, including the Touro-Shakespeare Home, Touro Infirmary, and Touro Synagogue, which bear his name.

Other notable Jewish citizens include:

- **Samuel Hermann,** builder of the Hermann-Grima House on St. Louis Street;
- **Judah P. Benjamin** (1811-80), Confederate secretary of war and state who, after being exiled, lived in England and gained international fame as a lawyer;

- **Martin Behrman,** born in New York in 1864 and elected mayor of New Orleans in 1904, a post he held for seventeen years (not consecutively), a citywide record.

The Baroness de Pontalba and the Pontalba Apartments

Micaela Almonester was born in 1795, when her father, **Don Andrès Almonester,** was seventy years old. Almonester, a widower, married a French Creole, twenty-nine-year-old Louise de la Ronde, in 1787. Two years after Micaela's birth, her sister Andrea was born. Andrea died at the age of four, leaving Micaela the only heiress to her father's vast estate.

Micaela's name and fame have survived so many generations due to the apartment buildings she constructed flanking the Place d'Armes, and it would be well here to trace the history of that property. In the century and a quarter after de La Tour, the French military engineer who sketched the first plans for officers' lodgings on the Pontalba site in 1721, buildings rose and fell in that location. When fire, rains, or hurricanes destroyed the structures, they were quickly replaced: first, a barracks, used as a place of worship until the first parish church was constructed; a warehouse; quarters for employees of the Government House; a residence for the governor; and finally, barracks for French soldiers and sailors. After the Spanish flag was raised over the Place d'Armes, the residence of Don Andrès Almonester was built

Portrait of Micaela Almonester, Baroness de Pontalba, who built the apartments flanking Jackson Square, now a historical monument of the city (Courtesy Leonard V. Huber Collection)

on the site. Before his death in 1798, when Micaela was three, he acquired all the land on both sides of the square. It was the choicest real estate in the city, and its use would be determined by his widow and his daughter, the indomitable Micaela.

In 1804, Almonester's widow married **Jean Baptiste Castillon**, the French consul of New Orleans. He died five years later. Madame Castillon was now a wealthy woman, who controlled the estates of both of her former husbands by the community property law and also the properties they had given her or she acquired.

On October 23, 1811, when Micaela was sixteen, she was married to **Joseph Xavier Celestin Delfau de Pontalba,** her twenty-year-old cousin. He was the son of **Baron Joseph Xavier Delfau de Pontalba** of Mont L'Evêque, France. Celestin, or Tin-Tin, as he was called, came over from France for the wedding, having never seen his bride before. Both Celestin and Micaela were heirs to enormous fortunes as well as to a barony, and nothing else mattered. The wedding had been arranged by their parents.

The young couple went to Europe on their honeymoon, accompanied by both mothers. If ever a couple was suited to such an arrangement, it was Micaela and Tin-Tin. The Ursuline nuns had educated Micaela and she was therefore very sheltered. Never "pretty," she was strong willed and intelligent. At the time of her wedding, she was childish in her dress and habits. She wore her hair in pigtails until the day she married and played with dolls on her wedding day. Celestin was her exact opposite. He was handsome (prettier than the bride, some said) but a weakling. He was spoiled by his mother and ruled with an iron hand by his father. Once again, in marriage, he was to be dominated by a determined, headstrong personality: Micaela.

Celestin's father was born in Louisiana and educated in France. Like Almonester, he was a real-estate genius who accumulated a fortune in rental property.

Micaela loved the activity and gaiety of Paris far better than the quiet of Château Mont l'Evêque, which Celestin's father had built and considered the family home. During the early years of their marriage, Micaela had three sons: Celestin, Alfred, and Gaston. When she was pregnant with her first son, her husband requested that she sign a contract, a "project of testament" (prepared, no doubt, by his father), which put claims on her fortune in case she died in childbirth. She would not sign it. Arguments followed. This was the beginning of the end of the Pontalba marriage. Money and property had always kept the two families wary of each other.

Twice Celestin left Micaela. In 1831, she sailed to Louisiana without him and wrote that she was beginning proceedings for a divorce. Later, she returned to France, and her son, Celestin, now seventeen, ran away from military school to live with his mother. Hearing this, his grandfather, the baron, now eighty-one years old, dropped the boy from his will. In an attempt at reconciliation, Micaela drove to Mont l'Evêque on October 18, 1834. She lodged in a "little château reserved for the use of visitors."

The day after she arrived, the baron, waiting until she was alone, went into her lodging, walked upstairs and into her room, and locked the door. Immediately, he shot three balls into her chest, followed by two more, which missed. While he was priming the pistol, Micaela found the strength to open the door and run to the floor below, where she collapsed. The baron, thinking her dead, closed himself in the room once again and fired two shots into his heart, which proved fatal.

The scandal rocked Paris and New Orleans. Micaela, now Baroness de Pontalba, having inherited the title, received four chest wounds, two of which were serious, and lost two fingers of her left hand trying to protect herself; yet this incredible woman lived to the age of seventy-eight and was yet to accomplish her most memorable undertaking. In 1848, she returned to New Orleans to begin working on her buildings.

The buildings were designed by James Gallier. However, Gallier and the baroness disagreed, and in 1849, she turned over the contract to a builder named Samuel Stewart. The architect Henry Howard also played a part. The baroness, Howard said, was not altogether satisfied with the drawings; she called at his office to ask him to make a complete set of plans for the building. He asked for $500. She refused. He finally agreed to a fee of $120 without specifications.

The buildings were constructed of dark red brick with cast-iron-decorated balconies, probably the first in New Orleans. The design for the ironwork was done by Waldemar Talen, who had also done the ironwork for Nottoway Plantation on River Road.

The contract for the buildings called for sixteen houses fronting on the Place d'Armes on St. Peter Street for a price of $156,000 using Howard's plans with Gallier's specifications. Micaela designed the *A-P* (Almonester-Pontalba) monogram assisted by Talen, who made the drawings. The monogram is still prominent in the cast-iron railings.

The Pontalba Apartments have changed little since the baroness built them in 1849. (Photo by Kathy Chappetta Spiess)

When the uptown side was finished in the fall of 1850, the baroness and her two sons moved into the third house from Decatur Street. In 1851, the downtown side was finished at a cost of $146,000. She had talked the builders into accepting $10,000 less on the second contract.

The city undertook the renovations of the Place d'Armes, contracting for an iron fence, which still surrounds the square.

When the St. Ann Street apartments were complete, there were sixteen buildings on each side of the square, with party walls between them, to be used as stores downstairs and handsome residences above, as they still are used today. Each house had an entrance on the street leading to an inside staircase and to a courtyard and service area in the rear. The stores were generally rented to different tenants than the houses and had their own entrances. The second floor consisted of a *salon* with guillotine windows opening onto a balcony overlooking the square and a dining room. The third floor was designed for family bedrooms and the attic for servants' rooms.

To the baroness's good fortune, Jenny Lind visited the city just when the buildings were completed in 1851. P. T. Barnum, the circus impresario, was her sponsor; he arranged for her to do thirteen concerts in New Orleans. She arrived in New Orleans from Cuba on the steamer *Falcon,* and as her ship approached the wharf, cheering crowds, estimated at ten thousand people, gathered to see the famous singer. One of the Pontalba houses had been reserved for her use, complete with the silver nameplate on the door. They traveled in carriages from the wharf as the crowds pressed around them. Jenny Lind was delighted with her apartment, and she received applause every time she stepped out onto the balcony. After Miss Lind departed, Baroness Pontalba had the furniture from her apartment sold at an auction, bringing in a total of $3,060.50.

Jackson Square

While the second set of row houses was still under construction, improvements began on the Place d'Armes. In 1851, the name of the Square was changed to Jackson Square in honor of the hero of the Battle of New Orleans. In 1840, Jackson had visited New Orleans and laid the cornerstone where a monument to him was to be erected. A decade later, spurred on by improvements all around the square, the Jackson Monument Association renewed its efforts and the legislature appropriated $10,000 toward the project. In 1856, **Clark Mills'** equestrian statue of Jackson was unveiled.

Until the Baroness de Pontalba's apartments were built, the Cabildo and the Presbytère had only two floors. The old Spanish roofs leaked and needed repairs, so the City Council decided to add a third story to the two buildings with a mansard or French roof and dormers. Flatboat wood was used in the construction. This addition gave the entire square a more balanced effect.

In March 1852, the baroness and her two sons left New Orleans for France, never to return. She died in Paris in 1874. Her former husband outlived her by four years. They are both buried at Château Mont l'Evêque, near Senlis, France.

In 1921, the Pontalba heirs, seventeen in number, sold the buildings on St. Ann Street for $68,000 to **William Ratcliff Irby,** who willed it to the Louisiana State Museum. In 1920, the St. Peter Street building was sold to Danziger, Dreyfous, and Runkel for $66,000. They sold it in 1930 to the Pontalba Building Museum Association for $200,000. The association turned it over to the city.

The Pontalba Apartments are often called the first apartment houses in the United States, but there is no proof of this claim. They are beautifully designed and planned, an outstanding work of architecture and one of the nation's foremost historic monuments.

The Garden District

The land grant given Bienville when he was governor was an enormous territory bounded by the river and what is now Claiborne Avenue, Canal Street, and Nine Mile Point, the bend in the river beyond Carrollton in what is today Jefferson Parish (Stahl 2009).

Shortly after the Company of the Indies made the grant, however, Bienville was notified that such grants were no longer to be made to governors unless the land was used as a vegetable garden. Bienville immediately had a portion of the concession (from Common Street to Felicity Street) planted with vegetables, which reduced the size of his plantation. His house was near the present intersection of Magazine and Common streets.

Later, when Bienville left the colony for France, he gave his property to the Jesuit priests, who raised sugarcane in the area where the Jesuit Church (Immaculate Conception) is today on Baronne Street. In 1763, when the Jesuits were expelled, their property was confiscated and sold at auction in parcels. This is how the piece of land we today call the Central Business District came to be owned by Don Beltram (Bertrand) Gravier when the fire devastated the Vieux Carré in 1788. His subdivision of the property created the city's first formally developed suburb. Originally Ville Gravier, it was later named Faubourg Ste. Marie and then Faubourg St. Mary.

German families had settled to farm the rest of Bienville's original claim, but many left in the wakes of flood and fevers, headed for communities upriver. By 1740, many segments of this land had been sold in tracts, which became riverfront plantations belonging to the families of d'Hauterive, Broutin, Darby, Carrière, and Livaudais. These plantations became, in time, three communities called Nuns, Lafayette, and Livaudais. In 1832, the three communities were incorporated by an act of the state legislature into the city of Lafayette. Eleven years later, the city of Lafayette took in a small settlement on its upper edges, the Faubourg de Lassaiz, extending its boundaries as far as Toledano Street. Finally, in 1852, Lafayette ceased to exist as a municipality and became the Fourth District of the city of New Orleans. The city of Lafayette, in its brief lifespan, became a gracious area of antebellum homes as well as a hardworking, commercial riverfront territory.

In 1816, a crevasse formed in the river at the McCarty Plantation, several miles upriver from the Livaudais property in the city of Lafayette. Most of the plantations were flooded from the site of the crevasse to the city of New Orleans, including the property of François de Livaudais.

Livaudais married Celeste Marigny, daughter of Philippe de Marigny, the wealthiest man in Louisiana and one of the wealthiest in America. The Livaudais-Marigny wedding represented the merger of two great fortunes. After their marriage, the young husband and wife began the construction of a castle (on the site that would later be St. Thomas between Sixth and Washington), resembling those of their French ancestors. By 1825, however, they separated, and Madame Livaudais moved to Paris, where she was fêted by King Louis Philippe and his court.

In the settlement with Livaudais, she had received the Livaudais plantation, which extended from First Street to Ninth Street (now

Harmony Street) and from the river to St. George Street (now LaSalle Street). She sold it to a group of entrepreneurs for $500,000. At once, the plantation was laid out into streets and lots. All she kept was the tract with her mansion on it, which was one block wide from Washington Avenue to Sixth Street and from the river to LaSalle. Her mansion was so enormous that the blocks of the tract were cut wider all the way from the river to LaSalle, in order to conform to the width of her house on that one block.

Over a period of time, this unfinished castle was used as a residence for members of her family, a ballroom, a plaster factory, and a refuge for two old female hermits. It was called the haunted house of Lafayette until it was demolished in 1863.

The lots of the newly divided Livaudais plantation provided Lafayette with river frontage, good residential sites, and silt-enriched soil in which anything would grow. Flowers bloomed year round, attracting wealthy Americans and even a few daring Creoles in the second quarter of the nineteenth century. The area soon became known as the Garden District. It was a quadrangle bounded by Jackson and Louisiana avenues and by Magazine Street and St. Charles Avenue. Originally, Apollo (Carondelet) and Josephine streets were included as well.

During the period of Spanish domination, after 1763, when the embargo existed against all but Spanish vessels trading with New Orleans merchants, British "floating warehouses" sailed up the river on the pretext of going up to trade with British colonies at Manchac, Baton Rouge, and Natchez. Instead, they docked at Lafayette City, where they carried on a brisk commerce in cutlery, cloth, farming utensils, and slaves with New Orleanians. The Spanish turned their heads, pretending not to notice, until the American Revolution made anti-British sentiment a necessity. In 1777, Governor Galvez seized the British ships and stopped the illegal trade. However, it was British trade that had established Lafayette City as a commercial center of the riverfront.

The Texas cattle trails ended at Gretna, across the river from Lafayette. Cattle boats then transported the stock across the river to slaughterhouses, where they were unloaded in a noisy, odiferous, earth-shaking herd. The riverfront was lined with the establishments of tallow renderers, soap boilers, hide tanners and merchants, bone grinders, and other spin-off industries.

Cotton was brought to the docks by steamboats, which competed for wharf space with the flatboats that lined the riverfront in the 1840s. It was said that one could walk a mile on the tops of flatboats on the riverfront. By 1850, however, twenty piers had been specially constructed of thick planks to accommodate the steamers.

The earliest homes in Lafayette City were built close to the river. Gradually, however, there was a greater demand for lots "in the back part of the city," where the wealthy built mansions a good distance from the sounds and smells of the slaughterhouses.

In 1852, the population of Lafayette City was 12,651 plus 1,539 slaves. Greek Revival mansions rose along Nayades Street (now St. Charles Avenue) and in the Magazine Street area in the 1840s and 1850s.

A conflict arose between those who demanded the removal of the slaughterhouses and tanneries from the Lafayette City riverfront (because of the offensive odors and noises) and those who claimed that the city would lose as much as $1.5 million per year in trade by such an act. The City Council finally passed measures that removed the cattle landing.

The Yellow Fever Epidemic of 1853

The events of the yellow fever epidemic of 1853 in New Orleans are so horrible that we read them with disbelief, equating them with the horrors of the Black Plague in Europe in the Middle Ages. Today, it is difficult to imagine the reality of death on such a grand scale. It has been called the worst single epidemic ever to hit an American city.

We know today that yellow fever is a virus that damages the liver, preventing it from functioning. Yellow bile pigments gather in the skin; the victim's eyes look yellow and his skin has a yellow tone. Their temperature rises rapidly, their bones ache, and they vomit black matter, which consists of partly digested blood after hemorrhages have occurred in the stomach. Some victims go into a coma. Many die. Those who live have a lifelong immunity to the disease.

We now know that the disease is transmitted by the *Aedes aegypti* mosquito, which carries it from one victim to another. Both the disease and the mosquito almost certainly came from the Old World, probably from Africa on slave ships. The warm, humid climate and heavy rainfall of New Orleans made it susceptible to yellow fever. Open cisterns were perfect breeding grounds for the mosquito, whose eggs must first dry a bit, then hatch when moistened. New Orleans was an ideal host for such a cycle.

Epidemics began with the hot weather and ended with the frosts, which killed the mosquitoes. In the 1800s, it was believed the fever was caused by poisonous vapors in the atmosphere, water contagion, or droplet infection.

The first epidemic of yellow fever in New Orleans occurred in 1793, the last in 1905, and in the interval, twenty major epidemics struck (although the fever came every summer, to some degree). From 1793 to 1853, the epidemics grew increasingly worse and more numerous, culminating in the 1853 season. This has been attributed to a growing population of impoverished immigrants in a below-sea-level, unhealthy city that had lots of rain. From 1853 to 1905, the epidemics decreased in severity and number. The decline began during the Civil War, when Gen. Benjamin Butler put the unemployed of New Orleans to work scouring the city from top to bottom.

On the morning of May 28, 1853, a New Orleans newspaper editorialized about the glorious future of a disease-free city. There had not been a yellow fever epidemic in six years. However, that evening, an Irish laborer, recently landed on a ship from Europe, was admitted to Charity Hospital, suffering from the black vomit. He died within a few hours. The doctor hesitated to diagnose the disease so early in the season. Doctors of the period had a difficult time distinguishing between hemorrhagic malaria, yellow fever, and other diseases, especially when no epidemic was raging. Municipal officers and newspapers hushed rumors of the fever, so as not to discourage tourists and businessmen.

After a second death occurred, the doctor traced the origin of the disease to the ship *Augusta,* which had arrived from Bremen, Germany on May 17, 1853, with 230 European immigrants aboard. The *Augusta* had been in close contact with another ship, the *Camboden Castle,* on which several crewmembers had died of yellow fever while in Jamaica.

The public was, at that time, preoccupied with a sensational murder trial in the news. In June, rumors of a slave rebellion (which never materialized) swept through the city. No one was concerned that on June 1, an item in a New York newspaper told of a yellow fever epidemic in Jamaica and warned that the disease was being carried by sailors and dockworkers to distant ports. Today we know that the *Aedes aegypti* mosquitoes swarmed thickly in holds and cabins of ships and bred in their water barrels.

On June 22, the editor of the *New Orleans Crescent* commiserated with members of the "Can't Get Away Club," merchants and tradesmen whose business required their presence in the city during the summer months. New Orleans was a six-months-a-year town because of the heat and disease. Those who could afford to had already left the city. Those who remained settled down to wait out the unusual heat and the swarms of mosquitoes, "a barbarous horde of great, ugly, long-billed, long-legged creatures" (*New Orleans Crescent,* "Mid-Summer," 1853).

New Orleans was a city of 150,000 people. All told, 50,000 left the city that summer. Of the 100,000 who remained, 1 out of every 10 would die.

Gutters were filled with garbage, human waste, and refuse, which rains would turn into lakes of filth, spreading cholera and malaria. No one would drink the river water, choosing instead to use cistern water, which was a breeding ground for the yellow fever carrier mosquito. The heat, floods, and surrounding swamps all contributed to the unhealthy conditions. Mayor A. D. Crossman urged health measures. The City Council agreed to end private street-cleaning contracts and establish a municipal sanitation department, but more immediate measures were needed.

As the death toll mounted, hearses rolled incessantly into the cemeteries. Streets were deserted except for carriages of physicians. Every evening, artillery was fired to "clear the atmosphere." Flames and smoke from hundreds of tar barrels scattered throughout the city sent up dense clouds and lit up the streets with an eerie glow. This approach to preventing the spread of yellow fever worked only because it killed and repelled mosquitoes, but it did not eradicate the cause of the fever.

Doctors tried the time-honored cures: bleeding and purging. Vomiting did not have to be induced. However, without the knowledge of the cause, they could not cure the disease.

The worst day of the epidemic was August 20, when 269 people died. At this point, 200 people per day were dying in the city. The private and public hospitals were overflowing. Every home in the city was a makeshift hospital. In some homes, whole families died within the hour and there was no one to mourn them or make funeral arrangements.

Open wagons passed daily, the drivers calling, "Bring out your dead." Hearses, carriages, and wagons massed near the cemeteries. Inside the cemeteries, the rotting corpses "were piled by the fifties, exposed to the heat of the sun, swollen with corruption, bursting their coffin lids" (*New Orleans Crescent,* "Down," 1853).

The dead were buried in shallow graves in the cemetery ground, covered with no more than fourteen inches of mud. When the rains came, the soil washed away, revealing grotesque, decaying bodies.

In desperation, the mayor offered five dollars per hour for gravediggers in order to remove such signs from public view. The *New Orleans Bee,* August 9, 1853, reported:

> Upon inquiry yesterday, we ascertained that the festering decaying of bodies which had been deposited in the Lafayette Cemetery had at last been consigned to mother earth. The eyes will no longer be pained and the nostrils offended by the further continuance of the horrible neglect. The Mayor . . . secured the labor of the chain gang, and set them immediately to work.

The epidemic took the lives of 10,000 people in the summer of 1853. Through the little mortuary chapel on Rampart and Conti streets passed the bodies of thousands of Catholics who had died of the fever. Funerals in the St. Louis Cathedral had been banned since 1827 for fear that disease would spread. The wardens of the Cathedral ordered the erection of the chapel near St. Louis Cemetery No. 1, so that the Catholics might be properly (though speedily) blessed before burial during yellow fever epidemics. After the Civil War, the ban on cathedral funerals was lifted, and the mortuary chapel became a parish church. That church, now called Our Lady of Guadalupe, still stands on the corner of Rampart and Conti. It is the oldest church in New Orleans, older even than the present St. Louis Cathedral. The current cathedral is the third structure of the same name to stand on the Place d'Armes.

It was another half-century before the cause of yellow fever was discovered. In 1900, in Cuba, **Walter Reed** of the United States Yellow Fever Board identified the germ and demonstrated the carrier role of the mosquito. Control measures followed, eliminating the disease as a

Our Lady of Guadalupe was originally a mortuary chapel where all Catholic funerals were held (near St. Louis Cemetery No. 1), from 1827 to 1860. It is the oldest church building in New Orleans. (Photo by Kathy Chappetta Spiess)

menace in the Panama Canal Zone. In 1964, the United States began a million-dollar program to eliminate the *Aedes aegypti* mosquito.

It is astounding to relate that in the fall of 1853, the tragedy that had struck New Orleans just weeks before seemed to be forgotten. Trade and commerce were as brisk as ever on the Mississippi, filling warehouses and boardinghouses. Immigrants crowded into customs houses. Newcomers replaced those who had been lost, and the city carried on with the booming prosperity of the 1850s.

The Emergence of Political Parties

Soon after the Louisiana Purchase, it became evident that the population of New Orleans was divided into three distinct groups. It was within these divisions that they would organize politically: the *ancienne population,* the New French, and the Anglo-Americans. In the period between 1820 and 1850, the *ancienne population* and the New French usually joined the Whig Party. Throughout the nation, Whigs were generally aristocrats; in the South, they were also slave-owners. Anglo-Americans in New Orleans were almost all Democrats. The Democratic Party had represented the rise of the common man since the elections of Andrew Jackson in 1828 and 1832. The hero of the Battle of New Orleans was popular in the city.

New Orleans voters made political decisions on many levels. A presidential candidate would be supported as a Democrat or a Whig, according to party allegiance. A gubernatorial, legislative, or mayoral candidate would win votes as a spokesman for either the Creole or the American factions.

The influx of Irish and German immigrants in the 1830s and 1840s complicated things. The Irish were clannish, but they were quick to be naturalized and they loved involvement in politics. Since the Irish were in such great numbers in the city as early as 1830 (when they tipped the scales for mayoral candidate Denis Prieur), both political parties began to work hard to win the Irish vote.

From 1828 until the coming of the Irish famine refugees in 1846, the arguments between the "nativists" and the "foreigners" dragged on. Nativists complained that the immigrants followed their party leaders blindly; they organized into bands of foreign soldiers, armed, equipped, and bearing a foreign name; they celebrated feast days of their own country's patron saints; and they generally were considered a degraded population, men without education, principle, or patriotism.

Since the Irish, and immigrants in general, had anti-slavery propensities, they were the political targets for the prominent, wealthy, slave-owning Whigs. Although hostility existed between the Irish and the black population (mostly due to competition for jobs), the Irish had been oppressed too long by the British to support an institution that fostered oppression. Paradoxically, many old, established Irish business leaders, who had married Creole women, were not only Whigs but also slave-owners. This was also true of some well-established Anglo-Americans.

The Democratic Party dominated national politics from 1801 to 1860. During this period, the opposition party had been called, at different times, Federalists, National Republicans, and Whigs.

As we have seen, the city split into three municipalities in 1836 and reunited in 1852. When they reunited, the Creoles wanted a common council, which, in allegiance with the Third District immigrants, they could control. The Americans wanted consolidation and annexation of the city of Lafayette, which would support them on basic issues. The latter plan was accepted.

To obtain the support of the Third District immigrants, many of the Creoles in the Vieux Carré joined the Democratic Party. The Americans in Faubourg St. Mary, both by choice and necessity, joined the Whig Party.

Just before the Civil War, the National Democratic Party split into the Northern Democrats and the Southern Democrats; the Whigs, divided over the same issue, began to disintegrate. The nation saw the emergence of a new political party, the Republican Party, in 1854 through 1856. With their candidate, Abraham Lincoln, the Republicans won the presidential election of 1860.

The Northern Whigs *opposed* slavery, but in New Orleans, Whigs *supported* slavery. This led to their demise. Those who had been Whigs and wished to retain their anti-Democratic identity joined the "Know-Nothings," rabid nativists whose main objective was to break the power of the immigrants in politics. It was easy to make the change from Whig to Know-Nothing. Whigs were wealthy and powerful. The nativist doctrine of the Know-Nothings, which oppressed the immigrants, suited their purposes.

Throughout the summer of 1854, reckless remarks by Know-Nothings convinced many of the Irish immigrants that the Americans were going to burn down St. Patrick's Church and slaughter Irish immigrants as they slept.

For ten days in September, armed gangs of Irish and Americans marched endlessly, causing needless destruction. On the evening of September 11, the Americans gathered at Lafayette Square and the Irish at St. Mary's Market. A fight ensued on Camp Street. Two were killed and many were wounded. Hostile feelings flared.

Just before the mayoral election of 1858, the Know-Nothings in New Orleans split. The independents nominated **Maj. P. G. T. Beauregard** and went after the old Whig vote; the American Party nominated **Gerard Stith,** a printer, and went after the labor vote. Two days before the election, the Creole-immigrant group formed a vigilante committee to guarantee a peaceful election. They recruited 500 men, mostly Irish, who occupied the arsenal and the municipal buildings at Jackson Square. The Americans formed an organization that camped at Lafayette Square. Peace was achieved by compromise, without the use of violence.

From 1860 to 1864, during the War Between the States, political parties had no purpose. Municipal government, as we shall see, gave way to military rule. Then, during Reconstruction, only two political parties remained, the Republicans (the members of the Federal army of occupation and the blacks) and the Democrats (the defeated Southern whites). For more than half a century, the South was referred to as the Solid South because of the total and predictable adherence of the whites to the Democratic Party and its policies.

CHAPTER VII
Customs, Carnival, and Cemeteries

Customs

When New Orleans became American in 1803, the port city became a refuge for the world. Immigrants came down the Mississippi and from across the Atlantic, bringing with them customs and traditions, which were to be their lifeline to a world they left behind.

In a city that was predominately Catholic and known for its love of festivity, it is not surprising that as many as twenty-five Holy Days per year, besides Sundays, came to have their own special celebrations.

On **Christmas Eve,** a peculiarity of the area is the lighting of bonfires all along the levee of the Mississippi. It is a very old tradition, supposedly begun by the Acadians, who were "so far from home that they had to guide 'Père Noel,' so he could find them." For weeks in advance of Christmas, river dwellers begin erecting pyramids of logs in graduated sizes in preparation for the fires. The sight of the line of bonfires from the opposite side of the river on Christmas Eve is one of the most memorable spectacles the area has to offer.

This tradition is still celebrated along the Mississippi. Bonfire structures, however, have become bigger and more elaborate than the original pyramid structures.

Twelfth Night is King's Day, a religious holiday that honors the day when the three wise men are said to have visited the Christ Child. It is the twelfth night after Christmas. It is celebrated in New Orleans by the baking and eating of "king cakes," circular coffeecakes sprinkled with colored, granulated sugar. Inside the cake, a tiny doll, bean, or ring is hidden. The guest who finds the object gives the next party, and so it goes weekly until Mardi Gras.

A forerunner of this charming party custom was the *Bal de Bouquet,* which originated in the nineteenth century. It was given by a bachelor, chosen at the beginning of the Carnival season, at the home of the young lady whom he designated as his queen. At the party, the bachelor would crown her with a wreath of flowers. After a few quadrilles at the party, the king (the bachelor) led the queen to the center of the floor, where she crowned him with a wreath of flowers. The ritual was repeated weekly until Mardi Gras. (The similarity to today's king cake parties can easily be seen.)

Carnival is so special in New Orleans and has such a history of its own that it will be described in a separate section of this chapter.

With the city's large Irish population, it is unsurprising that **St. Patrick's Day,** March 17, is celebrated in a big way in New Orleans and in the usual fashion. In addition to the obligatory green beer, wearing o' the green, and dances, several parades roll throughout the area. The krewes toss out green beads but also potatoes, carrots, and, of course, cabbages: just about everything you need to make your own Irish stew.

St. Joseph's Day, March 19, is observed by the building of St. Joseph Altars in the homes of Italians as well as churches and schools in thanksgiving to the saint for favors granted. The altars originated in Sicily during the Middle Ages, when famine threatened the island, and the people prayed to St. Joseph. One crop, the fava bean, survived to save them, and in thanksgiving, they cooked food and laid it out on an altar for the needy. New Orleanians of Sicilian descent still commemorate the day in the same way.

Today, the altars are elaborately decorated with bread baked in the shape of wreaths, crosses, and hearts. Italian cakes and cookies are decorated with praying hands and Bibles. Baskets of fava beans and St. Joseph medals are placed on the altar to be distributed to visitors, as they did in the old days, to ward off famine in the coming year. No meat is placed on the altar in keeping with the Lenten penance, but there are dishes of fish, stuffed lobsters, crabs, vegetables, fruits, and pasta of many kinds.

On St. Joseph's Day, children dressed as Mary and Joseph take part in a little ceremony commemorating their search for shelter in Bethlehem. The Italians invite them in to share the wealth of their altars. Then, the food is shared with friends and neighbors or is donated to a needy organization.

On St. Joseph's Night, the Italian community gives a parade through the French Quarter with floats, horses, bands, and marchers.

An interesting side note of the St. Joseph feast is the tradition of the parades of the Mardi Gras Indians. Only twice a year, on Mardi Gras Day and St. Joseph's Night, do they appear in their colorful, elaborate costumes, with the ornate beadwork and the enormous feather headdresses. Tribes such as the Wild Magnolias, the Black Eagles, the Yellow Pocahontas, or the Wild Squatoolas compete in a colorful display of costumes. It is believed that their appearance on this particular feast day dates back to their veneration of St. Joseph in their voodoo rituals of the late nineteenth century.

Easter Sunday is a movable feast, celebrated on the first Sunday following the first full moon after the spring equinox. This, of course, is a worldwide holiday. But in New Orleans, Germaine Cazenave Wells, a descendent of Count Arnaud (founder of Arnaud's Restaurant), arrived at the St. Louis Cathedral on Easter Sunday for several decades in an extravagant *chapeau,* after having led an Easter parade through the French Quarter. Today, the Germaine Wells parade continues and is followed by another at noon, led by French Quarter entertainer Chris Owens.

The **Spring Fiesta** is an acknowledgment of the beautiful season of spring and a tribute to the cultural heritage of Louisiana. Begun in 1947, the Spring Fiesta is a tourist-oriented celebration. For nineteen days, beginning on the first Friday after Easter, young ladies of New Orleans dressed in antebellum costumes escort groups of tourists by candlelight through the French Quarter patios and the beautiful old homes of the Garden District. Plantations along Bayou Teche, River Road, Bayou Lafourche, and Feliciana offer similar tours of private homes.

All Saints' Day, November 1, has a very special meaning to New Orleanians. Since the water table of the city made aboveground burials a necessity, residents took the opportunity to erect elaborate tombs and mini-mausoleums to house their dead. The upkeep of these properties was a way of life and a year-round occupation. Special pains were taken in preparation for All Saints' Day, which included whitewashing tombs, pulling weeds, sweeping sidewalks, and bringing vases to the burial site. In the old days, tombs and headstones were draped with flags or black crepe. Ground plots were edged with painted shells, China dogs, and pig banks. In addition, on the day itself, thousands thronged to the cemetery to bring flowers and pray for their loved ones in these cities of the dead. The first All Saints' Day

New Orleanians decorate the tombs of their dead for All Saints' Day (Courtesy Leonard V. Huber Collection)

activities celebrated the reopening of St. Peter's Cemetery in 1742 and the completion of the fence surrounding it. Materials had been paid for by the rich and labor was the gift of the poor.

Street Vendors

Since the earliest days, New Orleans street vendors sang in cadences as they advertised their wares. In colonial times, plantation owners sent older slaves who could no longer work in the fields out to sell the surplus products of the plantation. The owners had to buy licenses for their slaves but increased their annual income by thousands of dollars.

Street vendors endured well into the 1960s, and even today, an occasional truckload of fresh vegetables or fruit may still be seen in the residential areas of town. At the turn of the twentieth century, the housewife depended almost entirely on street vendors and went to market only if she needed meat, an item that did not appear daily on the supper table, and it was within walking distance.

The sight of the mule-drawn vegetable wagon was a welcome one, for it was a break in the day's routine, and the sound of vendors' melodious "Water-melon! Red to the rind!" or "Ah got ba-na-na, lay-dee!" was music to the ear of the housewife. The rendition of the vendor's songs and chants was limited only by his imagination and talent. "Black-ber-rees! Ah got black-ber-rees!" might be warbled into the morning air with the pathos of a tenor of the Metropolitan Opera House.

Many vendors walked, carrying baskets filled with a variety of vegetables on their heads. Their produce was fresh, and the cost of any item was subject to discussion. Each season saw the appearance of its own specialties. In early summer, there were strawberries, followed later on by watermelons and by wild ducks in the fall. During Lent, there were always fish and oysters. Milk vendors, ice cream vendors, and bread and cake vendors sang the familiar "Calas! Tout chauds!" Familiar faces included the Corn Meal Man, the Hot Pie Man, the Waffle Man, the Candy Man, the Broom Man, the Clothespole Man, the Chimney Sweep, the Bottle Man, the Knife Sharpener, the Umbrella Man, and Zozo La Brique, who sold brick dust to scrub stoops and walks in certain neighborhoods. There were also the spasm bands of small black boys who did a slapfoot dance with makeshift instruments, hoping for a handout from passing pedestrians.

Since 1791, Choctaw Indians sold sassafras and other roots and herbs in the French Market. Black women in tignons sold rice cakes, molasses, and pralines. In the markets everything was available from chickens to fish to oysters to live canaries in cages. Even women in search of a day's work were singing out their trades, waving their washboards above their heads.

Superstition

Due to the demographics of the population, superstition ran rampant throughout the city. The Irish brought over their own superstitions, most of which were considered comic, or at least not taken too seriously. The blacks, because they so long adhered to the voodoo cult, feared gris-gris (ritual objects such as crossed sticks, circles of salt, roosters' heads) as evil omens. Gamblers, with which the city abounded, were natural adherents of superstition. Many played the lottery and consulted their "dream books" for the numbers they should play, depending on whether they had dreamed of fire, death, rain, or even red beans.

The Creoles, gamblers or not, all believed that dreams had

meanings. For example, a dream of pulling a tooth meant death was coming and dreams of trees presaged joy and profit. They also feared the following omens: rain or tears at a wedding meant bad luck; flowers out of season brought bad luck; the transplanting of a weeping willow brought about violent death; spitting in a fire would draw up your lungs; and sleeping with the moon in your face would draw your mouth to one side and make it crooked. They were also well known for the Creole Mirror superstition: if three men look in a mirror at one time, the youngest would die; if three girls look in a mirror at one time, the eldest would marry within a year.

There were hundreds of such omens and superstitious beliefs from all immigrant populations.

Jazz

New Orleans is the birthplace of jazz. Jazz first gained national attention around the turn of the twentieth century, although its beginnings reach far back into history. When slaves were first brought to America, they carried memories of the music they had learned in West Africa or acquired in the Caribbean Islands. The slaves chanted as they worked, and their songs spoke of love, anger, longing, joy, and despair. Under the liberal French and Spanish governors of New Orleans, slaves were allowed the freedom to sing and dance together, which was not always a possibility in other parts of the United States. They made their own musical instruments—banjos from gourds or reeds to blow or pluck—and played music to accompany their dancing in Congo Square and at the many picnics, parades, and other celebrations in or around the city. Many musicians were needed in a city of so many festivities.

Free men of color often had an entirely different culture from that of slaves. Some were even sent by their white fathers to European schools, where they studied classical music. People considered the birth of jazz (or ragtime, as it was originally called), around 1887, to be nothing more than European music played badly. Innovations in music, such as syncopation, staccatos, and timbres, later viewed as revolutionary, were considered by these trained musicians to be mistakes. Variations on a theme became improvisations, which were called "jazzing it up." The raw-talent jazz musician would take a melody that consisted of just a few notes, such as that of "When the Saints Go Marchin' In," and play it in every possible variation. By the standards of European-trained musicians, these jazz musicians either could not or would not play music as it was written. Nice young ladies were discouraged from playing jazz. It was considered disorderly music, "closet music," rebellious and untraditional. The *Times-Picayune,* in 1918, called an attraction to jazz a "low streak in man's taste" ("Jass and Jassism").

Jazz was not born in Storyville but grew up and came of age there (1897-1917). The product sold in the bordellos was not music. Music was an accessory, paid for by the tips given to musicians. With its many dancehalls and bars, Storyville employed many jazz musicians. The audience at the bordellos was generally mellow and agreeable to whatever was played, which allowed the musicians ample opportunity to experiment and improvise.

"Spasm bands" appeared in the 1890s. They played homemade instruments on street corners. Emile "Stalebread Charley" Lacombe, who got his start with his Razzy Dazzy Spasm Band, became one of the jazz greats.

Storyville proved to be the melting pot that blended the perfect ingredients for jazz: the technical training and knowhow of the downtown black Creole musicians and the raw-talent improvisation of the uptown black American musicians. Here, the two were forced to mix. Their disparate heritages were wed and soon gave birth to jazz. Alan Lomax, in *Mister Jelly Roll: The Fortunes of Jelly Roll Morton, New Orleans Creole and "Inventor of Jazz,"* expressed it this way: "Creoles who played in Storyville were compelled to accept blacks as equals, and this was bitter medicine" (1956).

Paul Dominguez, a black Creole violinist, explained in the same biography: "See, us downtown people, we didn't think so much of this rough uptown jazz, until we couldn't make a living otherwise. That's how they made a fiddler out of a violinist—me, I'm talking about. A fiddler is not a violinist, but a violinist can be a fiddler." As for his feelings about black American pure talent: "I don't know how they do it, but they do it. They can't tell you what's on paper. But you just play it. Then they play the Hell out of it."

This forced cooperation was especially important in building understanding between blacks and whites who played together when jazz was just beginning after the Civil War. Jazz played more than a minor role in the building of mutual respect and admiration between the races. "Piano keys opened doors to many white homes for black musicians," according to Al Rose in *Storyville, New Orleans: Being an Authentic, Illustrated Account of the Notorious Red-Light District* (1978).

Many New Orleans-born musicians, such as "King" Oliver, Louis Armstrong, and Jelly Roll Morton, achieved fame in Chicago or New York or on the West Coast after their start in Storyville.

Jazz funerals are still held. In these processions, musicians play sad, slow music on the way to the cemetery. But after they have "turned him loose," as they say, referring to burying their dead, they lead the mourners away to the beat of a gay and lively tune, such as "When the Saints Go Marchin' In," because they are celebrating the jubilation of a soul gone to its reward. They strut and twirl umbrellas, picking up

The Olympia Brass Band of New Orleans (Photo by Johnny Donnels)

second-liners (bystanders who join in the singing and marching) as they walk.

There are many clubs where jazz can be heard, such as: Fritzel's, the Palm Court Jazz Café, and Preservation Hall, to name just a few. Jazz is still alive and well and struttin' in New Orleans!

Streetcars

Streetcars have become associated with New Orleans, not because this was the only city in which streetcars ran but because, while they were being replaced by buses in other towns, they remained the primary mode of public transportation in New Orleans for many decades. New Orleans has a way of lagging behind in such things, as it did with gas-lit streets and other municipal matters. This lack of desire for change stems not only from lethargy, which might be blamed on a debilitating climate, but also from a habit of clinging to the old ways and its gracious, passing lifestyle.

The streetcars of New Orleans were the successors of its original railroad lines. The early railroads were extremely crude, nothing more than iron bars nailed to wooden beams laid lengthwise across ties approximately five feet apart. Riding the railroad was dangerous. The rails often worked loose and penetrated the floors of the coaches. Boilers exploded, flying cinders set fire to nearby crops, floods washed out bridges, and cars jumped the rails.

The earliest railroad in New Orleans was the Pontchartrain Railroad, chartered in 1830, which ran on Elysian Fields from the river to Lake Pontchartrain. It ran 5.18 miles with horse-drawn cars, replaced in 1832 by a steam locomotive, the Smoky Mary. The line (probably the second to have been built in the United States) ran for 101 years until 1932.

St. Charles Streetcar Line

The St. Charles Streetcar Line succeeded the New Orleans and Carrollton Railroad. It is the oldest continuously operating street railway in the world. The line was incorporated as the New Orleans and Carrollton Railroad Company on February 9, 1833, by the Louisiana legislature and continues to operate today. It ran from the business district of the city up St. Charles Avenue (then Nayades Street) through the Garden District on its way to the city of Carrollton.

As far back as 1834, a spur route turned off St. Charles and came out Jackson Avenue to the river along the city's most elegant thoroughfare. This had been a mule-car railroad. The rate of travel could not exceed four miles an hour. The N.O. & C.R.R. was later a steam-driven railroad, and by 1900, it was all electric. Originally, the N.O. & C.R.R. terminal was roughly at the end of St. Charles Avenue. In 1846, the town of Carrollton began to extend Carrollton Avenue back through the swamps to a navigation canal known as the New Basin. The roadway was complete in 1862, and an omnibus (Latin for "for all") line was initiated.

After the Civil War, in 1866, Gen. P. G. T. Beauregard and some of his associates leased the N.O. & C.R.R. for twenty-five years. Many new omnibus and street railway companies were formed in the late 1850s and 1860s. These included the Pontchartrain Railroad.

By 1876, the New Orleans City and Lake Rail Road started running steam "dummy" trains along the route of the New Basin Canal from the city to the lake. An amusement park called West End Park arose in 1880. The railway line, electrified in 1898, was a six-and-a-half-mile ride from New Orleans on West End trains, which consisted of a motorcar pulling several open-sided trailers that thrilled thousands.

In 1909, the New Orleans Railway and Light Company acquired a site known as Spanish Fort. The fort had existed as a resort well before West End Park, and the two parks on the lakefront were long to be competitors for the business of lake enthusiasts. Electric cars ran out to the resort in 1911. The railway company rebuilt and reopened the amusement center, which had been abandoned when the railway service was discontinued in 1903.

By 1953, only two streetcar lines, the St. Charles Line and the Canal Line, remained in operation in New Orleans. Ten years later, New Orleans Public Service removed the Canal Line and replaced it with buses, accompanied by loud, vehement protestations.

On May 31, 1964, the St. Charles Streetcar became the last streetcar line in New Orleans. The electric streetcars now operating on the route (which provides visitors with a tour of the New Orleans business district, the mansions of the Garden District, the University area, Audubon Park, and the Carrollton area) are typical of the streetcars in use in the early part of the twentieth century.

The Perley A. Thomas Car Company streetcars still operate on the St. Charles Line. It is the oldest continuously operating street railway in the world and is on the National Register of Historic Places. (Photo by Kathy Chappetta Spiess)

The car itself was designed and built by the Perley A. Thomas Car Company of High Point, North Carolina, in 1923 and 1924. It is known in New Orleans as a streetcar, not a trolley, and it is treasured by the city. Over the years, modifications have included replacement of the mahogany sash and canvas roof with metal. Eventually, exact-change fare boxes and metal automatic doors were installed to facilitate one-man operations. The most nostalgic features are the exposed ceiling lightbulbs and the rich wooden seats. The seats can be reversed, depending on the streetcar's direction, and have brass handholds on their aisle corners. The historical character of the streetcar is painstakingly maintained. In 1973, the streetcar line was placed on the National Register of Historic Places by the Department of the Interior, 140 years after it was organized.

Through 1987, free transportation was provided on public transit to the nuns of the city, because, so the legend goes, the Ursuline nuns had prayed so unceasingly for victory in the Battle of New Orleans in 1815, when victory seemed impossible.

Canal Street and Riverfront Line

In 1988, seven vintage streetcars painted red with gold trim became

The "Ladies in Red" run along the Canal Street, Carrollton, and Riverfront lines. (Photo by Kathy Chappetta Spiess)

operational along the riverfront. These **"Ladies in Red,"** the first to begin running since 1926, run almost two miles connecting the many riverfront attractions.

At one time, Canal Street was one of the great "streetcar thoroughfares" in North America, having as many as six tracks through downtown. The line was converted to buses in 1964 but returned to Canal Street in 1999 with a short line running six blocks.

Two streetcar lines were rebuilt and put back into operation in 2004. The Canal/Cemetery Line runs the length of Canal Street, and Canal/City Park/Museum runs from Canal Street and North Carrollton Avenue to the entrance to City Park.

In 2005, 80 percent of New Orleans flooded following Hurricane Katrina. Fortunately, thirty-five streetcars in the Carrollton streetcar barn in uptown New Orleans were spared damage. The Canal Street car barn, however, was not so lucky. The Canal and Riverfront fleet of twenty-four cars sustained extensive damage from the flooding.

With a grant from the Federal Emergency Management Agency (FEMA) and state-contributed funds, they were repaired. Costs would run $800,000 to $1 million per car.

The St. Charles Line resumed operation by December 2005. The Canal Street and Riverfront lines were back in operation in 2011 (U.S. Streetcar Systems 2011).

Carnival

Most customs, as we have seen, were based on the celebration of feast days of the Roman Catholic Church, although they were not all religious celebrations. The most famous of these is **Mardi Gras,** part of the Carnival season, which is the farthest thing from a religious holiday. *Mardi Gras* is French for "Fat Tuesday," a name that hints at the feasting and partying that continues until midnight of that day, ending the Carnival season that started on January 6, the Catholic feast of the Epiphany. *Carnival* is derived from the Latin, meaning "farewell to the flesh."

Mardi Gras is celebrated the day before **Ash Wednesday,** when the forty-day season of Lent officially begins, and Catholics fast and do penance. The feast of Mardi Gras was brought to America by Iberville and Bienville, when they christened the bayou they discovered on March 3, 1699, Mardi Gras Bayou. They had found it on Shrove Tuesday, the day before Ash Wednesday.

In the years between 1806 and 1823, after Louisiana became American, laws forbade masking and balls, so private clubs were founded instead. In 1827, some students returning from their studies in Paris donned costumes and danced in the streets as they had seen maskers do in Paris. They threw flowers to the crowds watching them. (Later on, they threw flour on the crowds.)

The first parade was held in 1837. Because hostility existed between the Irish and the blacks over jobs and violence was likely, masks were forbidden. In 1839, the first float, a papier-mâché creation, appeared. On it, a design called chanticleer (a name given to a rooster) flapped its wings and crowed. On this occasion, it seems, lime was thrown on the crowds instead of flour. Trouble was brewing in the tempestuous heterogeneous population, more and more activities were becoming dangerous, and the press was calling for an end to Mardi Gras celebrations. A small group met soon after to form a secret society that would restore order and dignity to the New Orleans celebration.

In 1857, the **Mystik Krewe of Comus** was born, the organization that was credited with saving the institution of Carnival. Their tableau was an ambitious one based on *Paradise Lost.*

In 1870, the **Twelfth Night Revelers** emerged, staging a tableau with the nebulous theme of the Tide of English Humor—quite a sophisticated project for a population reputed to be uneducated!

Rex, the king of Carnival, whose parade takes place on Mardi Gras Day, held his first reign in 1872. The *New Orleans Bee* newspaper referred to the organizers as "swine-eating Saxons," an insult directed at their English heritage, although there were undoubtedly some French Creoles among the organizers. In the same year, the **Knights of Momus** debuted. Other krewes soon organized, each with its own special parade and ball date.

Rex had been organized by forty enterprising men in just a few weeks, to honor the visit of the Grand Duke Alexis Romanoff Alexandrovitch of pre-revolutionary Russia, who made an amorous pursuit of Lydia Thompson, a singer, in New Orleans. Miss Thompson had sung a song in a burlesque show, *Bluebeard,* entitled "If Ever I Cease to Love," which the bands at the Mardi Gras balls obligingly played and which became the theme song of the holiday. Although its lyrics include such nonsense as "If ever I cease to love, may oysters have legs and cows lay eggs," it nevertheless remains the theme song of Mardi Gras to this day.

Also introduced by Rex were the Mardi Gras colors: purple for justice, green for faith, and gold for power. The most plausible explanation for their selection is that they were colors of the king's costume in the production of Richard II, enacted by Lawrence Barrett, which was playing in the city at the time.

On the first day of Rex's reign, the king rode a bay charger. Boeuf Gras, fatted beef (the symbol of Mardi Gras), was represented by Old Jeff, a bull from the stockyards. The krewe was masked as playing cards. The following year, there was such a demand for invitations to the Rex Ball that 4,000 were mailed, and the ball had to be held in the Exposition Hall. In 1874, Rex arrived in the city by steamboat at the foot of Canal Street on the Monday before Mardi Gras. All the ships in the harbor tooted their whistles in greeting. To this day, there is a river parade. Rex is the only king not masked. The original Rex was made up to look like Richard II in the play, and the krewe continues the tradition.

The "Arrival of Rex" on the Monday before Mardi Gras began in 1874. This old print from Frank Leslie's Illustrated Newspaper *shows Rex's arrival near the Robert E. Lee statue for the 1879 Carnival.* (Courtesy Leonard V. Huber Collection)

The **Zulu Social Aid and Pleasure Club** was founded in 1916. It is known for its black-faced krewe members wearing grass skirts. It is primarily an African-American Carnival club. The krewe parades on Mardi Gras morning. Its signature "throw" is a hand-painted coconut.

The organizations are now so numerous that it takes two full weeks for all parades to roll, frequently several on the same date, and the balls now begin before Christmas, so that all may fit on the social calendar. Each organization pays for its own parade and ball. The parades are a gift to the people of the city; the balls are private parties for the entertainment of the friends of the krewe members.

The most prestigious krewes are those of Comus, Momus, Proteus, and Rex, but only Rex holds both a parade and a ball. The Twelfth Night Revelers, founded in 1870, is the oldest non-parading krewe. Other organizations that date back to the nineteenth century are the Atlanteans of 1890, the Elves of Oberon of 1894, Nereus of 1896, and Mithras of 1897. In 1871, the Twelfth Night Revelers established two Carnival traditions: a queen was introduced for the first time at a Carnival ball and the throwing of trinkets was begun by a member of the organization dressed as Santa Claus. Both traditions remain to this day in almost all Carnival organizations.

Bacchus and Endymion, both started in 1968, are organizations that have broken with tradition. Instead of selecting their monarchs from lists of social and civic leaders, they choose famous personalities such as Drew Brees, Will Ferrell, and Kelly Ripa. Entertainers such as Maroon 5 and KISS are on hand annually to play for the krewe members and their friends. These organizations are now big business and are often referred to as superkrewes.

The doubloon, which is struck in the image of a particular Mardi Gras organization, is a modern innovation begun by the Rex Krewe in 1960. That year, the Rex doubloon was designed by H. Alvin Sharpe. Today, dozens of organizations throw doubloons to the spectators, and many have become collectors' items.

The Rex and Comus jewels (crowns, scepters, necklaces, etc.) were, at one time, made in Paris, by an old firm of worldwide renown. They were imported duty free because of the public nature of the celebrations. Kings and queens were allowed to keep their royal treasures. Today, however, the jewels are passed from one royal couple to the next, being replaced every few years.

In all parts of the Greater New Orleans area, Mardi Gras flags fly before the homes of former kings and queens of the various Carnival krewes.

The expansion of Mardi Gras into the suburbs of Metairie, Chalmette, and the West Bank in the 1960s and 1970s and the Northshore communities of Covington, Mandeville, and Slidell opened participation to more neighborhoods. Superkrewes such as Bacchus and Endymion helped modernize the festivities.

Parading krewes traditionally admitted new members of their own choice until 1992, when a ruling was passed by the New Orleans City Council restricting the use of city streets for parading only to organizations admitting any and all applicants. Three of the city's oldest krewes—Momus, Comus, and Proteus—discontinued parading, although they continue to hold their Carnival balls. Others, such as Rex and Hermes, complied with the new regulation and they continue to parade. Orpheus, a beautiful parade, began to roll in 1994, replacing Proteus on its traditional Lundi Gras (Monday) night before Carnival.

Mardi Gras has become more than just the "greatest free show on earth." It also has a tremendous economic impact on the city. Thousands of people participate in approximately thirty-one parades in New Orleans, spending $2,000-$2,500 on costumes, throws, and fees. The celebration brings hundreds of thousands of visitors to the city. According to a study done by Tulane University professor Toni Weiss, the direct economic impact of Mardi Gras on New Orleans in 2014 was estimated at $164 million, with an indirect impact of $465 million (Weiss 2015). Consequently, it takes a tremendous event and much thought by city leaders and krewes to cancel the party. Mardi Gras celebrations were canceled for two years during World War I, for four years during World War II, and in 1951 during the Korean War. The last time Mardi Gras was canceled was in 1979, when the Police Association of New Orleans (PANO) went on strike.

Cemeteries

Some visitors to New Orleans are astonished at the sight of more than forty cemeteries of aboveground burial. This type of interment reflects French and Spanish burial customs and accommodates the high water table, which is the result of both climate and terrain. Heavy rains are common, and because the city is largely below sea level, coffins would rise to the surface of the ground unless properly anchored.

Early in the eighteenth-century, mortuary architects began building six-foot-thick brick walls to keep deadly diseases inside the cemetery. Later, the walls contained casket-sized niches called ovens, available as year-and-a-day rental tombs. A coffin was placed in an oven, and an inscribed marble (or wooden) slab closed off the opening. Walls of ovens surrounded the first cemeteries and are still found in St. Louis Cemeteries Numbers 1, 2, and 3 and in other old cemeteries such as Lafayette Cemetery and St. Roch Cemetery.

Cemeteries were traditionally built on the outskirts of town. Because of this, we can trace the growth of the city by the dates and locations of its main cemeteries: St. Louis No. 1 on Basin Street in 1789, St. Louis No. 2 on Claiborne Avenue in 1824, and St. Louis No. 3 at the end of Esplanade Avenue near Bayou St. John in 1854. Each marks the expansion of New Orleans.

The first cemetery in the city was St. Peter's Cemetery, dated 1724.

The first Protestant cemetery was on Girod Street, built in 1822. Many others followed, and by 1860, there were fourteen cemeteries at the end of Canal Street.

The city was growing in population and wealth, and in the thirty years after the opening of St. Louis Cemetery No. 2 in 1824, the new cemeteries were filled with private family tombs, many of which were elaborate and beautiful. The Avet and Lazzize tomb and the Pilié tomb in St. Louis No. 2 are among the most striking examples of iron craftsmanship to be found.

J. N. B. de Pouilly, who came to New Orleans from France in 1833 and designed the St. Louis Exchange Hotel and the present St. Louis Cathedral, brought scale drawings of tombs from Père Lachaise Cemetery in Paris, the best examples to be found of Greek Revival design. From these sketches, de Pouilly built such beautiful burial places as the Plauché tomb in St. Louis No. 2, which is of Greek Revival design. He created a style of mortuary architecture that continues in New Orleans to this day.

Metairie Cemetery was built in 1872 on Metairie Ridge on the grounds of the Metairie Race Track by a syndicate of New Orleans businessmen. During the Civil War, a portion of the track area was converted into Camp Miller, an army training camp, for a short time. It became the largest and most elaborate burial ground in the city. There are more than four thousand aboveground vaults and tombs and just as many in-ground plots spread out over 150 acres, with the mile-long track as the roadway.

Josie Arlington, a famous Storyville madam, has a tomb in Metairie Cemetery. She bought it in 1914. Because of a stoplight's reflection on her pink marble tomb, it seemed that Josie, even after death, was still in the red-light district.

Daniel Moriarty built a magnificent monument to his wife, who died in 1887. The tall shaft of the Moriarty monument stands just to the left of the entrance, graced by the statues of four life-size female figures at its base. The statues are simple stock figures placed on the monument for effect by the builder, but the story is told that the famous humorist Irving J. Cobb, when visiting the cemetery in the 1920s, asked about the identity of the four females, his cab driver answered, "Faith, Hope, and Charity." Cobb then asked, "And the fourth?" to which the cabby replied, "And who else but Mrs. Moriarty?" (In fact, the fourth represents Memory, carrying a wreath of immortelles.)

L. Kemper Williams, president of F. B. Williams Cypress Company, is buried in an Egyptian temple.

P. B. S. Pinchback, Louisiana's only black governor during Reconstruction, was buried in Metairie Cemetery in 1921.

Metairie Cemetery is one of the showplaces of the city, with its beautiful landscaping, paved walks, lagoons, and many fine trees. Its main aisle fronts Bayou Metairie and it was the location preferred by prominent citizens. Bayou Metairie is now Metairie Road.

In the center of a large green mound surrounded by palm trees is the handsome granite shaft, the Army of Northern Virginia Monument commemorating the Confederate general Stonewall Jackson and the men of the Louisiana Division of the Army of Northern Virginia who fought under him. Above the mausoleum, in which 2,500 men are buried, rises the granite monument, thirty-two feet in height. Atop this is a statue of Jackson.

Within the walls of this cemetery lies an interesting collection of New Orleans characters, including seven governors, six mayors (including Martin Behrman, who closed Storyville and rests as the eternal neighbor of Josie Arlington), and forty-nine kings of Carnival.

In the 1800s, because of the abundance of cypress in the area, New Orleans was the coffin capital of the United States, a fact that must have been both reassuring and profitable during the many yellow fever epidemics.

Funerals and Mourning

The care of these burial sites was a subject of great concern to New Orleanians, as were the rules and traditions that governed mourners. Death notices were tacked to poles and fences in the neighborhood of the deceased, giving the date and time of the interment and inviting friends to attend. Horses, pulling shiny black hearses, were draped with black and decorated with black plumes on their heads. White was used for children, and lavender or grey for the middle-aged. The horses had been trained to march, taking a single step with each note of the music.

At the hour of death, all clocks in the homes were stopped, mirrors were covered, and a crepe was hung on the front door. A huge wake coffeepot was brought out, since wakes were held in the home. All the women wore black clothing, which could be bought secondhand or rented for the occasion. Undertakers provided a service of redecorating poorly furnished homes and providing chairs for the visitors. A few touches of black crepe transformed the houses to honor the passing. "Mourning Hangings and Catafalque" were advertised at moderate prices or on moderate terms. "Coffin Furniture" was also offered at reasonable prices, and the cast-iron furniture we now use in our gardens was first designed for cemetery use to accommodate visitors. At wakes and funerals, mourning was to be restrained. Lamentations were revered. To New Orleanians, the care one took of the family burial site was the measure of his or her respect for the dead and the grief he or she still bore. Creoles especially kept an eye on burial sites close to their family tombs and were quick to comment on the lack of care given this vault or that plot.

New Orleans:
Yesterday and Today

1881. This building at 423 Canal Street, completed in 1881, served as the U.S. Custom House. Since 2008, it has been home to the Audubon Institute's Insectarium. (Courtesy Library of Congress)

Undated. The Orleans Ballroom was home to the famed Quadroon Balls, where young free women of color were introduced to wealthy French suitors as part of the plaçage system. Later the Orleans Ballroom and the adjacent Orleans Theater were purchased by the Sisters of the Holy Family and turned into a convent, school, and orphanage. Part of this complex was demolished; it was later rehabilitated to house the Bourbon-Orleans Hotel—717 Orleans Avenue. (Courtesy Library of Congress)

1857. Parlor of Gallier House, 1134 Royal Street, built by architect James Gallier, Jr., for his home in 1857. Today the building is a museum property of Tulane University. (Photo by Susan Gandolfo)

1939. Convent of Notre Dame, 835 Josephine Street, photographed in 1939. (Courtesy Library of Congress)

1934. View of Spanish Fort looking west across Bayou St. John at Lake Pontchartrain. (Courtesy Library of Congress)

1929. The lighthouse at Lake Pontchartrain, built in 1838, guarded Milneburg and offered a signal for ships from the lake's north shore. The light was extinguished in 1929 and the lighthouse turned over to the Levee Board. It found itself high and dry in 1935 when WPA money helped pump sand from the lake bottom to create lakefront property.

1984. Entrance to the Louisiana World Exposition. Seminude figures reminiscent of the City Park statues once again caused a furor in the city but remained from May to November 1984, to welcome visitors to the Centennial Plaza.

1936. Gallery corner of Le Pretre Mansion, 716 Dauphine Street, looking southwest on Orleans Street, photographed in 1936. (Courtesy Library of Congress)

1935. First skyscraper, 638 Royal Street. (Courtesy Library of Congress)

1923. King Oliver's Creole Jazz Band. Sitting, left to right: Baby Dodds, Honore Dutre, Louis Armstrong, Johnny Dobbs, and Lil Hardin (Armstrong's second wife). Standing, left to right: King Oliver and Bill Johnson. (Courtesy Hogan Jazz Archives, Tulane University Library)

1835. The U.S. Mint, designed by William Strickland in the Greek Revival style in 1835, is the only building in America to have served both as an American and as a Confederate mint. (Photo by Kathy Chappetta Spiess)

1884. The Sugar Exchange, designed by architect James Freret and built in 1884, was the center of business for the sugar industry in the nineteenth and twentieth centuries. Located at North Front and Bienville streets, it was demolished in 1963 (the date of this photograph). (Courtesy Library of Congress)

1788. The original Madame John's Legacy burned to the ground in the early 1780s; it was rebuilt on the same site, 632 Dumaine Street, in 1788. The building represents eighteenth-century Louisiana Creole residential design and is on the National Register of Historic Places. Photographed in 1940. (Courtesy Library of Congress)

1920. Grandstand at the Fair Grounds Race Course.

1993. On December 17, the century-old Fair Grounds Clubhouse on Gentilly Boulevard was razed by fire. (Photo by Chris E. Mickal, New Orleans Fire Department Photo Unit)

1929. Canal and Baronne before the Canal Street Beautification Project of 1930-31. Buildings include Liggett's Drug Store, the Strand Theater, the Exclusive Shop, Miller Brothers, the Godchaux Building, and parlor stores for rent. (Courtesy E. H. Gebhardt)

1950s. The river at Canal Street, with pedestrian ramp to Algiers Ferry. Note Poydras Street Wharf (lower left) and Louisiana and Nashville Railroad shed (right of ramp).

1960. Civil Rights picketers walk in the rain outside Woolworth's Five-and-Dime on Canal and Rampart streets. (Courtesy the Marion James Porter Collection, New Orleans Public Library)

1960. Civil Rights sit-in at lunch counter at Woolworth's. (Courtesy the Marion James Porter Collection, New Orleans Public Library)

1967. Canal and Baronne on Mardi Gras Day. Left: Walgreens Drug Store (where parlor stores were for rent in the 1929 photo), Graff's Men's Store, Cine Royale. Right: Maison Blanche (behind Rex sign), Audubon Building, Kress Five-and-Dime (with white façade).

1988. On May 11, the Cabildo, where the Louisiana Purchase was signed in 1803, was set afire by a roofer's torch. The third floor and cupola were destroyed and many artifacts water damaged. (Photo by Chris E. Mickal, New Orleans Fire Department Photo Unit)

1994. On February 27, the Cabildo reopened after an $8 million renovation.

2016. Faulkner House, 624 Pirate's Alley, is now the site of a rare bookstore, Faulkner House Books. It is the headquarters of the Pirate's Alley Faulkner Society and the literary magazine, the Double Dealer Redux. (Photo by Kathy Chappetta Spiess)

2001. Le Boeuf Gras, *one of the early floats in the Rex parade, represents the last meat eaten before Lent.* (Photo by Kathy Chappetta Spiess)

2014. Designed by architect Paul Andry, this neoclassical, open-air pavilion was built for parties in 1907 and is still a popular venue for celebrations and weddings. It sits on the banks of a City Park lagoon. (Photo by Kathy Chappetta Spiess)

2015. Most of the old cemeteries have wall vaults. These vaults were used when a tomb was not available, such as when a family burial was within a year and a day of the last burial. The coffin was placed in a wall vault until the family tomb could be opened and the coffin placed inside. Eventually, these vaults were sold outright to families. (Photo by Kathy Chappetta Spiess)

2016. Aboveground burial is common in New Orleans. While the myth is that the dead are buried aboveground because the city is below sea level, the tradition is also common in France and Spain, from where many early settlers immigrated. (Photo by Kathy Chappetta Spiess)

2016. Convention business is one of the city's major industries. Built on the site of the 1984 World's Fair, the Ernest N. Morial Convention Center provides 1.1 million square feet of exhibit space. (Photo by Kathy Chappetta Spiess)

2016. The Crescent City Connection consists of two bridges spanning the Mississippi River. (Photo by Kathy Chappetta Spiess)

Samples of the Architecture in New Orleans

2015. Pitot House, built in the eighteenth century on Bayou St. John. (Photo by Kathy Chappetta Spiess)

2015. Holy Rosary Rectory, nineteenth century. (Photo by Kathy Chappetta Spiess)

2015. "Tara House" on St. Charles Avenue. (Photo by Kathy Chappetta Spiess)

2016. Built in the 1832, the Malus-Beauregard House overlooks the Chalmette field where the battle of New Orleans took place. Originally called Bueno Retiro, it was designed by James Gallier, Sr. (Photo by Kathy Chappetta Spiess)

2015. This Creole cottage at 1234 St. Claude was built in 1832 of briquette-entre-poteaux construction. It was restored in 1993. (Photo by Kathy Chappetta Spiess)

2016. Confederate Memorial Hall, established in 1891, commemorates the military history and heritage of the South. It houses one of the largest collections of Confederate memorabilia in the U.S. The building was designed in the Richardsonian Romanesque style, developed by New Orleans architect Henry Hobson Richardson. (Photo by Kathy Chappetta Spiess)

2015. Victorian house in uptown New Orleans. (Photo by Kathy Chappetta Spiess)

2015. Bienville statue on Chartres Street in the French Quarter. Plaque reads: "In commemoration of the 250th anniversary of the founding of New Orleans, a wreath was placed here by his excellency, Charles Lucet, ambassador of France to the United States, and the honorable Victor H. Schiro, mayor of New Orleans, on May 9, 1968." (Photo by Kathy Chappetta Spiess)

2015. Jefferson Davis was the only president of the Confederacy. His statue stood at Canal Street and Jefferson Davis Parkway until it was removed in 2017. (Photo by Kathy Chappetta Spiess)

2016. The Army of Tennessee Memorial contains forty-eight crypts (including that of Gen. P. G. T. Beauregard) in a tumulus (grass-covered earthen mound). On top of the memorial is a sculpture of Albert Sidney Johnston sitting on his horse, Fire Eater. The sculpture was done by New York sculptor Alexander Doyle. The memorial was dedicated in 1887. (Photo by Kathy Chappetta Spiess)

2016. A statue of Gen. Robert E. Lee stood on top of a sixty-foot Doric column until 2017. The statue was sculpted by Alexander Doyle and the marble column by John Roy. The monument was created in 1884 and erected at what was then called Place du Tivoli. It was renamed Lee Circle in 1877. (Photo by Kathy Chappetta Spiess)

2015. This fountain, in the Carousel Gardens at City Park, was donated to the "little children of New Orleans" by Sara Lavinia Hyams. Mrs. Hyams left her jewels to Audubon and City parks with the instruction that they be sold and a testimonial built to her love of New Orleans. (Photo by Kathy Chappetta Spiess)

2007. The statue of Andrew Jackson in Jackson Square is the work of sculptor Clark Mills, erected in 1856. It is one of four identical statues in the country. (Photo by Kathy Chappetta Spiess)

2015. This statue in Lafayette Square honors John McDonogh, benefactor of New Orleans public schools. A slaveholder, McDonogh devised a manumission system by which his slaves could buy their freedom. (Photo by Kathy Chappetta Spiess)

2016. Monument honoring the lives lost an# buried at the site of the New Basin Canal. By th# time the canal was finished, eight thousand t# twenty thousand (the exact number is uncertain# immigrants, mostly Irish, died. Construction o# the canal started in 1832 and took six years t# complete. The plaque on the monument read# "In memory of the Irish immigrants who dug th# New Basin Canal, 1832-1838, this Celtic Cros# carved in Ireland has been erected by the Iris# Cultural Society of New Orleans." (Photo b# Kathy Chappetta Spiess)

2015. The fountain in Jackson Square was erected in 1960 to commemorate the visit of Gen. Charles de Gaulle, president of France. (Photo by Kathy Chappetta Spiess)

2016. Piazza d'Italia, designed as an urban public plaza by Charles Moore and Perez Architects, was completed in 1978. (Photo by Kathy Chappetta Spiess)

2016. The old and the new stand side by side in the Central Business District. (Photo by Kathy Chappetta Spiess)

2016. Beautiful Crescent. The curve of the Mississippi River at New Orleans. (Photo by Kathy Chappetta Spiess)

CHAPTER VIII
New Orleans, an Occupied City:
1862-76

A picture of New Orleans in the decade before the Civil War is prerequisite to an understanding of why certain events took place *here* rather than elsewhere. In 1860, New Orleans was the largest city in the South and the largest cotton market in the world, handling in that one year two million bales of cotton. Thirty-five hundred steamboats docked at its wharves that year, and its total trade amounted to $3.24 million. The Crescent City was a transshipment center for all exports coming down the Mississippi, and the port held a virtual monopoly on trade in the interior of the country.

New Orleans was slow in building railroads. The region had only eighty miles of rails when the war began.

Because the city was surrounded by swampland, the Mississippi River was the main corridor for shipping merchandise into New Orleans. The steamboat made its first voyage earlier in the century, but there were still impediments to shipping, such as snags and low water points, especially at the mouth of the river. The service of bar pilots was unsatisfactory, and the rates for towing were prohibitive.

New Orleans, with a population of 168,000, was sixth in size among cities in the nation. An urban aristocracy existed by the middle of the nineteenth century, to which one belonged by virtue of birth or property. Citizens whose ancestors had been in the city several generations called themselves "Creoles," a term whose definition is still much in dispute. According to *Jewell's Crescent Illustrated,* the local directory of 1873, it meant simply to be "born here." If this is so, in 1860, there were Creole French, Creole Irish, Creole Jews, and Creole blacks.

The middle class included businessmen, skilled workers, clerks, and grocers. The proletariat consisted mainly of Germans and Irish, who arrived too recently in the city to have earned places among the upper classes and were considered a laboring class of the lowest level. In the fourth social class were the blacks, who enjoyed considerable freedom in New Orleans in the twenty years before the Civil War. Many were skilled workers or house servants. If they were slaves, they could be hired out by their masters; if they were free, they could easily get work. Free blacks included small businessmen and skilled artisans, many of whom were well to do. As the slavery issue grew more conflicted, the state legislature put more restrictions on free persons of color and finally forbade manumission in 1857, causing some free blacks to immigrate to Haiti and all blacks who remained to welcome the Federals when they arrived in 1862.

In 1853, as we have seen, the worst yellow fever epidemic ever to hit New Orleans took the lives of 10,000 people. But yellow fever was not the only "sickness" from which the city suffered. Drinking was widespread, prostitution was accepted and even advertised, and gambling a way of life. Political corruption and illegal voting, especially among immigrants, was tolerated.

And yet, it was a city of contrasts. The architecture in the richer parts of town was beautiful, the homes of the wealthy exquisitely furnished, the cuisine superb. Pleasures abounded during the Mardi Gras season. There was a regular opera season, and at any time of the year, there were plays at the Théâtre d'Orléans. Staged concerts featured well-known artists. There was horseracing at the Metairie Track and hunting and fishing within easy reach of the city. Blacks, whether slave or freemen, enjoyed their Sunday afternoons at Congo Square, where they danced uninhibitedly. Most citizens were Catholics. Others were Episcopalian, Methodist, or Jewish. Fraternal organizations had already been formed to assist the immigrants in coping with their difficulties of adjusting to a new country.

New Orleans's citizens were opposed to secession. This was not because they opposed slavery. On the contrary, they defended it vehemently. But they were afraid that secession would destroy the city's trade with the upper Mississippi Valley, which was paramount to the region's prosperity.

To New Orleanians, secession did not seem to be necessary to protect the institution of slavery. When Abraham Lincoln was elected, sentiments changed rapidly. Lincoln said that he favored non-extension of slavery. The handwriting was on the wall: eventually, Lincoln would end slavery. In 1861, Louisiana had to decide whether to follow the other Southern states and make a final break with the Union or attend a convention of Southern states to make one last attempt at compromise. On January 26, 1861, delegates to the Louisiana Secession Convention voted 113 to 17 to secede.

The problems of the Confederacy were numerous. There was no organized government. A Confederate cabinet had to be appointed, agencies set up for coordination, and decisions made for strategy. The Confederacy had few ships and not many guns, war materials, or uniforms. There were no factories to produce these necessities. Pres. Jefferson Davis decided, for this reason, to fight a defensive war.

Battle of the Forts

The fall of New Orleans began with the Battle of the Forts at the mouth of the river in April 1862. When Vicksburg fell in July 1863, the conquest of the Mississippi River was complete. The events of the intervening fifteen months were disastrous to the people of New Orleans.

No Confederate-held area in the country was so exposed to Union attack as the lower Mississippi Valley, where there were no mountains, but the mouth of the river was thought to be well protected by forts that had existed for a long time. There were shallow areas in the river that were hard to navigate and swamplands that were difficult to penetrate. New Orleanians felt that their defenses were impregnable.

Even when the flotilla of Union Flag Officer **David G. Farragut** crossed the bar at the mouth of the river in April 1862, the *Times-Picayune* newspaper announced that "Forts Jackson and St. Philip had 170 guns . . . that navigation of the river was stopped by a dam about a quarter of a mile from the forts . . . that no flotilla on earth could force the dam in less than two hours, during which time it would be within cross range of the 170 guns of the highest calibre." Many New Orleanians were not in the city but fighting in Virginia, since no one had expected an invasion from the "well-protected" mouth of the river. The remaining able-bodied men built breastworks around the city, giving special attention to the Chalmette Battlefield. They sunk obstructions in the bayous leading into the city. They prayed their defenses would hold.

But disasters were to befall the city. When Farragut's flotilla came to the area of the forts, the Union guns were discovered to be too small and their shells fell short. Confederate defenders had built a dam, or "boom," of cypress logs across the river. The dam was broken by the rising water, which was soon to be in flood stage. The Union fleet simply cut through the rebuilt boom and sailed on toward New Orleans. Ironclads under construction in the South were not finished in time for Farragut's arrival. There were more Union losses than Confederate losses at the Battle of the Forts, but the fleet continued to New Orleans.

On April 24, the day before the city fell, state officials moved the city's archives by railroad and steamer to other cities. On the levee, citizens burned 15,000 bales of cotton to prevent them from falling into the hands of the Yankees. The dry-docks on the Algiers side of the river were sunk by order of Gen. Mansfield Lovell, and privately owned steamboats were set on fire by their owners to drift downriver. On Canal Street, a bonfire blazed, burning the records of the Custom House. Normal business ceased, and the poor looted warehouses on the riverfront of sugar, molasses, and food. That night, the governor and other state officials left the city by steamer and railroad, abandoning the residents.

On the morning of April 25, General Lovell sent his small force to Camp Moore, seventy miles north of New Orleans, near what is now the town of Kentwood, to prevent the bombardment of the city. He believed that the fort had fallen and that it would be absurd to confront a flotilla of forty vessels equipped with more than one hundred large-caliber guns with less than three thousand militia armed with shotguns. Mayor John T. Monroe urged storekeepers to open their shops. People gathered on the levee to watch the flotilla sail up to the docks. Farragut disembarked and joined the mayor to make his demands.

After a week of unsuccessful negotiations between Mayor Monroe and Captain Farragut, the U.S. flag had still not been raised before the U.S. Mint, the Custom House, or City Hall. Farragut had no desire to bombard the city. For one thing, he would not have had enough ammunition left for his attacks on Baton Rouge and Vicksburg.

What brought matters to a head were the actions of an irresponsible and impulsive group of New Orleanians, who could not resist showing open defiance to the Yankees. On a Saturday morning, a week after the arrival of the flotilla, the captain of the *Pensacola* took a small

party ashore and raised the U.S. flag over the Mint, at the end of
Esplanade Avenue near the river. He warned the mob that his ship
would fire howitzers loaded with grapeshot if the flag was molested.
Almost immediately, **William B. Mumford,** a local gambler, went
up to the roof and lowered the flag. He and his friends dragged the
flag to Lafayette Square, where they tore it to bits and distributed the
pieces as souvenirs. Farragut replied with an ultimatum to remove the
women and children from the city within forty-eight hours.

The City Council protested that bombardment was inhuman and
that it was impossible to evacuate in so short a time. Then, Farragut
received word that the forts had fallen. The Southern provisions ran
low, so the Fort Jackson garrison mutinied and left in small boats. The
men at Fort St. Philip did the same. Gen. Benjamin Franklin Butler's

*Battle of the Forts, April 1862. Map shows position of Confederate forts Jackson
and St. Philip as Flag Officer Farragut passed beneath their fire, leading his
flotilla toward New Orleans.*

troops could now sail up an undefended river and take command of the city.

Mayor Monroe now agreed to the raising of the American flag at City Hall, and the military occupation of New Orleans began. It was to last fourteen years, the longest amount of time any American city was ever occupied by a hostile power. Loss of control of the Mississippi River and of the largest city in the South was a major blow to the Confederacy. The defeat boosted Northern morale and had a tremendous effect on the attitude of Europe. England and France otherwise might have recognized the independence of the Confederacy or even entered the war for economic reasons due to a cotton embargo.

Gen. Benjamin Butler, Commander of the Department of the Gulf

Of all the traditional villains in Southern history, none are painted blacker than William T. Sherman, who marched through Georgia, and Gen. Benjamin Butler, who served as military commander of New Orleans for seven months in 1862. Since there were no precedents to follow, commanders of occupied territories arbitrarily created policy as they went along, using as a guide the legislation passed in Washington, such as the Confiscation Act of 1862 and the Emancipation Act of the same year.

General Butler, forty-two years old at the outset of the war, was a fat man with a brilliant mind and a driving political ambition who had made a name for himself in Boston fighting for the rights of labor and later representing men of great wealth. Energetic, shrewd, and often unscrupulous, he decided from the beginning that he would employ harsh treatment toward the Rebels, as he considered them traitors and felt that he had been robbed of the glory he deserved as Occupation Commander of New Orleans, since it was Farragut who had lowered the Confederate flag over City Hall before he left the city. Butler was determined to make his power felt.

He entered the city as the new commander of the Department of the Gulf with 18,000 troops of mostly infantry but some cavalry and artillery. When urged by Gen. George B. McClellan to occupy only Algiers and the city of Carrollton, since the rest of the city had enough Union sentiment to control it, Butler said:

I find the city under the dominion of the mob. They have insulted our flag, torn it down with indignity. This outrage will be punished in such manner as, in my judgment, will caution both the perpetrators and the abettors of the act so that they will feel the stripes if they do not reverence the stars of our banner.

On another occasion, he declared, "New Orleans is a conquered city. It has been conquered by the forces of the United States and by the laws of nations, and lies subject to the will of the conquerors" (Evans 1899).

The municipal government was allowed to continue its many functions, but martial law was to prevail. All persons in arms against the United States were to surrender themselves and their equipment. Those who wished to pledge their Oath of Allegiance to the United States would be protected in person and property; violation of this oath was punishable by death, and those who refused to take the oath would be treated as enemies. The American flag was to be respected by all. Citizens were to go on about their business as usual. All assemblages, private or public, were forbidden. Only federal taxes and those for sanitation could be collected. Fire companies were to continue to operate. Military courts would try those accused of major crimes or of interference with the laws of the United States. Minor crimes and civil suits would be handled by city authorities. The press was to submit all copy to military censors. The army took over telegraphic communications. Butler stated that he would prefer to administer the government mildly, but if necessary, he could be ruthless.

Mayor Monroe wanted to suspend the municipal government at once, but the councilmen objected. There was a division of authority between municipal and military for two weeks, after which the general had the mayor arrested and forced the councilmen out of office by insisting they sign the Oath of Allegiance. After the municipal government of New Orleans was overthrown, Butler appointed federal officers to act as mayors, judges, and provost marshals for the duration of the war.

The Woman Order

The women of New Orleans had their own way of protesting the military occupation. If they met federal officers on the sidewalk, they would lift their skirts and move out into the streets. If federal officers got into a streetcar or a church pew they were occupying, they would leave at once. They were also insulting. It was after one woman spat in the face of two officers that Butler passed **General Order No. 28** on May 15, 1862. It read as follows:

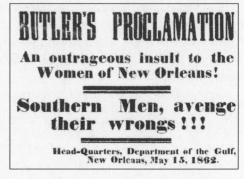

Citizens' newspaper ad protesting Butler's proclamation

As the officers and soldiers of the United States have been subject to repeated insults from the women of New Orleans in return for the most scrupulous non-interference and courtesy on our part, it is ordered that hereafter, when any female shall, by word, gesture, or movement, insult or show contempt for any officer or soldier of the United States, she shall be regarded and held liable to be treated as a woman of the town plying her avocations. (Butler 1892)

Southerners considered the order an open invitation for Yankee soldiers to ravage women of all ranks, and Butler's chief of staff warned him that his own officers might take the same meaning. Butler referred to the women of New Orleans as "she-adders." The women responded to the order by restraining themselves but continued to express dedication to the Confederacy by singing the "Bonnie Blue Flag" at every opportunity. It is said that prostitutes in the city put Butler's picture in the bottom of their "tinkle pots."

The Hanging of Mumford

Three weeks after the Woman Order, on June 7, 1862, Mumford, who had torn down the flag at the Mint, was hung at the scene of his crime. One week earlier, a military commission had pronounced his execution. Immediately thereafter, criminal elements had threatened to assassinate Butler if he went through with the execution. But Butler refused all pleas, including that of the prisoner's wife. Butler was thereafter called the "Beast."

Compared with other Southern cities, New Orleans was not treated as badly as many of its residents thought. The city was never bombarded. It was governed efficiently, and the physical comfort of the citizens was better during the federal administration than it had been under the Confederacy.

Mayor Monroe and the City Council, by *not* cleaning the streets, had hoped to hasten the coming of a yellow fever epidemic, which they believed would have killed off many of the federal army, while the Southerners, who were immune, would survive. Also, by *not* providing food for the poor, they forced Butler to do so, and by *not* restraining crime, they forced him to keep more troops in the city.

For the safety of his own men, as well as that of the city, Butler suppressed the crime levels. He allowed food to be brought into the city from Mobile. He allowed the sale of some army provisions to civilians. He helped the poor for a time using federal funds and forced the city to hire 2,000 unemployed men to clean the streets. His preventive measures kept the city free of yellow fever during the war and for some time thereafter. He collected "donations" of $350,000 from individuals and firms, which were spent on public works or given to Charity Hospital.

Another epithet by which the general was known was "Silver Spoons" Butler, referring to the profits he allegedly amassed through confiscation of personal property under the protection of the Confiscation Act. First, he claimed in the name of the government all property belonging to the U.S. government, such as the U.S. Mint and the Custom House. Then, he seized many private homes for the use of the military, usually those of Confederates off fighting in the war.

The Second Confiscation Act of 1862 provided for the seizure of all property (including slaves, since they were considered property) belonging to officers of the Confederacy and to all Rebels who continued to resist signing the Oath of Allegiance for sixty days after the law was passed. When this grace period ended, some three thousand citizens still refused to sign, forfeiting their property. They were classified as irreconcilables but were allowed to leave the city if they chose. Their homes and personal effects were sold at auction for low prices.

Who is to say if Butler's actions during this brief term of office were legal? A state of war existed, and there were no rules to follow. Laws were made up as the war progressed. They could be enforced only within a

Gen. Benjamin Franklin Butler headed the occupation of New Orleans for seven months during the Civil War. He was loathed by the natives, who called him "Beast" Butler and "Spoons" Butler. (Courtesy Lloyd W. Huber for the late Leonard V. Huber)

Union-occupied territory, and it was always possible that they might be countermanded by the president and his cabinet. The hanging of Mumford (the only New Orleans citizen killed during Butler's administration) inspired fear as well as hatred, perhaps resulting in the saving of many lives and the prevention of many prison sentences.

Many New Orleanians volunteered for military service early in the war and were sent to Virginia in various troops, such as the Crescent Rifles, the Louisiana Guards, and the Washington Artillery. They were the aristocrats. From the slums and the underworld came the Louisiana Tigers Battalion. The Sixth Louisiana Infantry was composed of Irish laborers and free blacks and were used for militia duty only.

New Orleans was the recruiting and debarkation center for the state. Troops on their way to somewhere else would stay at Camp Lewis in Carrollton and Camp Walker on the Metairie Race Track. By the fall of 1861, there were 23,000 men in the military from Louisiana. Many men volunteered for military service in the summer of 1861 because there were no jobs to be found in the city.

No one knew exactly what to do with the blacks in the occupied territories of the South. These territories were part of the Union, and the Emancipation Proclamation applied to all "slave states." Butler pleaded with Lincoln for guidance, but Lincoln told him to "get along" with the problems in the best way he could, trying not to insult either the Northern abolitionists or the Southern conservatives. Lincoln was having his own difficulties and hoped to win another election in 1864.

New Orleans, in any case, was no occupation commander's dream. There were not only black slaves, but also free people of color and maroons, who were escaped slaves seeking shelter in outside settlements. Thousands had rushed into the city as soon as it was captured, seeking security under the flag of the United States. Once here, they could not return to their owners: this had been ordered by an act of Congress. And Butler could not let them starve. He put them to work at rough labor or assigned them to work for his officers.

By the fall of 1862, Butler was supporting 10,000 blacks. Fearing an insurrection, he continued the curfew and refused to allow **Gen. John W. Phelps** to enlist black men in the army and give them weapons. He freed slaves belonging to the French and Spanish aliens and those in jail who had belonged to Confederate soldiers fighting in the war.

He allowed former slaves certain civil rights: they could testify in court against white men and ride in all streetcars. He used them as spies against their masters and did not allow jailers to whip black prisoners. In the fall he used blacks as free labor on confiscated plantations. It is a matter of record that he handled the situation as wisely as anyone could.

Fr. James Ignatius Mullon served the congregation of St. Patrick's Church as pastor from 1834 to 1866. An ardent Confederate, he often locked horns with Butler, the chief of military occupation. It was a daily custom for the congregation to unite in prayer after Mass for the success of the Confederate cause. Butler sent word for this to cease. Ostensibly, Father Mullon complied, but he told his parishioners to pray in silence. Once, when accused of having refused to bury a Union soldier, Father Mullon told the general that he stood ready to bury the whole Union Army, Butler included, whenever the occasion was offered.

On the evening of December 14, 1862, **Gen. Nathaniel P. Banks** arrived in New Orleans with papers assigning him as Butler's replacement. Shattered and disappointed, Butler went home to Lowell, Massachusetts.

Banks was a man of a different temperament altogether. He thought he could win over the people of New Orleans with conciliation, but the time was past when such an approach would succeed. If it ever had a chance, it would have been at the beginning of the occupation. By the start of 1863, New Orleanians no longer trusted any moves made by their federal occupiers.

Banks promised fair treatment for all and compensation for losses by acts of the United States, including slaves. The Episcopal churches, which had been closed under Butler, were reopened on Christmas Eve 1862. The sale of confiscated property was suspended, and more than a hundred political prisoners were released. Federal officers were forced to return houses they had seized. Banks promised to investigate cases of extortion, confiscation, and speculation. He and his wife began holding balls and inviting the élite of the city in the hope that these entertainments would win them over.

Taking this leniency as a sign of weakness, the Rebels responded by showing every manner of disloyalty. The women once again began insulting the federal officers. Teachers sang "Dixie" with their students. Newspapers refused to publish information submitted by federal officers.

In April 1863, Banks was forced to do an about-face. He issued severe orders, telling registered enemies of the Union to leave the territory within fifteen days, requiring the Oath of Allegiance of all who remained, and promising the death penalty to all who gave supplies to the Confederate Army.

From the start of the war, New Orleans was a garrison city. Though it was never attacked, it lay within a combat area. After Memphis and Baton Rouge fell to Union forces, Vicksburg surrendered on July 4, 1863. In April 1864, Banks's expedition against Shreveport started the bloodiest fighting in Louisiana, which took place at the Battles of Mansfield and Pleasant Hill. From 1862 to the war's end, there were two armies and two civil governments in the state.

The Federals blockaded the river, knowing that the Rebels depended on the incoming ships from Europe for food and staples. By the end of 1862, the port city was on the brink of starvation. In time, however, the Federals saw that they, too, depended on incoming vessels for their survival and lifted the blockade. Then the Confederates put up a blockade at Vicksburg, prohibiting free commerce on the river because it would have benefited the Union. The Federals depended on cotton and sugar for their economic recovery, and they had not captured enough of the farm area to bring this recovery about.

When the first blockade was lifted, merchandise coming from New England could be brought up the river from the Gulf, but there was no cotton or sugar to exchange for it. The goal of the Red River Campaign of 1864 was to capture Shreveport, which could be used as a base for a drive into Texas. There, the Union could acquire enough cotton to help bring about a Northern victory. But the campaign ended in disaster for the Federals, and Banks was removed from his command.

As long as the Confederates were able to keep Vicksburg cut off from the river, the progress of the Federals was slow, and the Rebels simply continued with their passive resistance to the Union. But once Vicksburg had been captured and the river was open to Federal traffic, economic progress resumed, and New Orleanians feared that Federal control of the region would become permanent. Then, when Banks was defeated in the Red River Campaign, hopes of a Southern victory were revived, and hostility against the Union occupiers sharpened once again.

In 1864, a free election was held under the supervision of General

Banks, and Michael Hahn was elected governor of Louisiana. Lincoln recognized Hahn as chief executive. At last, Louisiana had a civil government, however limited its powers.

Weaknesses of the South

The South's weaknesses during the war were its specialized economy and its dependence on external markets. Cotton, sugar, tobacco, and other staples had been sent to Europe and the North in exchange for manufactured goods and food. Cut off from these markets, the South could no longer continue to feed its own civilian population, to say nothing of a military force. The blockade hindered the importation of necessary goods, and economic depression spread. Men who worked in trade and transportation were now unemployed.

Before the war, New Orleans was one of the most commercial cities but had few industries. It had no rice mill, no flourmill, and only one sugar refinery, and even that was destroyed when Farragut was approaching the city in 1862. During the war, New Orleans was a city without industry.

After the capture of New Orleans, speculators from the North poured into the city expecting to make quick and easy money. Word of Butler's profits in confiscated property spurred them on, and they came in droves, expecting to grow rich within months. Southerners hated them because they took over functions formerly being done by the locals. Northerners hated them because they traded with the Rebels, transactions that only helped their enemies.

Actually, the only way speculators hurt the economy was by keeping prices high. That was inevitable in a time of war. But speculators were the only businessmen in the community with a supply of capital and the ability to direct business operations. However selfish their motives, they helped New Orleans out of the depression.

Lincoln had hoped to make Louisiana the model for all the Southern states. It was to be the first state to accept his plan for reentry into the Union. For this reason, he extended leniency whenever possible to the residents of the region. Life for the people of Louisiana was more comfortable than for most residents of occupied territories.

The upper classes suffered most, seeing their securities, their businesses, and their other assets diminish in value. Many suffered shortages of food; the ignominy of defeat; the sorrow of deaths of husbands, sons, and brothers; and the lack of social and cultural events. Women rarely went out. In 1863, General Banks forbade the observance of Mardi Gras, to the great vexation of the people.

The Yankees were no happier being in New Orleans than the citizens were to have them. They were bivouacked in tents at camps outside the city proper where the terrain was swampy. They suffered heat, rain, and flooded land, all of which brought on diarrhea and fevers. When in good health, soldiers sought relief from their misery and boredom. Food was scarce in the city, but women never were. Soldiers with venereal disease cost the Union in many ways.

Heavy drinking was the rule among laborers and soldiers on leave. Saloons were still abundant on Gallatin Street, Girod Street, and Thomas Street. On St. Charles Avenue, between Canal and Lafayette streets, forty-five places sold liquor within six blocks. In the saloons, if you didn't continue to drink, the proprietor threw you out; if you did, you usually wound up doped and rolled. Gambling was brisk with games of pitching pennies, shooting craps, or playing poker or three-card Monte.

On marches from Camp Parapet north of the city to Pass Manchac, Yankee troops saw everything from alligators to mosquitoes to snakes. Back in camp, they were at the mercy of lice. Cheap rooms in the city abounded with bedbugs and cockroaches.

Union officers, who were able to live in a better part of town, got a better impression of the city with its flowers and trees that flourished even in winter, its duck hunting, its theater, its French opera, and its beautiful (though rude) young women.

The war ended in 1865. By November of that year, the ex-Confederates were once again in control of the state. In most of the South, political reconstruction did not begin until the end of the war, but in Louisiana the issues had been debated and voted on long before Lee's surrender. Early in 1865, blacks, scalawags, and carpetbaggers formed the Republican Party, which, despite its first defeat, would soon gain control of the state.

According to the Congressional Act of 1867, Louisiana was occupied by Federal troops under Gen. Philip Sheridan, who interpreted the terms of the act so strictly that half of the white citizens could not vote at all, but all adult black males could vote. The Constitution of 1868 enfranchised the black population and gave them full equality of the races in public schools and on streetcars and railroads.

In the state election of 1868, **Henry Clay Warmoth** of Illinois, a carpetbagger, and his lieutenant governor, P. B. S. Pinchback, a mulatto, were elected.

In 1872, **William Pitt Kellogg** and **Caesar Carpentier Antoine** (another mulatto) replaced Warmoth and Pinchback as governor and lieutenant governor, respectively.

President Grant used Federal troops to install the new officials and to put his Republican supporters in control of the legislature. For the next four years, Louisiana had two governors and two legislatures.

In the presidential election of 1876, both the Republicans (Rutherford B. Hayes) and the Democrats (Samuel J. Tilden) claimed victory. Four states—Louisiana, South Carolina, Florida, and Oregon—had submitted two sets of electoral returns, one by the Democrats and one by the Republicans. The Electoral College gave the disputed votes to Hayes, making him the winner. The Democrats cried fraud and challenged the decision.

In January 1877, a fifteen-man Electoral Commission was appointed by Congress to make the final decision. In a private meeting, representatives from Louisiana, South Carolina, and Florida agreed not to oppose the decision of the Electoral Commission (which would be to name Hayes the winner) if in exchange, the states could be permitted to elect their own governors with no federal interference and if all Federal troops would be removed. As a result of this meeting, Hayes became president, ex-Confederate Francis T. Nicholls became governor of Louisiana, and the Federal troops were removed. After fourteen years as an occupied city, New Orleans was at last free again.

CHAPTER IX

Rebirth and Resurgence: 1865-1930

The years of Reconstruction were the darkest in the history of New Orleans. It was a time of violence, lawlessness, and corruption. Confederate soldiers, returning from war, found Unionists in charge of all civic affairs. Blacks, not knowing what to do with their liberties, crowded in the city under the protective wing of the Freedmen's Bureau. Carpetbaggers from the North came in droves to take possession of commerce and politics to whatever extent possible.

The Southerners tried hard, in spite of poverty, to regain their position in the city. Unionists feared that the Southerners might return to power, and carpetbaggers feared that they might be thrown out. Carpetbagger efforts to seat blacks in the legislature brought about the **Massacre of 1866** at the Mechanics Institute on Dryades Street (now University Place), when 44 black and 4 white men were killed and 160 others wounded.

During the administration of Governor Warmoth, control of New Orleans was taken from the Democrats by a new form of city government, in which the governor appointed the mayor and seven administrators. New Orleans was virtually in the grip of a dictator. Warmoth appointed local police, registrars, and a returning board for the city.

Results of any election could be altered by Warmoth's returning board, which had the power to review the results and throw out whatever votes they chose. In fact, voting became dangerous. Fights broke out, leading to fatalities at every election. Saloons were wide open, gambling thrived, and robbery and violence were the order of the day.

The Battle of Liberty Place

The **Crescent City White League** was formed in 1874 for the defense of the rights of white citizens against the radical state government. On the morning of September 14, 1875, the White Leaguers met at the Clay Statue on Canal Street to make plans to take possession of the city and the state governments, thus breaking the power of the Metropolitan Police. Reassembling at Camp and Poydras streets in the afternoon, armed for an encounter, they advanced down the levee at four o'clock. However, the Metropolitan Police were stationed at several points throughout the city, with the main body under **Gen. Algernon Sidney Badger** at Canal Street and the river. The general saw the men of the White League coming and opened fire. The White Leaguers had no artillery, but they charged into the police and cleared the street. They drove the police back to Jackson Square, where both armies remained through the night. In the morning, the police surrendered the State House, the Arsenal, and Jackson Square. In the fray, a total of thirty-one had been killed and seventy-nine wounded.

Victory was short lived. The White Leaguers installed **Lt.-Gov. Davidson B. Penn** in the State House on September 15, 1874, but President Grant immediately sent reinforcements and demanded the reinstatement of **Gov. William Pitt Kellogg** without delay. The city was to remain in the grip of a Republican governor for three more years.

After the compromise in which President Hayes was elected, **Gen. Francis T. Nicholls,** the Confederate patriot, served as Louisiana governor from 1878 to 1880 and returned in 1888 for a four-year term. Nicholls lost his left arm in combat at Winchester and his left leg at Chancellorsville. (One cannot help but wonder how he fought at the Battle of Chancellorsville without an arm in the first place.) In placing his name in the nomination, Tay Goode of Terrebonne Parish said, "I give you all that is left of Francis Nicholls, because all that is left of him is right."

The Louisiana Lottery

In 1868, an institution known as the Louisiana Lottery Company was born in a corrupt era. Founder **Charles T. Howard** managed to obtain a twenty-five-year charter from the state legislature. This enabled the lottery to control the city, state, and even national politicians who were on its payroll. To mask its vice, the lottery made regular contributions to charitable causes such as Charity Hospital and the French Opera House and was always ready with cash in times of hurricanes and floods.

New Orleanians loved the lottery. For twenty-five cents, they could purchase a ticket and a dream of leisure and luxury. Tickets were sold in denominations as high as $40, for which the prize was $600,000. More than two hundred shops dotted the city, and there were branch offices in many other major cities. Drawings were held each day in public. Throngs gathered to watch as two Confederate heroes hired to give respectability to the proceedings, P. G. T. Beauregard and Jubal Early, drew the numbers.

The lottery was supported by many Republicans and Democrats. It was the subject of political debates for twenty-five years. Its charter was set to expire January 1, 1894. The United States Supreme Court spelled out the beginning of the end of the Louisiana Lottery when it affirmed the right of Congress to prohibit the lottery's use of the U.S. mail in advertising. The company continued in the state until it expired in 1894, but its back had been broken. The *New Orleans Delta* declared, "The Lottery is now like a postage stamp . . . licked and put in a corner." It was out of business by 1895.

New Orleans had reached its lowest period as a municipality in the early 1880s. It had surrendered all its franchises, duties, and privileges to private individuals or corporations. The only thing it still controlled was the police force, which was in the hands of the mayor, who administered it so that it was overrun with politics and filled with corruption.

Fast forward to 1990. The Louisiana legislature proposed a constitutional amendment to allow for a state-run lottery to generate income without raising taxes. The amendment was passed and in 1991 the Louisiana Lottery Corporation was incorporated.

In 1993, a second constitutional amendment was approved that would dedicate the corporation's proceeds to the Minimum Foundation Program, a process by which the state determines the cost to educate students at public schools and provides funding to school districts.

Mayor Joseph A. Shakspeare

Joseph A. Shakspeare served as mayor from 1880 to 1882 and returned to serve in 1888. Shakspeare knew that the blackmail and corruption in the city had grown out of the gambling business. He introduced the Shakspeare Plan, which was nothing less than a payoff to his office for police protection for gamblers. The amazing thing was that it succeeded. Gambling had always been rampant in the city. Statutes against it were impossible to enforce and gave the police an opportunity to collect graft. The mayor could not license it, since it was against the state constitution. Therefore, for a small monthly payment, Shakspeare, as chief of police, agreed to forbid his officers to arrest gamblers. The money thus collected was used to establish the Shakspeare Almshouse and to support other charities. It was ultimately abused, needless to say, and the Shakspeare fund gradually disappeared from the revenues of the city.

Shakspeare was defeated in 1892 by John Fitzpatrick, a candidate of the Regular Democratic Organization. Ever since the 1870s, municipal elections in New Orleans had been battles fought between the RDO (or Choctaw Club, as it was called), which held power most of the time, and a reform movement, whose purpose it was to wipe out the RDO or keep its candidates out of office. The first of these reform candidates was, surprisingly, Shakspeare himself. Another reform mayor, **Walter C. Flower,** took office in 1896.

The Seventeen Years of Mayor Martin Behrman

In between the terms of Shakspeare and Flower, John Fitzpatrick of the RDO held office. His protégé was a young man named Martin Behrman, who was orphaned at an early age and ended his formal education at St. Philip School, when Warren Easton was still the principal there. Living in Algiers, Behrman worked in a family grocery store until he was married at the age of twenty-two. Then, he became a clerk in the district assessor's office but lost his job when Shakspeare's reform administration replaced all RDO men with reform followers. When Fitzpatrick of the RDO defeated Shakspeare, Behrman was appointed clerk to three City Council committees and elected delegate to the Constitutional Convention in 1898 and state auditor in 1904. Later in 1904, he was nominated for mayor and won in a landslide.

Behrman was reelected in 1908, 1912, and 1916. The Regular Democratic Organization was the New Orleans version of New York's Tammany Hall, a political machine that was seemingly invincible.

As early as 1907, the Behrman organization was referred to as the Behrman Ring, and "Ring politics" grew stronger as Behrman won election after election. The anti-Ring leaders formed the "Good Government League." Nicknamed the "Goo-Goos," they supported **Luther E. Hall** for governor. The Goo-Goos hoped that Hall would replace the New Orleans mayor and councilmanic form of government with a commission system, which they thought would reduce Behrman's powers and eventually his popularity. Hall was elected and the change of government was made as promised in 1912. Ironically, and to the great disappointment of the "Goo-Goos," Hall's administration was under the control of the Behrmanites, who adopted the commission council form of government as their own.

John M. Parker, another reform candidate, was elected governor in 1920 and launched a movement to oust Martin Behrman, who had been asked by the Old Regulars (as the RDO was called) to run for mayor for a fifth term. Behrman lost the election to **Andre McShane** in 1920 but was reelected in 1925. His supporters changed their campaign rallying cry from "Papa's Coming Home" to "Papa's Back." Behrman died in office a year later, having served as mayor for seventeen years, the only man in the city's history to be elected five times as mayor.

During this period in the city's political history, T. Harry Williams, in his biography *Huey Long* (1981), wrote:

> Louisiana (and hence, New Orleans), politics, w[ere] speculative, devious, personal and exuberant, and highly professional. The objectives w[ere] to win, and in no other state were the devices employed to win— stratagems, deals and oratory—so studied and admired by the populace.
>
> Louisiana's people are accused of having a tolerance of corruption found no place else in the United States. This tolerance is described as "a Latin enclave of immorality set down in a country of Anglo-Saxon righteousness."

In spite of occasional riots, labor unrest, and corruption in local government in the late nineteenth and early twentieth centuries, business and community leaders managed to create a resurgence in the economy. The American Sector became a modern city with burgeoning commerce, and mansions mushroomed all along the main thoroughfares. People had time to turn their minds to a bit of leisure at one of the new amusement parks that were now available for their enjoyment.

Recreation and Amusement

West End Amusement Park offered swimming, picnicking, amusement rides, and outdoor movies, some of the first movies seen in the city.

New Orleanians took barges along the New Basin Canal to the site of the present Southern Yacht Club as early as 1838. Then, after 1876, when the New Orleans City and Lake Railroad started running trains to the lake, they traveled by train. At that time, a large wooden platform was constructed over the water, and a hotel, restaurant, and structures to house amusements arose. It was called New Lake End until 1880, when it was rechristened West End Park, and for the next thirty years, it remained a popular lake resort. In 1909, the city constructed a seawall 500 feet out in the lake and filled in the space between it and the old embankment to form the present thirty-acre West End Park.

Another lakefront amusement center popular at this time was **Spanish Fort**, which grew up around the site of the old colonial fort originally built by the French in 1701 at the mouth of Bayou St. John. Because it was rebuilt by the Spanish in 1779, it was called Spanish Fort. The fort never saw warfare but was used as an observation point in the War of 1812. The area around Spanish Fort was sold in 1823 to

West End Amusement Park, a gathering place for pleasure seekers at the turn of the twentieth century. (Courtesy Leonard V. Huber Collection)

Harvey Elkins, who built the Pontchartrain Hotel there. In 1874, the hotel was rebuilt around the same time that a railroad was constructed to connect the resort to downtown New Orleans. In 1878, Moses Schwartz bought Spanish Fort. He built a casino with a restaurant offering meals for one dollar and a theater featuring light opera and band concerts. In 1880, Otto Touché opened the Over the Rhine Bar and Restaurant, which could be reached by a winged footbridge across the bayou from Spanish Fort.

Spanish Fort became the site of an amusement park in 1883. It was abandoned for a time in 1903, when railroad service to the site was suspended. Its buildings burned down in 1906. The property was acquired in 1909 by the New Orleans Railway and Light Company, which rebuilt and reopened an amusement center that included a Ferris wheel and other rides, picnic pavilion, restaurant, and bathing facilities. Ownership of the property later reverted to the city. Plans were drawn in 1928 to develop the lakefront from West End to the airport, concluding the final chapter to Spanish Fort as an amusement center.

In 1928, the amusement park was relocated to the lake end of Bayou St. John on land already "filled" and its name changed to Pontchartrain Beach. Eventually, the Orleans Parish Levee Board decided to establish a permanent site for an amusement park several miles farther east and grant a twenty-year lease. The Batt family (headed by Harry Batt, Sr., president) acquired control in 1934, and in 1939, the new Pontchartrain Beach opened at the end of Elysian Fields Avenue. The Zephyr rollercoaster was the park's symbol. World War II created a boom for the park, bringing servicemen in droves to enjoy recreation. The park closed in 1983.

Another delightful outing at the turn of the twentieth century was a drive on Old Shell Road, which ran along the Metairie side of the New Basin Canal. The drive went past the New Orleans Country Club on Pontchartrain Boulevard and the new Metairie Cemetery on a trail lined with palms and oleanders and a view of pleasure boats on the water.

The Second Renaissance of the Vieux Carré: The Vieux Carré Commission

Baroness de Pontalba is credited with the first rebirth of the Vieux Carré in the mid-nineteenth century. It was a time when the wealthy moved out of the old part of town and built mansions on St. Charles Avenue. Her beautiful apartments flanking the Place d'Armes served as a catalyst, renewing interest in the French Quarter and pride in its history.

In the decades following the Civil War, there was a sharp decline in the commercial importance of the city to the rest of the nation. New Orleans remained impoverished. The city had no money for improvements and repairs. Once again, the French Quarter began to deteriorate. Families who could afford to move migrated to the newer parts of town. Jackson Square, at the turn of the twentieth century, was once again seedy. The Pontalba Buildings were derelict with vagrants for tenants, and the whole neighborhood was fast becoming a slum.

In 1908, an entire block of the finest buildings in the Quarter was destroyed to build the Civil Courts Building. The St. Louis Exchange Hotel with its majestic dome, once the pride of the Vieux Carré and the site of the State Capitol in 1874, fell into decay. It was badly damaged in the 1915 hurricane and eventually demolished.

New Orleanians who cared about preserving their historic treasures began to take note in the 1920s and 1930s that, unless something was done to protect what remained of the Quarter, it would soon disappear and be lost forever. The Vieux Carré Commission was established in 1921 and, by state constitutional amendment in 1936, was given the power to regulate architecture through control of building permits. Its purpose was to renovate, restore, and remodel the old buildings and put them to new uses so that the buildings might pay their own way. Thus began the second renaissance of the Vieux Carré.

Fortunately and unfortunately, President Roosevelt's Works Progress Administration almost simultaneously moved in with money and talent to recondition parts of the Quarter, giving special attention to the French Market, Jackson Square, the Cathedral, the Cabildo, the Presbytère, and the Pontalba Buildings. While no one would dispute the fact that a slum area was rehabilitated and that land values began to rise, it was equally true that progress, as envisioned by legislators in Washington, had a different definition in New Orleans. WPA "progress" involved the demolition of some of the city's earliest structures.

The Cotton Exchange Building, built 1882-83 on the corner of Gravier and Carondelet, was demolished in 1920. Statues on the third floor were moved to City Park for a brief stay. Two on the ground floor, called caryatids, now stand in the 100 block of City Park Avenue.

St. Charles Hotel, viewed from Canal Street circa 1925, the third on the same site. It was demolished in 1974. Today it is the site of Place St. Charles.

Opulent lobby of the third St. Charles Hotel, 1925

Chartres Street in the French Quarter, including the St. Louis Cathedral on the site of the first church built in the Mississippi Valley.

The WPA's main concern was to put food in the mouths of the hungry. Workers on those projects were earning fifteen to twenty dollars per week. The agency began "making improvements" by eradicating some of the French Market's oldest buildings. The Old Red Store (1830) was demolished and Gallatin Street on the riverfront, that "dark alley of mystery and murder," was wiped out altogether "to relieve the city of an area of human decay." According to Robin Von Breton Derbes, in *New Orleans Magazine* in 1976, this act was "the equivalent of demolishing Camp Street to get rid of Skid Row."

None of this was done without a fight. The powers that be in the WPA and the Vieux Carré Commission locked horns daily. The WPA argued that slum clearance was its first concern while the Vieux Carré Commission insisted that the French Quarter retain its distinctive character. But the WPA plowed forward.

Improvements were made and some would argue that they were for the better. Gallatin Street was replaced with the present air-steel sheds of the Farmer's Market.

Since a major restoration in 1975, the historic French Market's buildings, distinguished by graceful arcades and stately columns, offer a glimpse of a scene of activity that has existed in the same place since the early 1800s. The Halle des Boucheries (built in 1813), the Halle des Legumes (1822), and the reconstructed Red Store are all part of the rebuilt French Market complex that authenticates early French Quarter architecture. One end of the market is tucked into the bend of the river; the other is at Jackson Square.

Today, flagstone promenades, sparkling fountains, and old-fashioned benches add touches of a bygone era. At the Jackson Square end is Café du Monde, with its inimitable coffee and beignets (without which no visit to New Orleans is complete).

Just outside Café du Monde, the steps of the beautifully landscaped "Moonwalk," named for Mayor Moon Landrieu, are decorated with fountains, lampposts, and benches where one can watch the river roll past. To the right are the lighted spans of the Crescent City Connection and to the left is the French Quarter.

Street Patterns

The Mississippi's crescent course affected the entire way of life of the city's residents. Only the Vieux Carré, laid out in a grid pattern, has straight streets. Beyond the Vieux Carré, property lines extending back from the river date back to the earliest land grants ever to exist in the city. Property lines ran perpendicular to the levee in long narrow strips, for good reason: all landowners needed access to transportation, and transportation was the river. Also, the only dry, usable land was on the natural levees; its value diminished as it approached the backswamp.

The river wraps the city in concave and convex curves. On the land inside the convex curves, the streets were squeezed together. Cross-streets ran parallel to the river, running in straight lines toward the curve of the river, then shifting slightly in conformity with the curve as they crossed property lines, which later became boulevards: Melpomene, Jackson, Louisiana, Napoleon, Jefferson, Broadway, and South Carrollton.

St. Charles Avenue (originally called Nayades Street) was the great boulevard running parallel to the river. It was actually the rear boundary line of the original land grants. It was inevitable that such a wide boulevard, situated on a habitable part of the natural levee halfway between the noisy riverfront and the backswamp, would become the main residential avenue of the American section of the city.

Black and White Population Patterns

The street layout determined the patterns of black and white population settlements. In early New Orleans, in spite of social segregation, there was no geographical segregation of blacks and whites. Slaves lived in the homes of their owners. Free persons of color working for whites lived within walking distance of their employers, usually in small houses behind the big houses owned by the whites. When the boulevards were divided into blocks, neighborhoods developed with an affluent white perimeter, enclosing a small nuclear cluster of blacks. The architecture of these cluster houses was not conspicuously different from that of poor whites' homes. It was, in fact, a far less detrimental type of segregation than that which was found in most Northern cities.

Chinese in New Orleans

After the Civil War, when slaves were no longer available for work in the cotton and sugarcane fields, the Chinese began arriving in Louisiana. Many remained in New Orleans, and in the late nineteenth century there developed a Chinatown of sorts near the current site of the New Orleans Public Library and extending in the direction of the Joy Theater, opium dens and all.

Since weather was hot and humid in New Orleans, and since it was the style for businessmen to wear starched linen shirts and suits, Chinese laundries were popular with the male population and sprung up in every neighborhood. The Chinese also dried Louisiana shrimp, prepared in their own villages in the swamps below New Orleans. Many Chinese restaurants emerged. It is an ethnic group that has retained its own speech and culture.

New Orleans, a Railroad Center

After the Civil War, the mode of transportation in the United States changed from waterways and horse-drawn wagons to railroads. New Orleans, complacent in her leadership on the river, was caught unprepared for the competition. In the decade before the Civil War, New Orleans had only eighty miles of railroads. During and after the war, steam locomotives hauled goods across the continent from the West to the Atlantic, stopping in Chicago and St. Louis, both of which surpassed New Orleans in populations by 1865.

Between 1865 and 1945, New Orleans became a railroad center, almost in spite of herself. With her time-honored position at the junction of the Mississippi and the Gulf, she had the advantage of shipping goods not only out of the agricultural South but also from Latin America. The Latin American connection provided two products greatly coveted by Americans: coffee and bananas. New Orleans became a prime port of entry for both.

Bulk cargo, such as grain from the Midwest and coal from Illinois and Kentucky, continued to travel slowly down the river through New Orleans. Barges moved along, sometimes in a ten-to-one tow, like great floating islands. By the 1950s, trade on the river from the Midwest had increased and, in fact, exceeded that of antebellum days.

The Eads Jetties

Col. James Buchanan Eads, in 1879, completed a system of jetties at the mouth of the Mississippi River, making possible a deep-water channel that would revolutionize navigation on the river.

From the earliest days of settlement, the mouth of the river filled up with silt and logs, and engineers worked unceasingly to dredge it out to allow passage for ships. After the Civil War, larger ships were built. Often, they became stuck on a sandbar for days or weeks, holding up the passage of other ships. Clearly, something had to be done.

Eads visited the mouth of the river and declared that the way to open it to commerce was to build parallel dikes, or jetties, at the mouths of the passes, constructing a channel and causing the stream to flow faster. This faster current, he claimed, would scour its own deep-water channel. This provoked a storm of controversy. Eads took the proposal to Congress, where he struck a bargain with the legislators. He said he was so sure he could produce and maintain a twenty-eight-foot channel that he would ask for $10 million if he succeeded but nothing if he failed. After much debate, he was given a contract to build a jetty at South Pass for $5.25 million and a $100,000 maintenance fee for twenty years.

Work began in June 1875, and four years later, the channel was thirty feet deep and the bar was swept into the Gulf. Eads, gave new life to the river and saved the port of New Orleans, which had fallen from second to eleventh place in the nation. He also indirectly wrote the end to any plans for industrializing Lake Pontchartrain.

The World's Industrial and Cotton Centennial of 1884

The Cotton Centennial was an extravaganza organized by **Mayor Edward A. Burke,** state treasurer, lottery agent for Louisiana, and editor of the *New Orleans Times Democrat*. He convinced Congress to grant a loan of $1 million to the fair and give a gift of $300,000 for government exhibits. The city government donated $100,000, and the rest of the capital was provided by the sale of private stock.

The display covered 249 acres in a rural tract between the edge of uptown and the recently annexed city of Carrollton. Later, the site of the fair would be moved to Audubon Park. The site was about two miles long from the river to the backswamp, with St. Charles Avenue and the Carrollton Railway to Canal Street cutting squarely across its middle.

The fair boasted an area of fifty-one covered acres in the five main buildings and the most dazzling display of electric lights ever seen anywhere. It could be reached from Canal Street by six street railroads or by steamers on the river, which left the foot of Canal Street every half-hour. An electric railroad three miles long encircled the entire fairgrounds, and one of those cars passed every few minutes. In spite of art galleries, industrial displays, restaurants, railroads, and rolling chairs, the fair was a financial failure. Built at a cost of $2.7 million, it lost $500,000. The walkways for tourists became seas of gumbo in the New Orleans rains.

In 1915, the last of the World's Fair buildings were demolished by a hurricane. Now, the only remaining evidence of a fair at the site is a huge boulder in the middle of Audubon Park Golf Course. It resembles a meteorite but is actually a sample of iron ore from the state of Alabama. The fair entrance on Exposition Boulevard and St. Charles Avenue is still used as a path through the park to the former site of the exposition.

When the exposition ended, the state turned the fairgrounds on the river side of St. Charles Avenue (the site of the former Foucher and Boré plantations) into **Audubon Park.** It is today a 340-acre park abounding with ancient oaks and lagoons still enjoyed by walkers, golfers, and picnickers. On the other side of St. Charles Avenue, the land became the campuses of Tulane University and Loyola University. **Loyola University** at 6300 St. Charles Avenue was established in 1912, an outgrowth of Loyola College of 1911. **Tulane University,** financed in 1884 by a bequest from Paul Tulane, was a merger of the Medical College of Louisiana (1834) and the University of Louisiana (1947).

The effects of the fair, though not a profitable venture, are still very much in evidence in the city. A flourishing late Victorian architectural boom came in the wake of displays at the fair. The new park and university area was created, surrounded by one of the city's most affluent neighborhoods.

The Rebuilding of the Port

The **Board of Commissioners of the Port of New Orleans** was created in 1896. Known as the **Dock Board,** it had unprecedented authority as designated by the state legislature. It had complete jurisdiction over all water frontages in Orleans Parish and considerable portions of the river and canal frontages in adjacent parishes. It could expropriate property, demolish and rebuild structures, operate facilities, and lease them at will. A landmark law had created this autonomous body, because legislators realized that the port was New Orleans's number one industry, and the health of the port was the life of the city.

In 1901, the Dock Board began demolishing structures and rebuilding according to the latest standards. Within ten years, most of the port had been totally rebuilt with cotton warehouses, bulk storage facilities, and one of the biggest grain elevators in the world.

Italians Arrive in New Orleans

By the mid-1800s, New Orleans had a diverse population that included French, Africans, Caribbeans, Spanish, Creoles, Anglos, Isleños, Germans, Irish, and Italians.

Italians had been immigrating to New Orleans since the French colonial period, enticed by a climate similar to that of their homeland, affordable land, and a familiar religious community. Other large migrations occurred before and after the Civil War.

Those who came during the Civil War left Italy after its unification (1860-70) as exiled refugees and peasant farmers seeking better conditions. Many were uneducated and unskilled.

After the Civil War, Louisiana's economy was in a downward spiral. Plantations suffered with the loss of slave labor. While some freed slaves worked the land as tenant farmers, there was nothing keeping them from abandoning the fields and migrating to the North or West. A cheap work force was needed.

Italians arriving after the Civil War were recruited by Italian merchants and steamship agents (supported by the Italian government) as laborers for the sugar plantations of Louisiana, public improvements, and railroad construction. This was a profitable endeavor not only for the agents, who received a commission, but also for the plantation and construction-company owners, who thus obtained cheap labor. From the plantations, many of these Italian laborers found their way to New Orleans.

The Italians aligned with the Populist Party and disagreed with common discrimination practices against blacks. They even traded and went into business with former slaves. Consequently, they were subjected to prejudice and hostility and were relegated to an inferior position in New Orleans society.

As experienced by other poor immigrants, the Italians faced discrimination, animosity, and violence. In Louisiana, tensions were especially high between the Irish and the Italians. They vied with the Irish and freed slaves for low-paying jobs. But they thrived. They established several benevolent societies, which helped keep the Italian culture alive, even as they helped the immigrants to assimilate.

Living in the Vieux Carré, the Italians worked primarily with the importation, distribution, and sale of citrus fruit, mostly in the French Market. Their business interests later extended to wine, liquor, and truck farming in communities outside of the city.

According to the census of 1850, Louisiana had 924 Italian-born residents, the largest concentration of Italians in North America. In 1910, the French Quarter was 80 percent Italian.

After the Italian Massacre of 1891, racial conflicts between Italian and Anglo ethnic groups grew worse. Italians found refuge in their own benevolent organizations, which sought to treat ill health with a free medical clinic and provide financial assistance for a religious orphanage and school. The Italian Hall on Esplanade Avenue served as the social and cultural center of Italian activities through the 1950s.

By the twentieth century, the Italians in Louisiana had established themselves in businesses and occupations that contributed to economic success for themselves and future generations.

The Mafia

The Mafia arrived in New Orleans in the late 1800s. Giuseppe and Bernardo Provenzano controlled the New Orleans underground from 1879 to 1881. They dominated commercial shipping from South America as well as the grocery and produce business.

In the late nineteenth century, Charles and Antonio Matranga established the first "real" crime family in the Crescent City. They operated saloons and brothels in addition to racketeering and extorting "tribute" from Italian laborers and dockworkers. By 1889 they were strong enough to challenge the Provenzanos.

Eventually, the two families were at war with each other. Giuseppe Provenzano tried to broker a peace between the families, but the killing of Vincenzo Ultonino escalated matters and attracted police attention, especially from Chief David Hennessy. Ultonino was a key player in the New Orleans underworld who often brokered peace between the factions but was not a member of either family.

The Italian Massacre

On October 15, 1890, **Police Chief David Hennessy** was shot while walking along Girod Street. He died the next morning. The chief, appointed as part of Mayor Shakspeare's reform program, had ruthlessly pursued members of the secret Sicilian murder associations in the city.

For some time, a war had been in progress between the Provenzano and Matranga families to control the produce business on the city wharves. Hennessy met with the families to demand that the violence be stopped. But there was a vendetta against Hennessy that dated back to the beginning of the 1880s, thus making his efforts futile.

In 1881, Hennessy captured the Sicilian bandit Giuseppe Esposito, who was then in New Orleans, and returned him to New York, from whence he was extradited to Italy. Indicted for eighteen murders and other crimes, Esposito was sentenced to death, but his sentence was later commuted. Vendettas against all who informed on Esposito had been carried out. Hennessy's role in these events had never been forgotten.

After Hennessy's assassination, nineteen Sicilians and Italians were arrested and indicted. Ten were later charged, and nine named as accessories. On March 13, 1891, the jury acquitted some defendants and declared a mistrial for the rest. The people of the city were incensed.

At this time, two ships arrived in port with 1,800 Sicilian immigrants. Stories spread throughout the town that the Italians would take over the city. On Friday, March 14, 1891, the morning paper announced that all good citizens were to meet at the Henry Clay statue on Canal Street (now in Lafayette Square) in order to remedy the failure of justice. The crowd assembled for speeches and a march to the prison on Treme Street behind Congo Square (now part of Louis Armstrong Park).

The sheriff left the prison. His subordinates locked in all other prisoners but opened the cells of the Sicilians, telling them to hide wherever they chose. The mob battered down the wooden gate and found the Sicilians crouching and begging for mercy. The maddened crowd shot the Sicilians one by one, dragged them out, and hung one from a lamppost at Treme and St. Ann streets and another, who had shammed death in a pile of corpses, from a tree in front of the prison on Orleans Street. The affair became an international incident, arousing conflicting opinions across the nation. Pres. Benjamin Harrison called the massacre "deplorable and discreditable," and the United States government paid an indemnity of $25,000 to the Italian government (Moore 2006). The people of New Orleans fumed, but the matter was ended.

The incident resulted in the condemnation of the entire Italian community in New Orleans, most of whom were law-abiding citizens, as frightened of the Mafia as was the rest of the population.

Crowds gather around Parish Prison on Treme Street after the execution of Italians in 1891. (Courtesy Leonard V. Huber Collection)

The Matranga family came out on top in this fight and was the dominant crime family in the Crescent City until the beginning of Prohibition.

In 1922, Sylvestro "Silver Dollar Sam" Carolla took over from the Matrangas and turned the family business into a "modern crime organization." Carolla was arrested in 1930 for shooting a federal narcotics agent and was jailed for two years. When he got out of prison, he was instrumental in bringing slot machines to Louisiana after negotiating a deal with New York mobsters Frank Costello and Phillip "Dandy Phil" Kastel and Sen. Huey Long.

In the late 1940s, Carlos Marcello, a known criminal and member of Carolla's organization, took over the gambling network in Louisiana. He eventually became the leader of the Mafia in New Orleans and was investigated in the assassination of John F. Kennedy.

In 1981, Marcello was convicted of attempting to bribe a federal judge and, in 1982, was convicted of racketeering. After he served six years, his conviction was overturned and he was released. He died in 1993.

After Marcello was convicted, the New York and Philadelphia families expressed interest in expanding their business to New Orleans. When Marcello was boss, he wouldn't allow other families into his territory. Frank "Fat Frank" Gagliano, the underboss succeeding Marcello in the mid- to late 1980s, reportedly told Philadelphia Mafia capo Albert "Reds" Pontani, referring to the Marcello organization, "Sure, go ahead. Come on in. They're finished. They don't mean nothing around here anymore" (John H. Davis 1989).

By this time, organized crime was on the decline in New Orleans, but the Marcello family could not be counted out . . . yet. In 1994, members of the Marcello family, along with the New York Gambino and Genovese families, were involved in two gaming businesses, Worldwide Gaming of Louisiana and Louisiana Route Operations, Inc. These companies were set up to sell, distribute, and receive revenues from the newly legalized video-poker machines in Louisiana. The families schemed to skim money from the proceeds before taxes and funnel those funds to the families. Unfortunately for them, the FBI heard about the scheme and they, along with the Louisiana State Police, raided and arrested high-ranking mobsters and their front men. All served prison time and paid hefty fines to the gaming industry. This crippled the New Orleans organization (mafia.wikia.com, n.d.).

Mafia activities appear to have subsided in New Orleans, with barely organized street gangs taking the place of the Mafia dons.

Storyville

Perhaps the best-known "reform" during the administration of Mayor Walter C. Flower from 1896 to 1899 was the establishment of Storyville. The ordinance creating Storyville, an area bounded by Basin Street and running down cross streets Iberville, Bienville, Conti, and St. Louis, did not declare it an area of legalized vice. Instead, it specified the only area where prostitutes could live and work.

Prostitution was therefore illegal outside of Storyville but, according to the wording of the ordinance, neither legal nor illegal within it.

A license for prostitution issued in 1857

Since everyone knew it was there, the city obviously had a right to control it.

Prostitution in New Orleans had existed since the foreign reigns of Louis XIV and XV. Those monarchs had sent hundreds of prostitutes to the colony. The Mississippi Company of John Law had a reputation for kidnapping "women of bad repute" and shipping them to Louisiana as colonists.

After the Louisiana Purchase in 1803, Mississippi River commerce increased enormously, bringing into the city the rough, bawdy keelboatsmen with their pockets full of money, ready for their whiskey and women. To fill this demand, a stream of prostitutes converged upon New Orleans. Such women were barred from living or working in the city itself (the Vieux Carré), so they moved outside the city to the basin of the Carondelet Canal, where "with their own hands and the help of levee loungers and General Jackson's forces, they dug a drainage ditch, erected shacks and shanties for themselves, and hung out their red lanterns. 'Basin Street' was opened for business" (Rose 1978).

Other tenderloin areas existed in the city, such as the "swamp" on Julia and Girod streets and the two-block-long Gallatin Street at the river called the "port of missing men." These areas abounded with cutthroats, dance-house operators, fight promoters, thieves, thugs, and pimps. There were dance halls, brothels, saloons, gambling rooms, cockfighting pits, and rooming houses. Police mortality in these areas was high. Gallatin "was the center of narcotics traffic, as well as the home of dealers in stolen goods" (Rose 1978).

In 1898, **Alderman Sidney Story** introduced the ordinance calling for a "restricted" red-light district, hoping to wipe out all other areas of vice and control the restricted area. The document was discreetly worded so as to be legally acceptable, and it passed. The area of brothels that bore his name was both a backhanded honor and a bitter pill for him to swallow.

Celebrities from all over the country visited Tom Anderson's saloon and bawdy houses, such as Josie Arlington's, which, in time, became "sporting palaces" with furniture, draperies, and chandeliers equal to those in the mansions of St. Charles Avenue. Mardi Gras was a profitable season for brothels, and the inhabitants of the demimonde had their celebrations just as the "society" people did.

Beginning in 1882, before there was a Storyville, the Ball of the Two

Basin Street in Storyville, looking from Bienville to Canal Street. Right to left: Mahogany Hall (Lulu White's mansion), Martha Clarke's, Josie Arlington's, Jessie Brown's, Lizette Smith's, Marie sisters', Hilma Burt's, and Tom Anderson's Annex. The little house is typical of the pre-Storyville era. (Courtesy Tulane University Special Collections)

Well-Known Gentlemen became the focal point of Mardi Gras for all the creatures who frequented the area: the bartenders, prostitutes, musicians, politicians, and policemen. Word spread about these festivities, and nice young women begged their husbands and fiancés to get tickets to the affair, so that they could see with their own eyes (well hidden behind masks) how these brazen creatures carried on. In 1906, Josie Arlington, aware of their curiosity, arranged a police raid in which every lady present would be arrested unless she was carrying a card registering her as a prostitute in good standing. This caused untold embarrassment to a number of high-society women, who were carted off to the police station for not being prostitutes.

Tom Anderson, the Mayor of Storyville

Tom Anderson, the richest and most powerful "business man" in Storyville, was an Irishman without equal in flair and raw nerve with regard to the annals of Old New Orleans. Born in 1858 of a poor Irish Channel family, he sold newspapers as a child, became an informer for the police, and added to his earnings by delivering cocaine and opium to two local bagnios. In 1892, he opened a bar and restaurant on Basin Street, which were an immediate success. The well-known brothel owner Josie Arlington became his consort, and he rebuilt her house and reopened it for business in 1901, renaming it the Arlington Annex.

In time, through friendships made across the bar with policemen and politicians, the blue-eyed, red-haired Anderson boasted two titles, which he juggled admirably. He was both mayor of Storyville, that tenderloin of crime and corruption; and Hon. Tom Anderson, representative in the Louisiana legislature of a large and important district of New Orleans. From *Collier Magazine,* February 1908: "Tom Anderson overtops the restricted district; he is its lawgiver and its king; one of the names for it is 'Anderson County' . . . saloons with their wide-open poker and crap games; the dives where Negroes buy for fifty cents five cents worth of cocaine . . . when a woman of Anderson County commits robbery [not an uncommon occurrence in the brothels], and when the victim complains loudly enough that she has to be arrested, Tom Anderson comes down and gets her out. He doesn't even have to give cash bail . . . [she] may be released on parole of any responsible prominent citizen."

The Settlement of Mid-City: 1890-1930

At the turn of the twentieth century, available high, dry land was scarce on the two-mile area of natural levee of New Orleans. Three options were available if the city were to accommodate more people: expand toward the lake, expand farther and farther along the levee, or crowd more people onto the same land.

Lakeward expansion was out of the question, in spite of the New Basin Canal and the amusement parks at West End and Spanish Fort. The backswamp, which lay midway between the lake and the river, were uninhabitable because of flooding.

Expansion along the river had its limits, too. On the uptown end, at the boundary line between Orleans and Jefferson parishes, there was a protection levee running from the river to the lake; on the downtown side, expansion was limited by the simple fact that parts of Faubourg Marigny were regularly under water after rains.

What remained, then, was the obvious alternative of packing more people into the same space. New Orleans resisted residences with more than two stories because of the fear that the spongy soil of the area would not bear the added weight.

The homes most typical of New Orleans architecture at the turn of the twentieth century were the shotgun houses. The shotgun was a string of rooms lined up one behind the other, usually without a hallway. It afforded no privacy and little ventilation. It was the cheapest house on the market. Tradition has it that these houses were called shotguns because one could fire a shotgun from front to back without hitting an obstruction.

The bungalow, or double tenement, was as popular as the shotgun. In reality, it was a shotgun, or a pair of shotguns, under one roof with party walls. To avoid flooding, builders set them five feet off the ground on piers. Others had "raised basements" built on the ground beneath the residences. Because of the high water table of New Orleans, in-ground basements were never built. Such houses were called raised bungalows. None of these houses were invented in New Orleans but were built to suit the city's needs. However, once they were embellished with favorite New Orleans touches—louvered French doors, floor-length windows, Carpenter Gothic cornices and brackets, and gables with stained-glass windows—they took on a personality of their own. They became "typical New Orleans."

At last, gifted engineer **A. Baldwin Wood** invented a heavy-duty pump, which could rapidly raise great quantities of water and carry it out of the city into Lake Pontchartrain. With this invention, New Orleans entered an era of land reclamation that would revolutionize its geography, and nothing would ever be quite the same again. Previously uninhabitable swampland would now be open to settlement. None of this was to happen quickly, however, or without great difficulty.

Draining the backswamp was a Herculean task, requiring both time and money. A system of drainage canals had to be built to carry the displaced water to Lake Borgne or Lake Pontchartrain. Levees had to be built to secure the newly drained land. Pumping caused the backswamp to fall considerably below sea level, making flood controls a matter of life and death. A series of dikes had to be built along the lake to keep out tidal surges. Even then, a line of inner protection levees was needed to connect the levee systems of lake and river. In 1899, Orleans Parish passed legislation to install its first pumping system. Within ten years, much of the backswamp had been pumped out. Even with this tremendous effort, nothing could be built on the newly drained land without driving pilings to considerable depths.

Drainage: Pumping Stations

Today, there are twenty-two drainage pumping stations in the city and thirteen underpass stations in New Orleans providing hurricane protection to the people who live in the fishbowl that is the Greater New Orleans area. The New Orleans drainage system includes ninety miles of open canals and ninety miles of subsurface canals, which can drain 29 billion gallons of water every twenty-four hours (Sewerage and Water Board of New Orleans 2016).

The Building of the Lakefront

In spite of the high cost of land, the city moved inexorably lakeward. By the mid-1920s, it became inevitable that something had to be done about the lakefront. The levee itself was inadequate, and the old lakefront was seedy and ugly with its fishermen's shanties and its two amusement parks connected to the city by streetcar lines. As early as 1873, **W. H. Bell,** city surveyor, suggested a plan for the lakefront combining flood protection with land development. Fifty years later, in 1924, the state legislature asked the **Board of Commissioners of the Orleans Lakefront (the Levee Board)** to design and carry out such a plan. The Board was to make the lakefront more beautiful with improvements that would pay for themselves. No one denied it was a large order.

The Levee Board, like the Dock Board, was a powerful body. It had been organized in 1890 and put in charge of 129 miles of levee, 27 miles on the river and 94 miles of inner-city levees. It could levy taxes, expropriate land, run rights-of-way through property owned by other public bodies, and maintain its own police force.

When the Levee Board at last revealed its plans for the lakefront, the residents of the city were astounded. A stepped concrete seawall, five and a half miles long, was to be built on the bottom of Lake Pontchartrain, approximately three thousand feet from shore. Lake waves could roll up and dissipate at the top. Backfill material would be pumped in from the lake bottom outside the seawall. Behind the seawall, the filled area would be raised five to ten feet above the lake levee, making it one of the highest parts of the city. When complete, the city would have a new levee and a whole new lakeshore with 2,000 acres of prime land to be disposed of by the Levee Board.

For 200 years the city cut itself off from the river by constructing warehouses, railroads, and docks. New Orleans was now discovering a new waterfront to be lined with beaches, boulevards, parks, and a municipal yacht harbor. The Shushan Airport, now the New Orleans Lakefront Airport, was constructed on a manmade peninsula at a cost of $4.5 million. Completed in 1934, it was one of the biggest and best in the country.

The Great Depression came, and with it came the Works Progress Administration, which managed public works of this magnitude. The residents of New Orleans thought of this as manna from heaven, for it offered employment to thousands.

To pay off its bonds, the Levee Board charged rent from the airport and the new Pontchartrain Beach Amusement Park, completed in 1939, just before World War II.

CHAPTER X
Growth in a Modern City:
After 1930

The late twenties and early thirties brought the city of New Orleans unemployment, soup lines, and deflated bank accounts. Like all other cities in the United States, New Orleans was suffering from the effects of the Great Depression. The people were without hope, and a hero was needed.

When **Huey Pierce Long** was elected governor of Louisiana in 1928 and to the U.S. Senate in 1932, Louisianans felt that they had found their hero. In Long, they saw the rise of the most colorful leader since Bernardo de Galvez.

The Kingfish

Long built up one of the most powerful political machines in the United States and, in the face of incredible obstacles, enacted his radical program by sheer exuberance of his personality. His doctrine was one of socialism, a revolution of the poor whites. "Every Man a King" and "A Chicken in Every Pot" were the slogans of his Share Our Wealth program. He believed and preached that no man should be allowed to earn more than one million dollars per year and that everything he earned over that should go into a general fund from which the needy would be taken care of. A faction in Louisiana and later around the U.S. hated him, but his power was such that his endorsement for any political office, state or city, was tantamount to election. His power over the state legislature made it possible for him to pass his entire legislative program.

He was virtually a dictator in Louisiana, and his power was felt most especially in New Orleans. In 1934, he sent the Louisiana National Guard to Lafayette Street to the Orleans Parish Registration Office

231

Huey P. Long promised "a chicken in every pot" to working men in the early 1930s. (Courtesy the Deutsche Collection, Earl K. Long Library, University of New Orleans)

across from City Hall. Troops broke the lock and took possession of the office. The militia had to be called out by **Mayor T. Semmes Walmsley** to try to prevent the seizure of the office. Military and police, heavily armed with rifles and machine guns, swarmed around the office and City Hall. Long was victorious, and the office was reopened under his supervision.

Long abused his right to use the State Police during his administration as well as the subsequent administration of his hand-picked representative, Gov. O. K. Allen, which he controlled. Because of this abuse, legislation was passed after his death between 1936 and 1938 restricting the jurisdiction of the State Police in the city of New Orleans until the late 1970s.

Long was considered a saint and a king to the poor and downtrodden, who heard from his lips the first sound of democracy in action. They had been used to only one kind of government, the aristocratic, one-party kind. If Long wanted to be their dictator, they were willing to go along with it in return for what he promised them. He rode into office on their backs.

Long found his political start after he finished an eight-month law course at Tulane University and passed the bar. On his thirtieth birthday, in 1923, he ran for governor and came in third. In preparation for running again, he made use of all the things that had needed attention in Louisiana for a long time: roads, literacy, school textbooks, healthcare, and a Mississippi River bridge. Promising all of these reforms, he was elected to the office of governor in 1926.

The Kingfish, as he was called, published his own newspaper, the *Louisiana Progress*. Later it became the *American Progress,* as his political aspirations had him looking at running for president. He wrote a book, *Every Man a King,* in which he outlined his ideas for putting an end to the Great Depression. Another literary effort, *My First Days in the White House,* was a futuristic exercise in political egomania.

During his term as U.S. senator, Long made a history-making, if unsuccessful, filibuster against a bill backed by Pres. Franklin D. Roosevelt. For fifteen hours and thirty-five minutes, he read the United States Constitution, the Declaration of Independence, parts of Victor Hugo's *The Laughing Man,* chapters of the Bible, a monologue on Greek mythology, and a recipe for fried oysters.

Long made many enemies in Washington and back home in Louisiana. A dozen or more senators would rise and leave the chambers whenever he stood up to speak.

Long was assassinated in the state capitol in Baton Rouge on September 8, 1935, allegedly by Dr. Carl A. Weiss, whose father-in-law Long had gerrymandered out of office. Weiss was then riddled with bullets by Long's bodyguards. Suspicion has lingered that it was Long's bodyguards who killed the Kingfish.

In spite of his strong-arm tactics, Long was a governor to whom New Orleans and Louisiana remain indebted. His achievements include the Shushan Airport (now the New Orleans Lakefront Airport), the extensive lakefront development, the Huey P. Long Bridge, the enlargement of Charity Hospital, the LSU Medical Center, and free schoolbooks in the public schools of Louisiana.

Some of the government boards that Long packed with cronies exist to this day, as well as taxes on the oil industry and social welfare programs he created.

His legacy continued after his death when his widow, Rose McConnell Long, and son Russell B. Long both succeeded him in the U.S. Senate.

Mayor Robert Maestri

In 1936, the city was on the verge of bankruptcy when Robert Maestri was elected mayor. In less than two years, he put New Orleans on a cash basis. Every morning, he drove around the city with an engineer, checking streets, sidewalks, drainage, and public buildings. Every afternoon, he sat at his desk, working to reorganize the archaic fiscal structure of New Orleans and to improve municipal services. In 1942, he was reelected almost without campaigning. In his second term, gambling and extra-legal activities increased, which alienated the clergy. Maestri began to spend all his time running the Old Regulars, which he had fused with the Earl Long state-government organization. This alienated the uptown establishment.

A story has always been told that Maestri entertained Pres. Franklin D. Roosevelt on his visit to the city by taking him to Antoine's for dinner. There, they dined on Oysters Rockefeller. Proud of the city's seafood, the articulate mayor asked the aristocratic president, "How ya like dem ersh-ters?"

Spillways

In the 1920s and 1930s, the Mississippi River threatened once again to divert its path, frightening New Orleanians. One threat of a diversion existed in a weak spot in the natural levee at a place called **Bonnet Carré,** where a crevasse had occurred more than once, carrying flood waters from the Mississippi to Lake Pontchartrain. If it had not been stopped, it might have gone directly on to the Gulf by way of the lake, instead of continuing its twisting path for 130 miles southward.

A second potential diversion was above Baton Rouge at a small town called **Morganza** on the west bank of the river. If the river had jumped its course there, it would have poured into the slot between the present Mississippi River levee and the ancient levee of Bayou Teche, a sluggish, swampy area twenty miles wide called the Atchafalaya River Basin, which flows slowly toward the Gulf. This was, by far, the most dangerous diversion the river could have taken, for if it would have strayed there, it would have stayed there, saving itself half the distance to the Gulf.

Bonnet Carré Spillway, dedicated December 13, 1935. Here the gates are open to divert the rising waters of the Mississippi River into Lake Pontchartrain and prevent the river from overflowing into the Greater New Orleans area. Men above the spillway use cranes to lift gates. (Courtesy Port of New Orleans)

The crevasses at both **Morganza** and **Bonnet Carré** have since been repaired. In 1931, the Army Corps of Engineers built giant concrete floodgates, which now prevent a breach on both levees. These gates can be opened if a flood crest approaches, allowing surplus water to pour into Lake Pontchartrain. The Bonnet Carré Spillway has been opened several times since it was built, but the Morganza Spillway has been opened only twice since it was built. In 1973 and 2011, the Morganza Spillway was opened when the area experienced record-breaking flooding from high precipitation levels.

The Bonnet Carré Spillway and the levees make it possible to divert three million cubic feet of water per second into Lake Pontchartrain and, eventually, into the Gulf of Mexico.

During and After World War II: The Lakefront

World War II brought a shortage of labor, materials, and, consequently, a moratorium on residential building. It also cut a striking design into the lakefront area, making it the fringe of a mobilized city.

From West End to the Shushan Airport, the lakefront was lined with military installations beginning in 1942. At the western end, near the lighthouse, was the Coast Guard Station. This is the only installation that remains today. Moving eastward, in what are today the West and East Lakeshore subdivisions, were the U.S. Army (LaGarde) General Hospital (west of Canal Boulevard) and the U.S. Naval Hospital (east of Canal Boulevard).

After 1942 on the lake edge of the Lake Vista subdivision, which had been cut in 1938, was a second Coast Guard Station. Situated on the eastern bank of Bayou St. John, between Robert E. Lee and Lakeshore Drive, was a building housing the U.S. Maritime Commission.

The Naval Reserve Aviation Base occupied an area on the lakefront between the London Avenue Canal and Franklin Avenue, Lakeshore Drive, and Robert E. Lee Boulevard. Included in this area were an Aircraft Carrier Training Center and a Rest and Relaxation Center. This was a tent city from which the amusements of Pontchartrain Beach were within walking distance.

On Lakeshore Drive, on the western corner of Franklin Avenue, the War Assets Administration condemned a 750-foot tract of land, had it appraised, and bought it from the Levee Board. And according to maps held by the Levee Board, the Navy Assembly Plant was located here. Some of the engineers, however, recall the Consolidated Vultee Aircraft Company, which existed on the spot in the war years, with its ramp that allowed seaplanes to be launched. At that time, there was a fence crossing Lakeshore Drive, and no vehicular traffic was allowed along the lakefront. After the war, the federal government sold the property to Nash-Kelvinator, and it was later acquired by American Standard. The property now belongs to the Levee Board.

Continuing eastward between Franklin and Camp LeRoy Johnson Road stretched the barracks of Camp LeRoy Johnson. This area is shown on maps of the period as the U.S. Army Bombing Squadron. Another interesting feature of this area was the German Prisoner of War Camp on the far western lakefront corner (at Franklin Avenue and the lake).

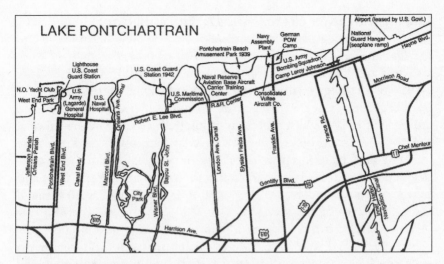

Lakefront during World War II. Most military installations existed from 1942 to the end of the decade. (Map by M. L. Widmer)

During the war, Shushan Airport (now Lakefront Airport) was leased by the United States government to house a National Guard hangar and a ramp for launching seaplanes. Also, along its western wall was an area occupied by the U.S. Army Bombing Squadron. Pan-American and Delta airlines planes used the administration building jointly with the government for limited commercial activities; Pan-Am moved to Moisant Airport (now Louis Armstrong International Airport) in 1947.

By the late 1940s, after the war, the face of the lakefront was changing to peacetime construction. Military installations were coming down and work was progressing on the residential area, which had been earmarked as such by the Levee Board. Lots were then sold to help pay off bonds. Plans had been on the drawing board since before World War II for five residential areas.

Once again, starting at the West End of the lakefront and moving eastward, the Coast Guard Station remains to this day at West End for the protection of boat enthusiasts. The Southern Yacht Club stands on the northernmost peninsula of West End, as it has for over a century. The Orleans Marina was built on the west side of the New Basin Canal.

East and West Lakeshore subdivisions, completed in 1953, include 352 residential lots on the sites of the old Army and Navy hospitals. The Mardi Gras Fountain is situated near the lake on the East

Lakeshore subdivision. The East and West Lakeshore are bounded by the lakefront and Robert E. Lee Boulevard, the New Basin Canal and the Orleans Canal.

The Lake Vista subdivision was completed in 1938, just before World War II began. It was laid out in the "City Beautiful" design of Radburn, New Jersey, with a central "common," pedestrian lanes, and cul-de-sacs to provide safe areas for children. Mayor Maestri called it the "poor man's project," but prices of land in this area of premium location and planning would prove the slogan absurd. It was to become one of the wealthiest areas in the city. Lake Vista is bounded by the lakefront and Robert E. Lee Boulevard, Bayou St. John, and the London Avenue Canal.

The next lakefront property moving eastward is now occupied by the University of New Orleans West Campus. Its boundaries are the lakefront, Leon C. Simon Boulevard, the London Avenue Canal, and Elysian Fields Avenue, bringing the total to 195 acres. In 1964, this land was leased to the Louisiana State University in New Orleans (LSUNO; it became the University of New Orleans)—UNO—in 1975) for ninety-nine years at one dollar per year.

Continuing eastward, the Lake Oaks subdivision has boundaries that are slightly out of line with the other lakefront developments. It lies between Lake Oaks Parkway, New York Street, Elysian Fields Avenue, and Music Street. Completed in 1964, it consisted of 290 home sites.

Pontchartrain Beach Amusement Park was located on a fifty-acre site on the lakefront from 1939 to 1983, abutting both the West UNO Campus and the Lake Oaks subdivision.

To the east of Lake Oaks, an additional 195 acres were leased to the LSUNO (now UNO) in 1964 for ninety-nine years at one dollar per year. This East Campus is bounded by the lakefront and Leon C. Simon Boulevard, Franklin Avenue, and Press Drive. On that site is also a multipurpose indoor sports arena with a seating capacity of 16,000. On the grounds between the arena and the lakefront, a beautiful altar was erected for the Papal Mass said by Pope John Paul II when he visited New Orleans on September 12, 1987.

The New Orleans Lakefront Airport, formerly Shushan Airport, is today a general aviation airport facility with three new runways that serve private, corporate, and military aircraft. The current FAA control tower was built in 1988. The main runway is 6,895 feet and is used by B-727s, C-130s, C-17s, and C-5s. Most commercial airlines now operate out of Louis Armstrong International Airport in Kenner.

The seawall at Lake Pontchartrain, built at a cost of $2.64 million, is the world's largest grandstand. Along its five-and-a-half-mile expanse, there is a yacht harbor, a boat marina, a university, public recreation areas, and an airport.

The Veteran Candidate

In 1964, when Mayor Maestri once again threw his hat in the ring, he was to find himself opposed by another reform candidate, the handsome, vigorous, thirty-three-year-old **deLesseps Story "Chep" Morrison**.

Morrison, part of the silkstocking crowd, returned from a tour of duty in Europe as a colonel in the U.S. Army. Before World War II, he had been in private law practice, worked in the labor-law section of the NRA, and become a member of the state legislature at age twenty-eight. He had been reelected to the legislature in 1944 in spite of his absence. Attractive to both female voters and veterans, he was a natural for politics. He agreed to enter the race, although he thought he had no chance whatsoever of victory. No one was more surprised than Morrison when he defeated Maestri in the first primary (with the possible exception of Maestri himself). Maestri had a saying, "I was shaved without soap," which meant that someone had gotten the best of him. He undoubtedly made that remark the morning after the primary.

Morrison's organization was the Crescent City Democratic Association. He was reelected for a second, third, and fourth term, serving all but the last year of his fourth term, when he resigned in 1961 to accept the post of United States ambassador to the Organization of American States, which had been offered to him by President Kennedy.

Morrison's terms in office signaled the end of a half-century of machine-dominated politics. On May 22, 1964, Morrison was en route to Mexico with his younger son, Randy, in a chartered plane on a combined business and pleasure trip, when his plane crashed into a mountain, bringing his career to an untimely end.

School Integration

In 1954, the U.S. Supreme Court, in its historical decision of **Brown vs. Topeka Board of Education,** ruled unconstitutional the "separate but equal" doctrine as applied to public education. New Orleans, like most Southern cities, never really implemented this segregationist doctrine, although it professed to do so. The Orleans Parish School Board had maintained for many years a distinctly inferior school system for black children.

The School Board fought the decision with delays, and the state legislature enacted a number of pro-segregationist statutes, all of which were cut down by the U.S. Supreme Court. Some thought it would be best to close down the public schools completely, as whites had done after the Civil War. Mayor Morrison remained silent on the issue, as he did not feel responsible under state law for the public schools, only for the keeping of law and order.

On November 14, 1960, federal marshals escorted four young black girls as they entered first-grade classes at two white schools. Crowds

A black girl enters the first grade in 1961, integrating McDonogh 11 School in Mid-City, after an order by Judge J. Skelly Wright in 1960. Pres. Lyndon B. Johnson signed the Civil Rights Act into law in 1964. (Courtesy Times-Picayune Publishing Company)

gathered, and some threatened the students and their parents. On November 15, **Judge Leander Perez** of Plaquemines Parish addressed 5,000 New Orleanians at the Municipal Auditorium, exploiting their prejudices and racial fears and urging them to stop the four black children from attending the white schools.

The following day, thousands rioted in the Central Business District, finally forcing action. The New Orleans Police arrested 250 people after much violence and vandalism, including attacks on the black community.

In time, the turmoil subsided with the help of church groups as well as the academic and business communities. School integration seemed, at last, somewhat accepted, and there was a return to law and order.

The Suburban Explosion

After the Mid-City and lakefront areas were well settled, the population of the city continued to grow, consuming the land like locusts, especially in the aftermath of World War II. By 1950, the swampland of the city from the river to the lake had been filled.

In the late 1950s, the population rolled like a wave beyond the Orleans Parish line into the East Bank of Jefferson Parish, following the direction of Airline Highway (which ran from Baton Rouge to New Orleans and was built by Gov. Huey P. Long between 1930 and 1932). Veterans Memorial Boulevard, which parallels Airline Highway, now became the main street of Jefferson Parish. Moisant Airport became New Orleans International Airport (later the Louis Armstrong International Airport). In 1957, the twenty-four-mile-long Lake Pontchartrain Causeway spanned the lake between Jefferson Parish and St. Tammany Parish. The world's longest bridge, it offered commuters the opportunity to work in New Orleans and reside in Covington, Mandeville, or Folsom. The second span of the Causeway was completed in 1969. The southbound span of the Causeway is a toll bridge.

Shopping centers in Jefferson Parish mushroomed: Lakeside Shopping Center, Clearview Mall, and the Esplanade Mall in Kenner all held shops and restaurants that siphoned shoppers away from historic Canal Street.

Because of the speed with which this expansion took place and the enormity of the area it covered, New Orleans has become, in the last half-century, a city within a city. At the center is the old New Orleans. On the outskirts is suburbia. In this respect, it is different from most big, urban communities and followed the national pattern of development and expansion.

New Orleans East

The land to the east of the city, originally marshy and uninhabitable, became usable once it was "reclaimed" in the 1900s, similar to what was done from the French Quarter to Lake Pontchartrain. The largest landholder, the Lake Shore Land Co., owned 7,500 acres. The company began to sell five-acre lots to citrus growers. But this reclaimed land didn't end up as fruitful as Mid-City and Lakeview.

World war and rough weather made the envisioned industrial-size orange-growing production go dark. By the 1940s, all that was left in the area were small citrus groves and farms. It became an area where people lived in raised wooden houses and quietly tended their land, hunted, and fished. Some middle-class residents of the city purchased land but it was for recreational purposes or camps.

Richard Campanella, professor and geographer at the Tulane School of Architecture, attributes five events in the 1960s that made New Orleans East what it is today. Hurricane Betsy hit the city in 1965, which was the impetus to build more substantial levees; NASA's Michoud Assembly Facility brought jobs into the area; whites fled the city into the suburbs after the war; the Mississippi River Gulf Outlet (MRGO— now closed) was built to enable oil companies' offshore drilling but accelerated coastal erosion and saltwater intrusion; and the construction of Interstate 10 allowed easier access to the area, which sparked housing developments (Campanella 2013). In 2005 another event occurred that deeply affected New Orleans East—Hurricane Katrina.

By the 1970s, the East was a vast suburban area waiting only for the completion of the Interstate 10 to follow the pattern of Jefferson Parish. New Orleans East began to feel a trickle of population growth as early as the 1960s. Houses and businesses had begun to crop up in an unorganized fashion along the newly built Chef Menteur Highway, which cut across New Orleans East in much the same way that Airline Highway cut across Jefferson Parish.

When African Americans came to political power in the 1970s, the white middle class left the East for adjacent parishes. They were replaced by middle- and upper-class African-American families. Beginning in 1975, Vietnamese immigrants settled in the area.

Land developers thought that the real estate along the route of the new I-10 would be worth its weight in gold. One can see their optimism in the stone monument announcing, "New Orleans East," which still stands along the interstate in the midst of forest and marsh.

In the 1980s, however, the bottom dropped out of the oil industry, and New Orleans East has since suffered from urban decay and disinvestment. Accelerating the decline is the fact that the land is sinking, leaving many of the subdivisions subject to flooding.

Hurricane Katrina in 2005 exacerbated the problem, wiping the area out in twenty-four hours.

New Orleans East suffered severe flooding from Katrina and the levee failures. Ninety percent of the homes were damaged beyond repair. Recovery was slow, and even now many areas still struggle. By 2007, only a handful of businesses had reopened and half of the area's residents had returned, with many of those still living in FEMA trailers. By 2010, the population of New Orleans East was just 70 percent of what it was in 2000 (Non-Profit Knowledge Work, n.d.).

Today more people have moved back and rebuilt, although abandoned houses still sit on partially populated streets. The area is seeing more businesses open and national retailers moving in.

After expansion to the east, there was only one more direction in which the population could move, and it rapidly did so in the early 1980s. That direction was southward from the west bank of the river in the direction of Bayou Barataria in Jefferson Parish.

The Mayors After 1961

When Morrison resigned in 1961, the City Council voted to make **Victor H. Schiro** interim mayor. Schiro was, at the time, councilman-at-large on the City Council. Born of an Italian father who was involved in the banking business in Honduras, Schiro spent much of his boyhood in Honduras, where he learned Spanish, a language that was of great value to him when he traveled in Central America representing the city as mayor.

As a young man, he attended Tulane University and graduated from Santa Clara University in California. He then spent three years in Hollywood, working under film director Frank Capra. In World War II, he served in the Coast Guard for three years. Returning to New Orleans, he worked as a program director and announcer for radio, entered the insurance business for Metropolitan Life Insurance Company, and then opened an insurance company of his own.

His first effort in politics was his vigorous support of a Home Rule Charter for New Orleans. Mayor Morrison endorsed him in his candidacy for City Council, and in 1950 he was elected commissioner of public buildings and parks. In 1954, he won a seat as councilman-at-large on the City Council, which had been established as part of the Home Rule Charter in 1954. He was reelected in 1958 for a four-year term, but took over the office of mayor when Morrison resigned in 1961.

Mayor Victor H. Schiro: Changes in Racial Tolerance

In the summer of 1961, when Schiro assumed office, he was immediately confronted with the problem of school integration, which was, as yet, far from solved. The episode of the previous fall, with the black children breaking the segregation barriers and the abusive bystanders jeering at and spitting on them, brought New Orleans to the attention of the nation, and criticism had been strong. Intent upon preventing such an incident in 1961, Schiro instructed the police to set up barricades to keep diehard segregationists a good distance away from the schoolchildren. In this way, additional demonstrations were avoided, and school integration proceeded more smoothly.

Schiro ended the segregation of restrooms at City Hall. He appointed the first black executive assistant to the mayor's office. He was the first mayor since the end of Reconstruction to sanction the appointment of blacks as heads of important boards and commissions.

These changes in racial tolerance and goodwill were no doubt exactly what the city needed to prevent the racial upheavals that occurred elsewhere in the 1960s. New Orleans was one of the few cities with a large black population where violence did not erupt during the period.

During Schiro's administration, the NASA space program brought thousands of highly skilled technicians, engineers, and administrators to Michoud Assembly Facility. This meant new households, growth in retail sales, and an expanded tax base. Schiro also sponsored the initial

Aerial view shows, left to right, the Civil District Courts Building, City Hall, State Office Building, State Supreme Courts, and New Orleans Public Library, 1960. (Courtesy New Orleans Public Library)

effort to plan the construction of a domed stadium (the Superdome).

When Hurricane Betsy (the most devastating hurricane to reach the mainland United States prior to Hurricane Katrina in 2005) struck New Orleans on September 9, 1965, Schiro's prompt and effective coordination of relief efforts played a major role in the city's recovery. Schiro was, however, a master of malapropisms and is unfortunately best remembered during that frightening time for his remark on television (hard hat and all), saying, as the storm gathered force, "Don't be afraid. Don't believe any false rumors until you hear them from me" (Haas 1990).

Mayor Maurice "Moon" Landrieu: Principle Before Expediency

Schiro was succeeded in 1970 by Maurice "Moon" Landrieu, a lawyer, a U.S. Army veteran, the father of nine children, and a representative in the state legislature. In the late 1950s, he became active in the Young Crescent City Democratic Association, an organization aligned with the Crescent City Democratic Association led by then-mayor Chep Morrison. It was with Morrison's endorsement that he won a seat in the State House of Representatives.

In November 1960, **Gov. Jimmie Davis** convened a special session of the legislature to consider a package of pro-segregationist bills to circumvent the federal court orders integrating New Orleans's public schools. The legislature could not nullify the federal judge's integration orders, but almost the entire legislature chose the path of least resistance rather than lose the segregationists' votes. Landrieu was the only member of the Louisiana House of Representatives to put principle before expediency. He voted against the bills. His action brought death threats, but in the late 1960s and 1970s, his support for equal rights proved to be a political asset. In 1965, he won a seat on the City Council as councilman-at-large. In 1969, he was elected mayor.

The new administration strove to deal with the city's fiscal problems on a long-term basis. Landrieu named the first black to head a department of city government. He chose qualified personnel, regardless of race. He was also responsible for the advancement of women in high places in city government. He promoted the growth of tourism through public improvements and renovation projects.

The Moonwalk, named in his honor and built during his administration, stretches out on top of the levee at Jackson Square, giving visitors an unparalleled view of the river, the West Bank, and St. Louis Cathedral.

From 1975 to 1976, Landrieu served as president of the U.S. Conference of Mayors, and he was nominated by Pres. Jimmy Carter as secretary of housing and urban development on September 24, 1979, an office that he held until the end of the Carter administration.

Mayor Ernest "Dutch" Morial: Trailblazer

Mayor Ernest "Dutch" Morial blazed trails and made history for his race as the first black mayor of New Orleans. In 1965, Morial was made the first black assistant in the U.S. attorney's office. In 1968, he became the first black man in the legislature since Reconstruction. In the 1970s, he became the first black juvenile-court judge and the first black elected to the state's Fourth Circuit Court of Appeals. He served as mayor from 1978 to 1986. Few people can claim such a collection of firsts.

Morial tried to bring a greater stability to the city's economy. During his administration, major improvements were made in the port's docking facilities. He also attempted to improve existing job training and vocational programs and to create new ones where they were needed.

His efforts to expand tourism included the $88 million Convention and Exhibition Center (now called the New Orleans Ernest N. Morial Convention Center) and offering the city as host of the World Exposition and Fair in 1984. Morial died on December 24, 1989. The 1.1-million-square-foot convention center sits along the river in the shadow of the Crescent City Connection between the riverfront and Tchoupitoulas Street, in an expanding hospitality district.

Mayor Sidney Barthelemy: Mayoral Landslide

Mayor Sidney J. Barthelemy won the race for mayor of New Orleans in 1986 by the largest landslide of a non-incumbent in the city's history. He had served as the director of the City Welfare Department and was the first black Louisiana state senator elected since Reconstruction. During his first year in office, he was elected president of the National Association of Regional Councils and was on the board of directors for the U.S. Conference of Mayors.

Mayor Marc Morial: Sweeping Victory

Marc Morial, at age thirty-six, became the youngest mayor in the city's history and the second half of a father-son mayoral lineup with former mayor "Dutch" Morial.

Morial served on the board for the Louisiana American Civil Liberties Union from 1986 to 1988 and served as a state senator from 1992 to 1994. He was elected to his first mayoral term on March 5, 1994. In his campaign, he promised a "safe" city and work opportunities. His achievements in reducing crime and police reform won him re-election in 1998.

He expressed a desire to run for a third term and petitioned for a change to the city charter to allow it, but voters defeated the effort. After leaving office, Morial was selected as president of the National Urban League, beginning in 2003.

Mayor C. Ray Nagin

A Republican who switched parties right before he ran for office, Clarence Ray Nagin, Jr., a cable TV manager, consultant, and entrepreneur, served as the sixtieth mayor of New Orleans, from 2002 to 2010.

His first few months in office were spent making good on a campaign promise to rid City Hall of corruption. His first target was the taxicab licensing and vehicle inspection department. A total of eighty-four warrants were issued, but in the end, the district attorney declined to prosecute fifty-three of them. This set the pattern of Nagin's tenure as mayor: ambitious plans derailed.

Nagin gained national attention in the days leading up to and following Hurricane Katrina in August 2005. He ordered the first-ever mandatory evacuation of the city on August 28, resulting in 80 percent of its residents evacuated by that evening. Unfortunately, that left the most vulnerable residents—the poor, sick, and infirm who could not evacuate—at the mercy of the storm. A day before Katrina was to make landfall, Nagin declared the Superdome a "shelter of last resort." But the Dome was ill equipped to handle the tens of thousands of people who would seek shelter there at what was basically the eleventh hour. (See more on Hurricane Katrina in chapter 12.)

In the aftermath of Hurricane Katrina, Nagin worked feverishly to get the city the disaster assistance that it needed. He was very vocal in his criticism of the slow federal and state response to his pleas. And he opposed those who proposed rebuilding only the most economically viable areas of New Orleans, the land above sea level, which as it happened was mostly populated by the white residents of the city. Much of the black population lived on the outer edges of the city, the areas that were more likely to be below sea level. In an effort to calm the growing concern of African-American residents about the rebuilding of the city, Nagin addressed a Martin Luther King Day crowd, saying, "This city will be chocolate at the end of the day. . . .

This city will be a majority African-American city. It's the way God wants it to be" (Nola.com 2006). Many people were not happy with that comment, believing it out of line, dividing, and inflammatory. Nagin later apologized for the remark.

Nagin was reelected in 2006, even though the election was held in the city with two-thirds of its citizens displaced after the storm.

His second term could only be characterized as dismal. The media criticized Nagin throughout the next four years. Crime increased as the city struggled to rebuild. Nagin's response to reports of increased crime in the city was that it "keeps the New Orleans brand out there" (Bohrer 2007). It was evident that Nagin had given up on the city. He spent an increasing amount of time lobbying in Washington, D.C. and on a speaking tour, reportedly to secure support for New Orleans.

Toward the end of his second term, the *Times-Picayune* alleged conflicts regarding trips Nagin took that were paid for by city vendors. This was the tip of the iceberg.

By the end of his second term, the Justice Department was amassing evidence of Nagin's participation in bribery, corruption, and securities fraud. The mayor who entered office promising to clean up City Hall was the first sitting New Orleans mayor to be indicted for corruption.

On February 12, 2014, C. Ray Nagin, former mayor of New Orleans, was convicted on twenty of twenty-one counts of bribery, corruption, and fraud and sentenced to ten years in federal prison. He currently resides as prisoner number 32751-034 at the Federal Correctional Institution in Texarkana. His earliest release date is spring 2023.

Mayor Mitchell "Mitch" Landrieu

Mitchell "Mitch" Landrieu, son of former mayor Moon Landrieu, had a successful law career for fifteen years before being elected to the state legislature in 1987, where he served for sixteen years.

Landrieu was elected lieutenant governor in 2003. He received 53 percent of the vote, avoiding a general election.

He ran for mayor in 2006 but lost the election to Ray Nagin. Landrieu said that he would not run for mayor in 2010; however, late in December of 2009, he changed his mind. Ultimately, he won the mayoral seat with approximately 61 percent of the vote.

When Landrieu took office, the city was having a difficult time. New Orleans was divided. It was trying to rebuild after Hurricane Katrina and had a rising crime rate and a depressed economy. Landrieu had one rallying cry when he took office: "One team. One fight. One voice. One city."

One tenet of his campaign was quashing corruption. He said, "If the city of New Orleans cannot reverse its culture of corruption, we have no chance of making the city great again. We have to make sure everybody has confidence that we're there to serve the public and not ourselves" (Monteverde, Donze, and Krupa 2011). Early in his first term, Landrieu announced contracting reform measures to allay long-held concerns about corruption and patronage in City Hall. This did not make him popular. Landrieu, however, does not appear to let the naysayers get to him. He continues his fight to better the city.

Landrieu won reelection in 2014 with 64 percent of the vote in a three-candidate race. Still, not everyone is happy with Landrieu, as he is accused of steamrolling over critics. He has tackled a few controversial issues and made enemies on both sides of the political coin (Gadbois 2010).

One hallmark of his term in office is getting the approvals and funds to build a new passenger terminal at Louis Armstrong International Airport. It is expected to open in 2018 as New Orleans celebrates its tricentennial. Landrieu's mayoral term ends in 2018, the 300th anniversary of the founding of the city.

CHAPTER XI

New Orleans in the New Millennium

Waterways still play an important role in the story of New Orleans. The Mississippi River and the business it brings are vital to the city, and so, the U.S. Army Corps of Engineers works to keep the river running past our door on its familiar route. The lakes and bayous used by the explorers are still important to commerce and recreation; for this reason, the Lake Pontchartrain Basin Foundation works to keep these waterways free of pollution and inviting to human and wildlife habitation.

The Vieux Carré remains the city's chief attraction. More pedestrians cross Jackson Square and its bounding streets each year than any other area of equal size in the entire United States. What keeps the attraction alive and existing aside from the beautiful architecture of the Jackson Square area? The French Quarter's buildings, while not a living museum such as those of the city of Williamsburg, have retained that European city look and that ancient Bohemian essence that makes it sui generis in North America.

New challenges and needs are being met as the city moves further into the twenty-first century and overcomes obstacles and disasters. From the days when cotton was king to the rise of the global economy, the Port of New Orleans evolves with the changing face of the world, and it remains one of the busiest ports in the United States.

The Crescent City Works Hard . . . and Plays Hard

The Greater New Orleans area has a diverse economic makeup. Some of its main sectors include the port, oil and gas, tourism, healthcare, and aerospace manufacturing.

The Port of New Orleans

In 1962, the **Port Authority of Greater New Orleans** (also known as the Dock Board) began a program of rebuilding made necessary by a change in the technology of shipping: the use of container vessels and barge-carrying ships. Container docks require large, alongside assembly areas; huge stuffing sheds; large yards for assembly of trucks and railroad cars; and cranes for moving containers from ship to vehicle. The extensive upgrade took three decades to complete.

The Dock Board started from scratch with a brand-new location, establishing the France Road and Jourdan Road river terminals, which have greatly increased the Port's general cargo and bulk cargo capabilities. By the year 2000, the Port retired twenty-nine wharves in downtown New Orleans and increased development in New Orleans East. For the first time since Bienville landed in the 1600s, New Orleans has a riverfront uncluttered by wharves.

Since the early 2000s, the Port of New Orleans has invested $400 million in new, state-of-the-art facilities. The Port offices are now located near the New Orleans Ernest N. Morial Convention Center.

Today the Port of New Orleans is a deep-draft, multipurpose

Governor Nicholls Street Wharf on the downriver side of the French Quarter. (Photo by Kathy Chappetta Spiess)

facility. It is at the very center of the Lower Mississippi River system, connecting New Orleans to markets in the U.S. and Canada via 14,500 miles of waterways, six Class-I railroads, and interstate highways. Many types of cargo pass through New Orleans, such as steel, coffee, chemicals, forestry products, and natural rubber, as well as more than a million cruise passengers ("Port of New Orleans" 2015).

The Intracoastal Waterway

Why was the Intracoastal Waterway built in Eastern New Orleans? The answer goes back to the 1920s when the Dock Board and the city collaborated to build a deep-water canal between the Mississippi River and Lake Pontchartrain. The **Inner Harbor Navigation Canal** is referred to by New Orleanians as the **Industrial Canal.** It was later linked to the **Intracoastal Waterway,** which led eastward to Lake Borgne and the Mississippi Gulf Coast. In 1923, the canal was connected to the river by locks. In 1934, on the west bank of the river, the Harvey Canal was finished, linking the Mississippi River, Bayou Barataria, western Louisiana, and the Texas Gulf Coast. Both the Industrial Canal and the Harvey Canal became links in the newly finished Intracoastal Waterway, which today stretches from the Rio Grande River to the Florida coast.

The Port of New Orleans experienced rapid growth in 2015 in bulk cargo such as steel and forestry products and containerized cargo. A new third passenger terminal in 2015 served international cruises and river cruises originating in New Orleans. The Centroport from Baton Rouge to the Gulf is poised for more growth with the widened Panama Canal in 2016. To bring in larger ships, the river was dredged an additional five feet in 2015.

Six major railroads, Amtrak and shortline, serve New Orleans. Major interstate highways connect both coasts and the Midwest. The region is linked by 19,000 miles of navigable waterways.

Mayor Mitch Landrieu announced construction of a new $650 million passenger terminal at Louis Armstrong International Airport. It is expected to open in 2018, in time for New Orleans's tricentennial celebration. The airport regained a bit of its former reputation as an international gateway with new flights to Panama and new routes to Europe.

The Central Business District and Poydras Street Boom

The Dock Board's decision to abandon and raze riverfront wharves helped revive the riverfront and the Central Business District. The Rivergate brought a large multi-use convention center to Canal Street in 1968. Later, the site would become the home of **Harrah's New Orleans Casino.**

The World Trade Center was completed in 1967 to house foreign consulates, trade offices, and the Top of the Mart rotating cocktail lounge on the thirty-third floor.

In the years after Katrina, the city, business community, and residents debated whether to preserve the building at 2 Canal Street or tear it down for other riverfront uses. In the end, a Four Seasons hotel was selected for development on this prime real estate.

Since the razing of the Rivergate Convention Center in 1995, dozens of new and refurbished hotels blossomed in the CBD. By 2015, they included: Courtyard by Marriott, DoubleTree, Embassy Suites, Hyatt Regency, Le Meridien, Le Pavillon, Loews New Orleans,

Curtis and Davis Architects and Planners designed the Rivergate Convention Center in collaboration with Edward B. Silverstein and Associates and Mathes Bergman and Associates. Built in 1968, it sat at the foot of Canal Street at the river. It was an innovative, modern structure. It was demolished in 1995 to make way for the land-based casino in New Orleans. (Photo by Kathy Chappetta Spiess)

JW Marriott, Sheraton, Omni Riverfront, Omni Royal Crescent, Ritz-Carlton, Roosevelt Hotel New Orleans, Westin Canal Place, and Windsor Court.

The **Superdome** generated a lot of activity in 1975, as did the **Louisiana World Exposition** on the riverfront in 1984, thereby opening this area for future development.

Poydras Street is a monument to the oil boom of 1981, when a record number of rigs (502) pumped off the shores of Louisiana. By 1986, only 92 remained. The culprit was the Organization of the Petroleum Exporting Countries (OPEC), which reduced the price of oil from thirty-five dollars per barrel to a low of ten dollars. The impact was devastating. Oil-related jobs disappeared. In 1983, major manufacturers such as Kaiser Chalmette Works, formerly one of the world's largest aluminum-reduction plants, shut down, causing 20,000 workers to become unemployed. The Port of New Orleans lost business to other ports, including Houston and Gulfport. People left the city. Houses were for sale, but values fell. By the mid-1990s, prices were back up and the oil companies survived.

Today, Poydras Street has become home to a variety of new industries—restaurants and hotels, apartments and condominiums, startup companies, and government offices.

Tourism

The New Orleans Convention and Visitors Bureau continues to capitalize on the city's living history. Tours offer visitors the opportunity to walk in the steps of city founders, entrepreneurs, musicians, and even ghosts on the haunted tours.

The Golden Age of steamboating on the Mississippi is recalled as ships, reminiscent of that earlier era, fill the river, dodging containerized freighters, ferries, cruise ships, ocean liners, and oil tankers, all vying for their space in the river.

Excursion boats allow the same view of St. Louis Cathedral and Jackson Square enjoyed by steamboat passengers in the 1900s. The *Natchez*, the largest sternwheeler built in the United States, offers cruises on the river, as do the *Creole Queen* and *John James Audubon*, names and designs evoking memories of the steamboat era. New Orleans keeps the old and just adds the new.

The Steamboat Natchez *still travels the Mississippi River.* (Photo by Kathy Chappetta Spiess)

The National World War II Museum draws from a national military interest, and Audubon Nature Institute continues to add exhibits to enthrall old and young visitors to the city.

The Crescent City took a hit in its tourism business in 2006, after Hurricane Katrina, but those numbers have steadily climbed. While not yet back to pre-Katrina levels, the city saw over nine million visitors, who spent more than seven billion dollars in 2015 (Nola.com 2016).

Casino and Riverboat Gambling

On June 11, 1992, the Louisiana legislature signed the Louisiana Economic Development and Gaming Corporation Act into law. This act allowed a single land-based casino in New Orleans near the French Quarter. It also legalized riverboat gambling on the Mississippi and other Louisiana waterways in 1991.

Harrah's opened a temporary casino in the Municipal Auditorium in

May 1995, while the only approved land-based casino was being built at the foot of Canal Street at the former site of the Rivergate Convention Center. The temporary casino declared bankruptcy in November of the same year and work on the new casino stopped.

Construction got back on track, and Harrah's permanent, land-based casino opened near the foot of Canal Street in November 1999.

The New Orleans area has two riverboat casinos, Boomtown Casino in Harvey, across the Mississippi River from the city, and Treasure Chest Casino in nearby Kenner.

Shipyards and Spacecraft

The Avondale Shipyards, founded in 1938 as Avondale Marine Ways, is across the river from New Orleans in Avondale, Louisiana. Today, the shipyard is part of Huntington Ingalls Industries. At one point, the shipyard employed more than six thousand people, making it the largest employer in the state. Huntington Ingalls closed down the shipyard in 2014 and put the property on the market in 2015.

The 832-acre Michoud plant called NASA Michoud Assembly Facility in Eastern New Orleans manufactured rocket boosters for flights in space. Martin Marietta manufactured the Space Shuttle's external fuel tanks under a contract to NASA. NASA retired the Space Shuttle program in 2010, but the facility continues to support projects for NASA's Space Launch System.

Louisiana World Exposition

From May to November 1984, New Orleans hosted the Louisiana World Exposition (also known as the World's Fair) on the riverfront between Poydras Street and the Greater New Orleans Mississippi River Bridge. The Fair's theme was "The World of Rivers—Fresh Water as a Source of Life." A 550-seat amphitheater provided a superb view of the proscenium stage with the magnificent Mississippi River as a backdrop for the international artists who performed there. An open-air aquacade extravaganza further carried out the water theme.

Although the World's Fair lost a great deal of money, it left a valuable legacy to the people of New Orleans in a developed riverfront, new hotels and parks, and improved roads. The **Riverwalk** houses a collection of outlet stores that attract millions of tourists annually. The **New Orleans Ernest N. Morial Convention Center** is the sixth largest in the nation.

New Orleans's Sports Teams and Their Home Turf

New Orleans Saints

On November 1, 1966, the New Orleans Saints became the sixteenth NFL franchise. John Mecom, Jr., was the majority stockholder and president of the franchise. Tom Fears was named the first head coach. The city was thrilled; the first day that tickets went on sale for the first game, 20,000 tickets were presold. Ticket sales for the Saints' first game totaled 33,400 tickets (Howell 2011).

The Saints played their very first game against the Los Angeles Rams and lost 16-7. Little did New Orleanians know that this would be an omen for the future of the team. But that didn't stop the fans from standing behind them—through all of the less-than-thrilling seasons when fans put paper bags over their heads, they still attended games of the "Aints."

In 1985, the team had a new owner. Tom Benson bought the team for $70.204 million (*Key Moments in Saints History* 2015). It wasn't until 1987 that the Saints made it to an NFL playoff game for the first time in their twenty-year history. The fans went wild!

In 2005, Hurricane Katrina severely damaged the Superdome. Knowing its importance to New Orleans and New Orleanians, the Dome was repaired in time for the Saints to play on their home field for the first regular-season game, lifting the spirits of the city at a time when it needed it most.

Then, in 2010, the city realized its hopes and dreams when the New Orleans Saints, under head coach Sean Payton, went to Super Bowl XLIV in Miami, where they beat the Indianapolis Colts, 31-17. More than forty years after the inception of the franchise, the New Orleans Saints were World Champions.

New Orleans Pelicans

In 2002, New Orleans got another pro sports team, the Hornets NBA basketball franchise.

Founded in 1988, the Hornets originally called Charlotte, North Carolina home. The team moved to New Orleans following its 2001-2 season. Its inaugural season as the New Orleans Hornets began with a home game on October 20, 2002. Hurricane Katrina forced the team to move temporarily to Oklahoma City, where they spent two seasons, returning to New Orleans in 2007 (Schott, n.d.).

In April 2012, Tom Benson, owner of the Saints NFL franchise, bought the team. With new ownership came a new name. The name "Hornets," according to Benson, "didn't mean anything to the community." He later added, "The pelican represents New Orleans, just like the Saints." In January 2013, the team became the New Orleans Pelicans (Associated Press 2016).

The brown pelican is the state bird of Louisiana. It was considered an endangered species until 1995.

Baseball in New Orleans

That New Orleans has a sports team named the Pelicans is not new. In 1865, the Pelicans Baseball Club was organized, but it wasn't until 1887 that New Orleans businessman Toby Hart obtained the baseball franchise for the city from the Southern League.

The New Orleans Pelicans played their first game on April 17, 1887, at Sportsman's Park, on City Park Avenue across from Greenwood Cemetery.

In 1908, Pelican Park opened on South Carrollton Avenue between Banks and Palmyra across from what is today Jesuit High School. The Pelicans played at this field until 1915. The team was sold to Little Rock in 1959.

Today, the city of New Orleans claims the **Baby Cakes**, a AAA baseball team, as its own. In 1993, Don Beaver bought a Milwaukee Brewers farm-club team and brought them to New Orleans, naming them the Zephyrs. The team played at Privateer Park on the University of New Orleans campus until 1998 when the club moved to the suburb of Metairie.

Superdome

The state of Louisiana owns the Superdome, locally called the Dome. It was built at a cost of $161 million and opened with a football game in August 1975. The most extravagant building in the world at the time, it boasted a seating capacity of 76,468, a diameter of 680 feet, and a height of 273 feet. Although it garners and reflects a Texas flavor, it outdoes the Houston Astrodome in size. The Astrodome could fit inside the Superdome with 30 feet above it to spare. The Dome towers over the site of the old railroad yard and is the most visible building in the city. With the opening of the Superdome, the city was announcing that it was officially open for business.

The Superdome is the home to the New Orleans Saints NFL team and the annual Sugar Bowl game.

In August of 2005, Mayor C. Ray Nagin designated the Dome a "refuge of last resort" for those citizens not able to evacuate the city for Hurricane Katrina. The Dome sustained severe damage during the storm. The latest renovation, completed in June 2011, cost $85 million.

The Superdome has hosted a number of Super Bowl games, including those of 1970, 1972, 1975, 1978, 1981, 1986, 1990, 1997, 2002, and 2013.

On October 4, 2011, Gov. Bobby Jindal and the New Orleans Saints announced that a ten-year agreement had been reached for renaming the Dome. The new name of the domed stadium became the **Mercedes-Benz Superdome.**

Mercedes-Benz Superdome (Photo by Kathy Chappetta Spiess)

Smoothie King Center

The Smoothie King Center, formerly known as the New Orleans Arena, hosts the NBA's New Orleans Pelicans, formerly known as the New Orleans Hornets.

Since the arena was built in 1999, it has hosted ice hockey (New Orleans Brass, disbanded), arena football (VooDoo, disbanded), concerts (seating nearly eighteen thousand), high-school basketball, and other events. Owned by the state of Louisiana, it was built at a cost of $114 million. It survived Katrina with far less damage than the Superdome.

English Turn

Another element was added to the sports picture in 1994 at English Turn. No longer just a bend in the river, it is now a country-club development with a Jack Nicklaus-designed championship golf course.

The Audubon Nature Institute

The Audubon Nature Institute is a nonprofit organization that operates the Audubon Zoo, the Aquarium of the Americas, Audubon Park, Woldenberg Riverfont Park, Freeport McMoRan Audubon Species Survival Center, Audubon Center for Research on Endangered Species, and the Audubon Insectarium. The Institute's attractions add $100 million annually to the local economy. It is in part supported by household and individual memberships. The Institute began as "Friends of the Zoo" in 1974.

Parks

City Park is one of the largest municipal parks in the United States and covers 1,500 acres of land. The original park was the Allard Plantation, bought at auction by John McDonogh, who willed it to the children of New Orleans. Allard lived on the land until he died and was buried beneath the one remaining Dueling Oak. The park tripled in size in the 1920s.

Audubon Park was once the plantation of Etienne de Boré and

Approximately 350 acres in uptown New Orleans, Audubon Park was the site of the Etienne de Boré plantation, the nation's first commercial sugar plantation. The park was named in honor of John James Audubon. (Photo by Kathy Chappetta Spiess)

the site of the World's Industrial and Cotton Centennial Exposition of 1884. It now boasts the **Audubon Zoo,** the South's largest zoo, at the juncture of Magazine Street and the Mississippi River. Besides alligators, swamp exhibits, and the world of primates, it features waterfalls and tropical vegetation that simulate a natural habitat for 2,000 animals.

Armstrong Park on Rampart Street between St. Ann Street and St. Peter Street is a square with an interesting history. Named in honor of the New Orleans-born jazz musician Louis Armstrong, who was the city's goodwill ambassador to the world, it is home to many festivals and celebrations. The city purchased the square from Claude Tremé in 1810 and subdivided the neighborhood. In this area, many free people of color and skilled black craftsmen lived side by side with white families who built the Italianate and Greek Revival homes.

After the Civil War, the square was renamed Beauregard Square in honor of the Confederate general P. G. T. Beauregard. In 1930, the Municipal Auditorium was constructed at the rear of the square. Its name was changed to **Morris F. X. Jeff Auditorium** in honor of the city official who helped provide recreation and sports activities for African-American children and was the location for operas, plays, concerts, and Carnival balls. It also housed the Harrah's temporary casino in 1995. The auditorium suffered damage from Hurricane Katrina in 2005. Future use of the facility is uncertain.

Woldenberg Riverfront Park, which opened in October 1989, provided the landscaping for the Aquarium, which opened the following year. The park is named for Malcolm and Dorothy Woldenberg, philanthropists who gave tremendous sums to Tulane University and to Woldenberg Village for the elderly in Algiers. The park consists of thirteen acres of green space featuring oak trees, magnolias, crepe myrtles, and a brick promenade along the river that connects Canal Street and the Aquarium with the Moon Walk and Jackson Square. A beautiful kinetic sculpture by a New Orleanian, John Scott, who won the commission in a contest sponsored by the Audubon Nature Institute, graces the area. The sculpture, called *Ocean Song,* is sixteen feet tall and made of mirror-finished stainless steel. Its top elements move in the wind.

The **Aquarium of the Americas,** part of the Audubon Nature Institute, opened in 1990 on a sixteen-acre site on the riverfront near Canal Street. It offers an up-close view of sea life, showing the aquatic worlds of the Caribbean, Amazon Rainforest, Gulf of Mexico, and Mississippi Delta. The zoo and aquarium, both on the Mississippi River, can be accessed by the *John James Audubon* **Riverboat,** which connects the uptown and French Quarter attractions.

Museums

The **New Orleans Museum of Art** (NOMA), in City Park, is the city's oldest fine art museum. The museum got its start with a $150,000 donation by Isaac Delgado. NOMA opened in December 1911 with only nine works of art. Today is houses over forty thousand works with notable collections in French and American art, photography, and glass, as well as African and Japanese art. In 2003, Sydney and Walda Besthoff donated over forty sculptures to the museum and the creation of the Sydney and Walda Besthoff Sculpture Garden. The garden exhibits more than sixty sculptures. In 2005, the museum sustained $6 million in damage by Hurricane Katrina, causing it to close for seven months. No collections were damaged by the storm.

The Historic New Orleans Collection at 533 Royal Street is a private, nonprofit organization established in 1966 by Gen. and Mrs. L. Kemper Williams to serve the public as a museum and research center for state and local history.

The **Cabildo,** 701 Chartres Street, built beginning in 1795, served as the seat of government for the Spanish colonies and the site of the signing of the Louisiana Purchase. Today the museum tells the story of Louisiana from the American Indians to the European explorers, slaves, and free people of color, as well as the French, Spanish, and Anglo-Americans who later shaped the city and state.

The **National World War II Museum,** originally called the National D-Day Museum, opened its doors on June 6, 2000. **Stephen**

The United States' official World War II museum houses a collection of artifacts covering the various theaters of the war. The museum was founded in 2000 as the National D-Day Museum but soon expanded to include the entire "war that changed the world." The six-acre campus now has five pavilions housing historical exhibits, dinner theater, and restaurants. (Photo by Kathy Chappetta Spiess)

Ambrose, historian and author, founded the museum as a way of telling the story of the American experience in World War II. The name was officially changed by Congress to the National World War II Museum in 2003. The museum, located at 945 Magazine Street, displays exhibits of film, documents, and artifacts of the war. The museum also features dining, entertainment, and shopping.

New Orleans has over forty-five museums, from art to voodoo.

There are a number of smaller, yet impressive museums scattered through the city, including the Presbytère, 1850 House in the lower Pontalba Apartments, the Old U.S. Mint, the Civil War Museum, the Pharmacy Museum, the New Orleans Jazz National Historical Park, the Louisiana Children's Museum, the American Italian Renaissance Foundation Museum and Research Library, as well as the Audubon Insectarium, to name but a few.

Destruction and Renovation of the Cabildo

On Wednesday, May 11, 1988, at 4:00 P.M., a fire broke out in the historic Cabildo and raged for ninety minutes, bringing down the cupola and the mansard roof, damaging a storehouse of historic furniture on the third floor. Artifacts on the lower floors were seriously water-damaged. New Orleanians and tourists watched as the fire department's hoses sprayed from all directions and firemen and volunteers made repeated trips into the building to salvage artworks. A possible cause of the fire was a spark from a welder's torch during repairs to the roof gutters. The St. Louis Cathedral next door remained unharmed.

Six years and $8 million later, on Sunday, February 27, 1994, New Orleanians saw the renovated building, improvements, and new exhibits for the first time. James F. Sefcik, director of the **Louisiana State Museum,** said the fire gave him the opportunity to present the comprehensive exhibition on the history of Louisiana that he already had in mind. The renovated building now includes carefully planned exhibits telling the story of Louisiana from the European explorers in 1877, with the emphasis on the American Indians, black slaves, and free people of color, instead of only the Spanish, French, and Anglo-Americans who controlled their politics.

Cuisine

The colonial French learned how to use roots and herbs, such as chicory and sassafras, from the Choctaw and Chickasaw Indians. The Acadians brought with them their one-pot dishes, which started with a roux (gravy made with browned flour). In the 1890s, the Italians came with their highly seasoned dishes.

Because of the variety of seafood and vegetables in and around New Orleans, much experimenting has been done with cooking, resulting in such delicacies as stuffed mirlitons, eggplants, and artichokes, as well as soups, sauces, stews, gumbos, and étouffées prepared with Creole tomatoes, onions, garlic, and green peppers. Red beans and rice is also a mainstay in the New Orleans family.

According to Tom Fitzmorris, well-known and longtime restaurant critic, there are 1,411 restaurants in the Greater New Orleans area, ranging from mom and pop po'-boy establishments to some of the country's oldest fine-dining restaurants. Fitzmorris's list does not include fast food, most national chains, takeout and delivery-only places, or food outlets (Fitzmorris 2016).

Some of the oldest restaurants in New Orleans still operate today: Antoine's (opened in 1840), Café du Monde (1862), Galatoire's (1905), Arnaud's (1918), and Broussard's (1920).

Other restaurants of note include: Acme Oyster House, Bayona, Bourbon House, Brennan's, Brigsten's, Central Grocery, Commander's Palace, Court of Two Sisters, Dickie Brennan's Steakhouse, Domenica, Dooky Chase, Emeril's Delmonico, GW Fins, Herbsaint, K-Paul's Louisiana Kitchen, Liuzza's by the Track, Mandina's, Mr. B's Bistro, Mosca's, Napoleon House, Pascal's Manale, Ruth's Chris Steakhouse, and Tujague's.

Reflecting the additions to our population, many ethnic restaurants are operating successfully in New Orleans today, such as those that feature Korean, Japanese, Greek, Cuban, Indian, Chinese, Vietnamese, Thai, and Turkish cuisines, to name a few.

The Music of New Orleans

Crescent City jazz pioneers include Louis Armstrong, Danny Barker, Buddy Bolden, Clarence Ford, the Humphrey Brothers (Willie, Earl, and Percy), Jelly Roll Morton, King Oliver, Alvin "Red" Tyler, and Dr. Michael White, among many others. It's also being played by brass bands such as the Dirty Dozen and Rebirth.

Ellis Marsalis came back to New Orleans in 1989 to a prestigious professional post at the University of New Orleans. His sons **Wynton, Branford, Jason,** and **Delfeayo** enjoy well-deserved success on an international scale. The same may be said for the multitalented singer-pianist-actor **Harry Connick, Jr.**

Ronnie Kole (1931-) continues to perform in New Orleans and internationally. Two of his mentors were **Al Hirt** (1922-99) and jazz legend **Pete Fountain** (1930-2016).

Rhythm and blues became an art form in the 1950s, when hometown hero **Fats Domino** topped the national charts. Another R&B artist was the late **Professor Longhair** (Roeland Byrd) (1918-80), whose Afro-Cuban rumba style bore evidence of the New Orleans connection to Caribbean culture. **Allen Toussaint,** singer, songwriter, producer, and pianist, was one of the creators of New Orleans rhythm and blues.

New Orleans's own Pete Fountain, one of the nation's greatest jazz artists

He began entertaining in New Orleans in the 1950s and was still performing up until his death in 2015. The R&B scene flourishes with stars still in great form, such as **Irma Thomas** and **Clarence "Frogman" Henry** (1937-).

The Grammy-winning **Neville Brothers** and **Aaron Neville** perform together infrequently and often solo. They and **Dr. John (Mac Rebennack)** have shared New Orleans R&B with the world.

Walter "Wolfman" Washington continues to perform R&B. Other legends included **Johnny Adams** (1932-98) and **Snooks Eaglin** (1936-2009). Some popular R&B nightclubs include **Tipitina's,** the **Maple Leaf Bar,** and the **House of Blues**.

Several New Orleans artists grace the rolls of the Louisiana Music Hall of Fame, including **Fats Domino, Jerry Lee Lewis, Little Richard, Cosimo Matassa, Louis Armstrong, Mahalia Jackson, Pete Fountain, Buddy Guy, Gov. Jimmie Davis, Ellis Marsalis, Lead Belly, Webb Pierce, Dale Hawkins, Louis Prima, Percy Sledge, Irma Thomas, Dr. John (Mac Rebennack), Jelly Roll Morton, Allen Toussaint, Al "Carnival Time" Johnson, Bill Conti,** and **Clarence "Frogman" Henry.**

The Grammy-winning Neville Brothers (1994) are native New Orleanians. Left to right: Cyril, Aaron, Charles, and Art. The older brothers got their start in the 1950s. These artists of New Orleans-style rhythm and blues are all now internationally popular.

The historic Orpheum Theater reopened in September 2015 with a $13 million renovation after Hurricane Katrina. The 1,500-seat Beaux Arts-style theater originally opened in 1915 with vaudeville acts. The Louisiana Philharmonic Orchestra is the anchor tenant.

Rock 'n' roll is alive and well as played by groups like **Johnny Sketch and the Dirty Notes** at places such as Tipitina's, **Carrollton Station**, the **Circle Bar,** and **Rock n' Bowl.**

Cajun music and zydeco, its African-American Creole counterpart, are unique to the local scene.

The Latin music scene still thrives in the music of **Vivaz, Los Po-Boy-Citos,** and the **Iguanas.**

Historic Universities and New Education

New Orleans is home to many universities and colleges, public and private: Dillard University on Gentilly Boulevard (1869), Tulane University on St. Charles Avenue (opened in 1884), Loyola University New Orleans on St. Charles Avenue (1912), Xavier University of

Tulane University, on St. Charles Avenue, established in 1884 thanks to more than a million dollars in land, cash, and securities for the "promotion and encouragement of intellectual, moral and industrial education" from Paul Tulane. (Photo by Kathy Chappetta Spiess)

Loyola University on St. Charles Avenue, on a section of the original Foucher Plantation purchased by the Jesuits in 1886. The college was established in 1904 by the Society of Jesus and chartered as a university in 1912. (Photo by Kathy Chappetta Spiess)

Louisiana on Washington Avenue (1915), University of Holy Cross on Woodland Drive (1916), New Orleans Baptist Theological Seminary on Gentilly Boulevard (1917), Delgado Community College on City Park Avenue (1921), Notre Dame Seminary Graduate School of Theology on Carrollton Avenue (1923), LSU Health Sciences Center New Orleans on Bolivar Street (1931), Southern University at New Orleans on Press Drive (1956), University of New Orleans on Lakeshore Drive (1958), and Nunez Community College in Chalmette (1992). Numerous independent and for-profit colleges operate satellite campuses or distance learning programs.

Government and Civic Center

The New Orleans government operates on the parish council system. Orleans Parish and the city of New Orleans share boundaries; therefore, the parish and city government are the same. A chief administrator and a city council made up of seven members, five from districts and two at large, assist the mayor in governing the city.

The Duncan Plaza Civic Complex was first envisioned by Mayor Chep Morrison in 1957. City Hall, originally located in Gallier Hall, moved into the new eleven-story building that was completed in 1959 at a cost of $7 million. The plaza was also to be the site of a state office building, court buildings, and the city library.

In 2004, the Louisiana Supreme Court left the area to return to the French Quarter, and its building was subsequently demolished. The **New Orleans Public Library Main Branch,** which won an architecture award in 1960, is still on Duncan Plaza, fronting on Loyola Avenue. The **U.S. Postal Service Main Post Office** is a few blocks away at 701 Loyola.

After Hurricane Katrina, many local and state agencies moved to **Benson Tower** at 1450 Poydras Street, owned by Tom Benson, owner of the New Orleans Saints and New Orleans Pelicans. The **Union Passenger Terminal** serves Amtrak and Greyhound passengers.

Medicine and Healthcare

Herbs and Prayers

As we've seen, eighteenth-century New Orleans had a tremendous need for medical care. Its below-sea-level elevation, proximity to the Gulf of Mexico, and semitropical climate provided an excellent environment for incubation of insects and disease. Diseases that most often affected the Crescent City were cholera, yellow fever, malaria, and smallpox (Louisiana State Museum 2016).

In the eighteenth century, physicians knew little about the cause of diseases, and cures spanned the gamut of ludicrous and dangerous to accidentally effective. Bloodletting was used to release "bad blood," smoke bombs were used to kill disease-causing vapors, and herbs and prayers were ever popular.

Because of the city's vulnerability to disease, New Orleans created its own board of health in 1817, which predated the state's board by nearly forty years. French-speaking physicians established *La Société Médicale de la Nouvelle-Orléans.* In 1820, English physicians founded the Physico-Medical Society. Both organizations worked to study diseases that plagued Louisiana, especially yellow fever. After the 1830s, Louisiana was the only Southern state to require medical licenses for physicians. The state established a board of health in 1855; it was the first state to do so in the U.S.

Hospitals in the Crescent City

The first hospital to open in New Orleans was the **Royal Hospital** in 1722. However, it was not open to everyone. Only military personnel and individuals in service to the king could be treated there. That left a great number of the colonists to be cared for by the Capuchin fathers, and this would prove to be an overwhelming task.

Charity Hospital

The colonists desperately needed a place to go for medical treatment. Their salvation came on January 21, 1736, with the death of sailor and boat builder Jean Louis, who bequeathed 10,000 French livres "to serve in perpetuity the founding of a hospital for the sick of New Orleans."

With those funds, *L'Hospital des Pauvres de la Charite* was established at the corner of Chartres and Bienville streets to provide medical care to the poor who could not afford care at the Royal Hospital.

Almost immediately, the original Charity Hospital proved too small. A second hospital was built in 1743, a third in 1785. A total of six buildings were constructed to house Charity Hospital. The Art Deco building on Tulane Avenue was built in 1939 and was adjacent to Tulane and LSU medical schools (Salvaggio 1992).

In 1970, Edwin Edwards, then a U.S. representative, battled to get a new Charity Hospital built to replace the 1939 structure, but the process never got past the planning stage. Consequently, the Art Deco building on Tulane Avenue remained in operation until 2005 when waters from the levee breaches following Hurricane Katrina flooded the hospital's basement. With the floodwaters came the excuse to pursue the long sought-after new facility with government support.

LSU developed a plan that would rebuild Charity Hospital as part of a vast new medical complex. A feasibility study conducted in 2008 concluded that the hospital, although damaged, was structurally sound and could be used to house the new facility. However, LSU was determined to build a new hospital, and over its many critics and a lot of political wrangling, the University Medical Center was planned to anchor the new BioDistrict of New Orleans.

The BioDistrict is a 1,500-acre site dedicated to bioscience and

Built in 1939, the old Charity Hospital was flooded following Hurricane Katrina in 2005 and closed. (Photo by Kathy Chappetta Spiess)

quality healthcare delivery. It features research facilities, workforce development initiatives, and an emphasis on attracting bioscience industry to the area.

University Medical Center

The University Medical Center is the successor to Charity Hospital and touted as a model for collaboration of industry, educational institutions, and private enterprise. At a cost of $1.2 billion, the glass-and-steel structure, designed by NBBJ architects, was completed in 2015. The world-class teaching facility can accommodate up to two thousand medical students and houses 426 private beds, 277 exam rooms, 5 trauma rooms and 56 Emergency Department exam rooms over its 2.3 million square feet (University Medical Center 2016).

New Orleans Veterans Affairs Hospital

The original Veterans Affairs Hospital opened on March 4, 1946, near the lakefront. By 2005, the sixty-year-old building had seen better days but kept on going. Then Hurricane Katrina hit the city, and the levees broke. Like many buildings in New Orleans, the VA Hospital sustained severe damage following the storm. And while the hospital was reopened within 100 days of the hurricane, a long-term solution needed to be put in motion in order to care for the many U.S. veterans in the area. Once approval to build a new hospital was received, the project, dubbed Project Legacy, began (U.S. Department of Veterans Affairs 2016).

The new 200-bed hospital located in the BioDistrict of New Orleans is ready to care for the 70,000 veterans in the Greater New Orleans area.

Louisiana Cancer Research Center

The third facility of the BioDistrict is the Louisiana Cancer Research Center, a collaboration of three universities' health sciences programs. Construction began on the $90 million facility in 2009. Designed by RMJM Architects of the United Kingdom, and the local firm of Lyons & Hudson Architects, the ten-story, 175,000-square-foot facility opened in 2012 at 1700 Tulane Avenue in Mid-City.

City Life

New Orleans is a fun-loving city where the party never ends. The taverns in the French Quarter are alive with laughter, music, and fun. People fill the streets, some of which are now pedestrian malls. They shop, sightsee, and enjoy the atmosphere as music spills out of the many establishments. Panoramic views of the city and river can be seen from the high-rise buildings, including the Westin Canal Place and other downtown hotels.

New Orleans, a Study in Contrasts

New Orleans is a study in contrasts: the Vieux Carré, the Garden District, the University area, Carrollton, the revitalized CBD, the old buildings, the Superdome, skyscrapers and high-rise hotels, uptown, downtown, back-o'-town, riverfront, lakefront, New Orleans East, New Orleans West, New Orleans North embraced by the lake, and New Orleans South hugged by the river.

Built on a site where no city should have ever been built, it went about its business of commerce, defying fires, floods, hurricanes, and epidemics, and it survived. New Orleans has drained half of its living area to make it habitable, has preserved its treasured heritage, and has achieved the rank of the sixth biggest port in the United States based on volume of cargo. Considering the problems it has solved in the past, those of today do not seem insurmountable.

The population is as diverse as ever, as the city continues to draw people of all cultures and backgrounds. The city has all the problems of an urban center but all the charms of an aging metropolis, spiced with a European and Mediterranean flavor.

Volumes can be written about New Orleans as the Queen of the Mississippi, and at the rate she's progressing, no one will ever write them all. She's romantic, aristocratic, decorative, scandalous, and old-fashioned, all at the same time.

There is something about New Orleans that gets in your blood. It is intangible. It roots in deep and stays with you. It fosters a love of the city and builds a loyalty like no other. It strengthens you. Floods, fires, and high winds cannot keep the city or its people down for very long. New Orleanians are survivors, loyal to their traditions and their way of life.

CHAPTER XII

Disasters: Natural and Manmade

A Short History of Hurricanes in Louisiana (Roth 2010)

In 1718, Bienville selected the site for the city of New Orleans, "at that beautiful crescent in the river, a spot half-way between Natchez [Ft. Rosalie] and Mobile [Ft. St. Louis] where the river almost touches the lake at Bayou St. John, a spot safe from Hurricanes and Tidal Waves."

1915 *September 29.* **Hurricane of 1915** lands near Grand Isle and causes serious damage to the city. Category 4. Causes $13 million (1915 dollars) in damage, 21 people die in New Orleans.

1947 *September 19-20.* **Hurricane #4** makes landfall in Louisiana. Jefferson Parish has flooding up to six feet in some areas. Category 1. Causes $110 million in damage, 51 people die in Louisiana.

1956 *September 24.* **Hurricane Flossy** hits Grand Isle, completely submerging the barrier island and causing severe coastal erosion. Category 2. Causes $22 million in damage, 22 people die.

1957 *June 27.* **Hurricane Audrey** hits the southwest coast of Louisiana, spreading devastation to most of Cameron Parish and parts of Vermilion, Iberia, and St. Mary parishes. One of the most destructive hurricanes to hit southwest Louisiana. Category 4. Causes $120 million in damage, 416 people die, mainly in Cameron Parish.

1965 *September 10.* **Hurricane Betsy** makes landfall at Grand Isle with a storm surge of 15.7 feet. In New Orleans the storm surge is 10 feet and causes the worst flooding in decades in

New Orleans East and Chalmette, with severe damage to the city and flooding in low-lying areas. Category 3. Causes $1.4 billion in damage, 58 people die in Louisiana.

1969 *August 17.* **Hurricane Camille** hits Pass Christian, Mississippi along the Gulf Coast near New Orleans. Category 3. Causes $199 million in damage, 3 people die in Louisiana.

1992 *August 26.* **Hurricane Andrew** hits south Louisiana near the Atchafalaya River. Category 3. Causes nearly $1 billion in damage.

2005 *August 29.* **Hurricane Katrina** makes landfall near the mouth of the Mississippi River and wipes out much of the Mississippi Gulf Coast and New Orleans; poorly built federal levees in New Orleans breach and 80 percent of the city floods. Category 3. Causes $81 billion in damage, 1,577 people die in Louisiana.

2005 *September 24.* **Hurricane Rita** hits near Johnson's Bayou in southwest Louisiana's coastal parish of Cameron, devastating an area spared by Hurricane Katrina just weeks before. Category 3. 1 person dies in Louisiana.

2008 *August 23-September 3.* **Hurricane Gustav** hits southeast Louisiana, causing a 9-10-foot storm surge that tops floodwalls and levees in New Orleans, but flooding was not widespread. Category 2. 7 people die in Louisiana.

2008 *September 12-13.* **Hurricane Ike** hits Point Bolivar, Texas. The primary impact to southeast Louisiana was a 3-6-foot storm surge, which increased to 17 feet by the time the storm hit Cameron. Category 1. Causes $19.3 billion in damage, 2 people die in Louisiana.

2012 *August 29.* **Hurricane Isaac** hits Southwest Pass and makes a second landfall just west of Port Fourchon. A strong storm surge of 6-11 feet causes flooding in unprotected areas of St. Bernard and St. Tammany parishes. Category 1. Causes $970 million in damage, 3 people die in Louisiana (Berg 2013).

Hurricane Katrina—August 29, 2005

"Tonight I also offer this pledge of the American people: throughout the area hit by the hurricane, we will do what it takes. We will stay as long as it takes to help citizens rebuild their communities and their lives. And all who question the future of the Crescent City need to know: there is no way to imagine America without New Orleans, and this great city will rise again."

This was Pres. George W. Bush's promise when he toured the devastated area on September 15, 2005.

It was bound to happen. The "Big One" was going to hit the city. Everybody knew it, but everyone prayed that it would not happen "this year."

New Orleanians have faced adversity since the city's founding in 1718, and they are certainly no strangers to hurricanes. People prepare as best they can—boarding up windows and doors, stocking up on bottled water and nonperishable food, and then hunkering down to ride it out. Some people evacuate, but not everyone has the resources to leave almost everything they own and hit the road. If you evacuated, it would only be for a few days. The hurricane hits and does its damage, and people clean up and repair and move on.

Such was not the case on August 29, 2005, when Hurricane Katrina hit southeast Louisiana. Hurricane Katrina was the "Big One" New Orleanians dreaded.

The Big One

Hurricane Katrina entered the warm waters of the Gulf of Mexico as a tropical storm in the early morning hours of August 26 and quickly strengthened. The National Hurricane Center predicted that Katrina would be a major hurricane. On August 28, the Center said that Katrina had the potential to be catastrophic. There would be a significant storm surge and flooding, and levees would probably be overtopped.

On the morning of August 28, New Orleans mayor C. Ray Nagin issued the first mandatory evacuation of the city. By this time, however, roads were already backed up with people from the city and surrounding communities trying to get out of town, even though the state implemented contraflow at 4:00 P.M. on August 27. No matter which direction you were going, it would take hours, in some cases days, to get there.

However, not everyone in the city had the means to evacuate. In 2005, almost 30 percent of the population lived below the poverty level. Tens of thousands could not evacuate. With the outer bands of the storm predicted to reach the city within hours, Mayor Nagin opened the Superdome as a shelter of last resort.

Katrina hit New Orleans on August 29, bringing 145 mile-per-hour winds and causing utility lines to snap, roofs to come loose, and debris to fly like missiles. Record storm surges overtopped the protection levees that surround most of the city. As rain poured down and levees were overtopped, a disaster within a disaster was occurring. The levees, built by the Army Corps of Engineers, began to deteriorate and break. In all, seven breaches occurred, allowing massive amounts of water into the city.

When it was all said and done, approximately 80 percent of the city of New Orleans was flooded due to the breaches in the federal levee system, leaving thousands stranded on rooftops and small islands of debris. Network and cable news programs broadcasted pictures of people waving from rooftops begging for help. Video showed the National Guard implementing air and water rescues of hundreds of people. Private citizens, using every available boat, went into flooded areas and rescued people and pets, while other people provided water and shelter.

Damage to Lakeshore Drive along the seawall caused by Hurricane Katrina

Ninth Ward house indicative of the surreal aftermath of Hurricane Katrina and the levee breaches felt throughout the city.

Hurricane Katrina destroyed many of the structures, some of which stood for decades, at West End, once the place to dine on fresh seafood in New Orleans. (Photo by Kathy Chappetta Spiess)

Scrap House *is a Hurricane Katrina memorial by artist Sally Heller. It sits across from the Ernest N. Morial Convention Center on Convention Center Boulevard.* (Photo by Kathy Chappetta Spiess)

After the Storm

The same news broadcasts that showed Katrina heroes rescuing people from rooftops also showed the world the Katrina victims, mainly African Americans and the elderly gathering at the Superdome, at the Convention Center, and in the streets. Storm victims, old, young, and sometimes dying, waited in the heat and humidity for help that was a long time coming. There was no water and no food.

In other areas of the city, civilization spiraled into chaos. Looting was rampant, fights and fires broke out, and assaults on already vulnerable people were occurring with greater frequency. Councilwoman Jackie Clarkson was reported as saying, "The looting is out of control. The French Quarter has been attacked. We're using exhausted, scarce police to control looting when they should be used for search and rescue while we still have people on rooftops."

Help . . . Finally!

Help was a long time coming. Terry Ebbert, New Orleans Homeland Security director, said, "We can send massive amounts of aid to tsunami victims, but we can't bail out New Orleans" ("Official: Astrodome can't take more refugees" 2005).

The Louisiana National Guard already had 3,000 men placed in New Orleans and surrounding parishes to prepare for the hurricane. After the storm, another 50,000 troops were deployed to the affected area. Ninety-six hours after Katrina hit, 30,000 additional troops arrived in Louisiana to assist with search and rescue, medical treatment, and security, bringing with them much-needed supplies (Orrell 2007).

Lt. Gen. Russel Honoré

The military sent Louisiana native Lt. Gen. Russel Honoré to lead its rescue efforts.

The priority of the Guard, according to Honoré, was to rescue the thousands still stranded in New Orleans days after Hurricane Katrina made landfall.

Arriving in New Orleans, General Honoré became the face of the military's recovery efforts. His mantra was "treat the residents like civilians, not criminals," and he instructed all soldiers to point their guns down. Honoré left the police work to the New Orleans Police Department while he got the victims safely out of the city.

His tell-it-like-it-is manner and his willingness to get his hands dirty made him a savior to those still in the city.

Rumor and Reality

With evacuations still ongoing, chaos seemed to reign in the streets of New Orleans following Katrina. While thousands were begging for help, bands of looters were helping themselves, ransacking businesses and abandoned homes. Some reports of these crimes were rumors; some were real.

The New Orleans Police Department was hampered by a broken-down command structure and sporadic communications. Officers on the streets were overwhelmed and shorthanded; more than two hundred police officers went AWOL during the storm. The officers left on the streets were fighting a losing battle against looters.

Reports of orders authorizing police officers to shoot looters circulated, but it is unclear where the orders came from. One video surfaced showing the police commander of the First District telling officers, "We have the authority by martial law to shoot looters." Another police captain told federal prosecutors he was ordered by the department's second-in-command to "take the city back and shoot looters." The Police Department denied these allegations (Shankman and Jennings 2010).

Tragic Deaths Unwarranted

No one really knows what was going on in the minds of NOPD officers in the days after Katrina. Communication between them was minimal; they were exhausted, frustrated, and scared. In hindsight, it seems inevitable that there would be civilian casualties of a police force gone haywire.

One such ruinous incident happened on the Danziger Bridge, which connects Chef Menteur Highway between Gentilly and New

Orleans East over the Industrial Canal. It was the scene of a police-involved shooting with innocent casualties.

According to the police report, an officer responded to a call of shots fired on the Danziger Bridge. Police officers said they were acting in self-defense when they killed two men, including a mentally retarded man who was shot in the back, and wounded four.

The families of the victims disputed the police report and filed federal civil-rights lawsuits against the city. After an investigation revealed an extensive cover-up by NOPD, five police officers were convicted of a cover-up and deprivation of civil rights.

New Orleans Recovery Plan—Cranes in the Sky

Mayor Nagin hired Ed Blakely, former professor at USC and UC Riverside, as the executive director of recovery management for the city of New Orleans, singing the praises of his accomplishments and experience in recovery planning.

In his recovery plan, Blakely identified seventeen recovery zones, which, he said, would jumpstart revitalization. He promised New Orleanians there would be cranes in the sky within two years of the storm. However, all he did was talk.

Blakely blatantly showed his disdain for New Orleans and its residents. He described the area as a Third World country and its inhabitants as buffoons. In addition, he alleged that officials reported a higher population than it was so it would not affect federal grants. The *coup de grâce* came in his comments in a televised interview when he claimed that New Orleanians were lazy and racist. This sparked widespread criticism of him and his efforts, or lack thereof.

Overblown promises, political missteps, and tactless comments about a city and its people trying to recover from devastation were the hallmarks of Blakely's tenure in New Orleans. He left the city at the beginning of 2009.

Laid Bare to the World

It was not long before federal, state, and local officials were pointing fingers at each other, placing blame for the debacle that was the Hurricane Katrina relief effort. Allegations were made and documents uncovered. What matters most is that 1,577 people in Louisiana lost their lives during the storm. Others perished during the recovery, waiting for evacuation or supplies. More deaths can be indirectly attributed to the trauma of surviving and rebuilding efforts that are still going on today.

As Katrina moved on and dissipated, the images of the people waiting for rescue at the Convention Center and the Superdome sparked nationwide discussions of the inequality of the evacuation and the "unseen" poor of the city. That debate is still going on.

Before Katrina, almost 30 percent of New Orleans's population lived below the poverty level. In 2014, that level, according to the U.S. Census Bureau, was 28 percent. Mayor Mitch Landrieu said in his 2015 State of the City Address, "The storm didn't create all our problems. Our issues are generations in the making and are shared by every other part of America."

Breach of Promise

Ironically, New Orleans was not devastated by Hurricane Katrina. New Orleans was devastated by the very structures meant to protect it. The Flood Control Act of 1965 gave the Army Corps of Engineers control over the flood protection system, specifically to protect south Louisiana from the worst storms. The ACE assumed full responsibility for the design of the levee system around the city and its construction.

An in-depth investigation into the levee breaches during Hurricane Katrina by the USGS proved the storm surge did not cause them. Levees were breached because of faulty engineering, being built of sheet pilings inadequate for the job they were supposed to do and inadequately installed.

300 Years Later

Most often, the people left behind in a disaster are the poor, disabled, and elderly. Disasters do not level the playing field; the disadvantaged suffer disproportionately in their wake. Katrina proved this statement.

Pockets of the city remain devastated. Front steps lead the way to empty lots; some houses inundated with water still bear the high-water marks. Homes still needing repair or rebuilding often continue to display the grim *X* codes, Katrina crosses, made by first responders as they cleared structures looking for survivors and identifying the dead during the first harrowing days after the storm made its way into the city.

The population has rebounded, but it is not where it was pre-Katrina. There has been progress. Rebuilding is still going on. New industry has come to the city and revitalized the economy to a certain extent. However, 28 percent of the population still lives below the poverty level.

The perception of recovery is relative. A survey conducted by the Manship School of Mass Communications at Louisiana State University showed that 80 percent of whites thought the state was mostly recovered. Sixty-three percent of blacks disagreed, illustrating that the African-American residents' recovery is quite different from that of white residents (Reckdahl 2015).

There is much to say about Hurricane Katrina, yet there are no words

Katrina cross (Photo by Kathy Chappetta Spiess)

This sculpture by Brian Hanlon features the likeness of New Orleans Saints safety Steve Gleason blocking a punt by Atlanta Falcons punter Michael Koenen on September 25, 2006. The play lifted the spirits of New Orleanians recovering from Hurricane Katrina. The piece was installed as a tribute to the reopening of the Superdome after Katrina and Gleason, who suffers from ALS, said, "The statue is about coming through adversity." (Photo by Kathy Chappetta Spiess)

to explain what New Orleanians experienced. It is not something that anyone can fully understand unless they have lived through it.

Deepwater Horizon Oil Spill

Five years after Hurricane Katrina, south Louisiana suffered another horrendous blow. On April 20, 2010, the Deepwater Horizon oil well exploded in the Gulf of Mexico, killing eleven men on the platform and injuring seventeen others. The Deepwater Horizon well was drilled on the BP-operated Macondo Prospect. The well was finally capped on July 15, 2010, after spilling almost five million barrels of crude oil. Federal officials declared the well effectively dead on September 19. The BP oil spill is the largest oil spill in the history of the oil industry, which sparked President Obama to issue a six-month moratorium on drilling in the Gulf of Mexico while new safety standards were developed.

The effects of the spill on the environment were so disastrous that the White House energy advisor, Carol Browner, declared the spill "the worst environmental disaster the U.S. has faced" (BBC News 2010).

The effects on the economy of New Orleans and all of Louisiana and the Gulf Coast were enormous, not only felt in the oil, tourism, seafood, and restaurant industries but also in downstream businesses, adding to an already devastated economy.

BP has made inroads into cleaning up the oil that spilled in Gulf waters and on the coast from Florida to Texas, but more work needs to be done and the long-term effects on the environment remain to be seen.

Coastal Erosion's Effect on New Orleans

New Orleans is 105 miles upriver from the Gulf of Mexico. This area and the area along the coast are part wetlands, part dry land. Since its earliest days, the land, with its wealth of vegetation, went far in protecting New Orleans from the full wrath of hurricanes and other gulf storms. However, the dry land is quickly eroding, leaving the city vulnerable as was evidenced during Hurricane Katrina.

The Louisiana coastline is disappearing at an alarming rate. As of 2004, Louisiana was losing land at a rate of sixteen square miles per year. As alarming as this is, in the 1990s, the rate was much higher at fifty square miles a year (Wernick 2014).

When Bienville sited his city, he set it on the high ground created by the natural levees alongside the Mississippi River. At that time, the river was still creating land along the coast from Mississippi to Texas, a process that started in the glacial age and ended when man tried to control the river by building levees.

To protect the fragile infant city, Bienville built up the natural levees on the river. In 1927, the entire Mississippi River Valley flooded after record-breaking rains. After the Great Flood of 1927, Congress put the Army Corps of Engineers in charge of protecting the valley from flooding. They built more levees to control the river. The consequences of this "solution" had a tremendously negative effect on the Gulf Coast of Louisiana. Because of the levees, the river can no longer deposit the silt to replenish the land.

In the 1930s, oil and gas exploration and production made an untenable situation worse, leading to unprecedented land loss.

With no laws in place to protect the wetlands, 50,000 oil wells were permitted in the coastal area and 10,000 miles of canals dredged to service them, resulting in unprecedented land loss.

From 1930 to 1990, as much as 16 percent of the wetlands were turned into open water, leading to saltwater intrusion into freshwater swamps and marshes. The saltwater killed plants and trees, whose root systems held the land in place. With nothing to anchor the soil, the shorelines crumbled, expanding existing bodies of water and leading the way to open water, subjecting the weakened landscape to stronger winds and tidal surge.

A direct effect of canal dredging is spoil levees. These are made up of the soil scooped up during the dredging. This soil piles up alongside the canals, sometimes as high as ten feet and twice as wide. The weight of the soil dumped on the swampy land causes the marshes to sink.

All of these factors affect the Louisiana coast. However, another factor significantly affects land loss.

Big Trouble from Climate Change

According to the National Oceanic and Atmospheric Administration, south Louisiana has "the highest rate of relative sea-level rise of any place in the country and one of the highest on the planet." The area is sinking under its own weight and it is expected to sink two to five feet by the end of the twenty-first century.

Virginia Burkett, senior researcher at the National Wetlands Research Center in Lafayette, stated, "The delta of the Mississippi River is the most vulnerable location in the nation to global warming, because it is sinking at the same time that the sea level is rising. And it's only going to get worse. This area is facing big trouble from climate change."

What Does This Mean for New Orleans?

Shifting soil strains brickwork and buildings, causing cracks in walls, peaks and valleys in sidewalks, and sinking soil under foundations. In some areas around the city, the land is sinking one inch every thirty months. By the end of the twenty-first century, New Orleans will have sunk three feet.

By that time, it is believed that the lower portion of the "boot" of Louisiana will be cut off and the Gulf of Mexico will be at New Orleans's door, leaving it vulnerable to even the mildest of storms. With the disappearance of the coastal lands, the buffer that protected New Orleans from the full punch of gulf storms is gone.

Today, all that stands between the city and extinction is the dwindling coastal area and a complicated system of levees, drainage canals, and pumps. How long will it be before the beautiful crescent becomes another Atlantis, lost to the sea?

No one really knows, but there is good news. New studies are being done to determine the state's current land-loss rate. Preliminary reports show the loss slowing since 2010, largely due to a number of natural events and manmade remediation efforts including fewer destructive storms, more coastal restoration projects, and a reduction of near-shore oil and gas development (Hammer 2017).

They say that the first step in overcoming a problem is to recognize that you have a problem. In April 2017, Louisiana governor John Bel Edwards declared a state of emergency over the state's dwindling coastline. Not only will this bring the issue to national attention; it may accelerate federal permitting for coastal erosion projects. Edwards also asked that Pres. Donald Trump declare Louisiana's eroding coast

The Louisiana boot loses its toe. The dark line indicates the predicted state coastline by 2050 at the present land-loss rate.

a national emergency and "provide appropriate federal attention and cooperation to the state" (Merrit 2017).

Residents of south Louisiana are crossing their fingers and toes that they can defy Mother Nature once again. In the meantime, we will enjoy the food, culture, music, and art that is New Orleans.

Mayors of New Orleans

Served in the Cabildo under American Domination

1803-4	Etienne de Boré
1804	Pierre Petit (succeeded as Mayor Pro-Tem)

Served the City of New Orleans, Incorporated February 17, 1805

1804-5	James Pitot de Beaujardière
1805-7	John Watkins
1807-12	James J. Mather
1812-15	Nicholas Girod
1815-20	Augustin Macarty
1820-28	Louis Philippe de Roffignac
1828-38	Denis Prieur
1838-40	Charles Genois
1840-42	William Freret
1842-43	Denis Prieur
1843-44	William Freret
1844-46	Joseph Edgard Montegut
1846-54	Abial Daily Crossman

Served in City Hall (Gallier Hall)

1854-56	John L. Lewis
1856-58	Charles M. Waterman
1858-60	Gerard Stith
1860-62	John T. Monroe

Served as United States Military Mayors (All Acting)

May 1862-July 1862	George T. Shepley
July 1862-August 1862	Godfrey Weitzel
August 1862	Jonas H. French
August 1862-September 1862	Godfrey Weitzel

October 1862-January 1863	Henry C. Deming
January 1863-September 1863	James F. Miller
September 1863-October 1863	Edward Henry Durell
November 1863-February 1864	James F. Miller
February 1864-March 1865	Stephen Hoyt
March 1864-May 1865	Hugh Kennedy
May 1865-June 1865	Samuel Miller Quincy
June 1865-March 1866	Hugh Kennedy
March 1866	J. A. D. Rozier
March 1866-May 1866	George Clark

Served as Mayors of New Orleans

1866-67	John T. Monroe
1867-68	Edward Heath
1868-70	John R. Conway
1870-72	Benjamin P. Flanders
1872-74	Louis A. Wiltz
1874-76	Charles J. Leeds
1876-78	Edward Pilsbury
1878-80	Isaac W. Patton
1880-82	Joseph Ansoetegui Shakspeare
1882-84	William J. Behan
1884-88	Joseph Valsin Guillotte
1888-92	Joseph Ansoetegui Shakspeare
1892-96	John Fitzpatrick
1896-1900	Walter C. Flower
1900-1904	Paul Capdeville
1904-20	Martin Behrman
1920-25	Andrew J. McShane
1925-26	Martin Behrman
1926-30	Arthur J. O'Keefe
1930-June 1936	T. Semmes Walmsley
June 1963-July 1936	A. Miles Pratt
July 1936	Fred A. Earhart
July 1936-August 1936	Jesse S. Cave
August 1936-46	Robert S. Maestri
1946-61	deLesseps Story Morrison

Served in the New City Hall, Dedicated 1957

1961-70	Victor Hugo Schiro
1970-78	Maurice "Moon" Landrieu
1978-86	Ernest N. Morial
1986-94	Sidney J. Barthelemy
1994-2002	Marc H. Morial
2002-10	C. Ray Nagin
2010-18	Mitchell "Mitch" Landrieu

Governors of Louisiana

Governors of Louisiana as a French Colony

1699	Pierre Le Moyne, Sieur d'Iberville (founder)
1699-1700	M. de Sauvolle
1701-13	Jean Baptiste Le Moyne, Sieur de Bienville
1713-16	Antoine de La Mothe, Sieur de Cadillac
1716-17	Jean Baptiste Le Moyne, Sieur de Bienville
1717-18	Jean Michel, Sieur de L'Epinay
1718-24	Jean Baptiste Le Moyne, Sieur de Bienville
1725-26	Pierre Sidrac Dugué de Boisbriand
1727-33	Etienne de Périer
1733-43	Jean Baptiste Le Moyne, Sieur de Bienville
1743-53	Pierre François de Rigaud, Marquis de Vaudreuil-Cavagnal
1753-63	Louis Billouart, Chevalier de Kerlérec
1763-65	Jean-Jacques Blaise d'Abbadie
1765-66	Charles Philipe Aubry

Governors of Louisiana as a Spanish Colony

1766-68	Antonio de Ulloa
1769-70	Alexander O'Reilly
1770-77	Luis de Unzaga y Amezaga
1777-85	Bernardo de Galvez
1785-91	Esteban Rodríguez Miró y Sabater
1791-97	Francisco Luis Hector, Baron de Carondelet et Noyelles
1797-99	Manuel Luis Gayoso de Lemos y Amorin
1799-1801	Sebastian Calvo de la Puerta y O'Fariel, Marquis de Casa Calvo
1801-3	Juan Manuel de Salcedo

Governor of Louisiana Before the Louisiana Purchase

1803	November 30-December 20. Pierre Clément de Laussat

Governor of Louisiana as a Territory

| 1803-12 | William Charles Cole Claiborne |

Governors of Louisiana as a State

1812-16	William Charles Cole Claiborne
1816-20	Jacques Phillippe Villeré
1820-24	Thomas Bolling Robertson
1824	Henry Schuyler Thibodeaux
1824-28	Henry S. Johnson
1828-29	Pierre Auguste Bourguigon Derbigny
1829-30	Armand Julie Beauvais
1830-31	Jacques Dupre
1831-35	Andre Bienvenu Roman
1835-39	Edward Douglass White
1839-43	Andre Bienvenu Roman
1843-46	Alexander Mouton
1846-50	Isaac Johnson
1850-53	Joseph Marshall Walker
1853-56	Paul Octave Hébert
1856-60	Robert Charles Wickliffe
1860-64	Thomas Overton Moore
1862-64	George F. Shepley (military governor within Union lines)
1864-65	Henry Watkins Allen
1864-65	Michael Hahn (elected governor within Union lines, resigned)
1865-67	James Madison Wells (succeeded Hahn within Union lines)
1867-68	Benjamin Franklin Flanders
1868	Joshua Baker
1868-72	Henry Clay Warmoth
1872	John McEreny (elected, but counted out)
1872-73	P. B. S. Pinchback
1873-77	William Pitt Kellogg
1877	Stephen B. Packard
1877-80	Francis Tillou Nicholls
1880-81	Louis Alfred Wiltz
1881-88	Samuel Douglas McEnery
1888-92	Francis Tillou Nicholls
1892-1900	Murphy James Foster
1900-1904	William Wright Heard
1904-8	Newton Crain Blanchard
1908-12	Jared Young Sanders

1912-16	Luther E. Hall
1916-20	Ruffin G. Pleasant
1920-24	John M. Parker
1924-26	Huey L. Fuqua
1926-28	Oramel H. Simpson
1928-32	Huey P. Long
1932	Alvin O. King
1932-36	Oscar K. Allen
1936	James A. Noe
1936-39	Richard Webster Leche
1939-40	Earl K. Long
1940-44	Sam Houston Jones
1944-48	Jimmie H. Davis
1948-52	Earl K. Long
1952-56	Robert F. Kennon
1956-60	Earl K. Long
1960-64	Jimmie H. Davis
1964-72	John J. McKeithen
1972-80	Edwin W. Edwards
1980-84	David C. Treen
1984-88	Edwin W. Edwards
1988-92	Charles Elson "Buddy" Roemer III
1992-96	Edwin W. Edwards
1996-2004	Murphy J. "Mike" Foster
2004-8	Kathleen Babineaux Blanco
2008-16	Bobby Jindal
2016-	John Bel Edwards

Statues and Monuments

Armstrong, Louis. Father of New Orleans jazz. At Armstrong Park at Rampart Street.

Battle of New Orleans. One hundred feet high. At Chalmette National Park.

Bienville Monument. Bienville, priest, and Indian. At 400 Decatur Street.

Cabrini, Francis Xavier. First American saint. At Harrison Avenue and Canal Boulevard.

Celtic Cross. Commemorating the Irish who died of yellow fever (1832-33). At New Basin Canal Park, between West End Boulevard and Canal Boulevard.

Churchill, Winston. Statue at the Hilton Hotel in downtown New Orleans.

Clay, Henry. American statesman. Stood at Canal Street and St. Charles Avenue from 1806 to 1901. At Lafayette Square since 1901.

Confederate Heroes. 1957. Features Colonel Dreux, first Confederate soldier from Louisiana to be killed in the Civil War (July 5, 1861); Gen. Albert Pike; and Fr. A. J. Ryan, poet-chaplain of the South. At Jefferson Davis Parkway and Canal Street.

Franklin, Benjamin. 1956. At Lafayette Square.

Galvez, Bernardo de. 1977. Spanish governor of Louisiana. Gift from Spain to New Orleans commemorating our bicentennial. Foot of Canal between ferry terminal and World Trade Center.

Haughery, Margaret Gaffney. 1884. Benefactor of orphans. White marble statue engraved *Margaret.* At the intersection of Camp, Prytania, and Clio streets.

Jackson, Andrew. 1856. Equestrian statue. Hero of the Battle of New Orleans (1815). By Clark Mills, sculptor. At Jackson Square.

Joan of Arc. Maid of Orleans. Gift of France to New Orleans. Originally at

Rivergate, then at the foot of Canal Street when Rivergate was demolished. Now at Decatur Street, near Café du Monde.

King, Martin Luther, Jr. Civil Rights leader. At Martin Luther King Boulevard and South Claiborne Avenue.

Krewe of Poydras. 1982. Twenty-foot welded-steel structure by Ida Kohlmeyer. Painted in enamel. At 1515 Poydras Street.

Latin American Heroes. Features Simon Bolivar, liberator of South America (gift from Venezuela, 1957); Benito Juarez, hero of Mexico (gift from Mexico, 1965); and Gen. Francisco Morazon, Central American idol (gift from Honduras, 1966). At Basin Street.

McDonogh, John. Benefactor of public schools. At Lafayette Square.

Molly Marine. 1943. Monument inscribed *Free a Marine to Fight.* At Elk Place and Canal Street.

Monument to the Tile Makers. 1884. Dedicated to historian Charles Gayarré. First shown at the Cotton Exposition. At the intersection of Bayou Road, Tonti Street, and Esplanade Avenue.

Monument to Vietnamese and American Veterans of the Vietnam War. 1988. At the intersection of Basin Street and Iberville Street.

Ocean Song. 1989. Sixteen-foot kinetic steel sculpture by John Scott. At Woldenberg Riverfront Park.

Piazza d'Italia. Italian Plaza. Reminder of the contributions of Italians to New Orleans. At the intersection of Poydras Street and Tchoupitoulas Street.

Seton, Elizabeth. First native-born American saint. At Tulane Avenue.

Spanish-American War Veterans. Honoring the Louisiana armed forces from 1898 to 1902. At Poydras Street and Loyola Avenue.

Spring, Summer, Winter, Fall. At the four corners of Jackson Square.

Vietnam War Memorial. 1987. At the Mercedes-Benz Superdome at Poydras Street.

Wading Pool Sculptures. By Enrique Alferez. At City Park.

White, Edward Douglass. Chief justice of the U.S. Supreme Court. Louisiana native. At the Louisiana Supreme Court building.

Wright, Sophie B. 1988. Sculpture by Enrique Alferez. At Sophie B. Wright Place and Magazine Street.

Noted Personalities

Alferez, Enrique (1901-99). Mexican-born Louisiana artist who served with Pancho Villa in the Mexican Revolution before coming to New Orleans. Many of his sculptures can be seen around the city.

Almonester y Roxas, Don Andrès (1725-98). Spanish grandee who provided funds for rebuilding St. Louis Cathedral after the great fire of 1788 and who built the Cabildo. Father of Baroness de Pontalba.

Ambrose, Stephen (1936-2002). Author and historian who spent decades researching and writing about World War II, D-Day, Eisenhower, and Nixon. Founder of the D-Day Museum, renamed the National World War II Museum in 2003.

Armstrong, Louis "Satchmo" (1901-71). One of the most famous musicians in the history of jazz. More than 1,500 recordings, several movies, and TV performances. Born in New Orleans. Known as an unofficial goodwill ambassador for the United States.

Audubon, Jean-Jacques Fougère (John James) (1785-1851). Ornithologist and artist whose *Birds of America* and *Ornithological Biography* are still highly regarded. Explored Louisiana, Mississippi, Alabama, and Florida bird life and taught at Oakley Plantation near St. Francisville.

Barelli, I. T. (1800-58). Planner of the tomb of the Italian Mutual Benefit Society in St. Louis Cemetery No. 1. He and architect Pietro Gualdi were the first two to be buried there. It was afterward known as the "Hex Tomb."

Beauregard, Pierre Gustave Toutant (1818-93). Creole Confederate general at whose command the first shot of the Civil War was fired at Fort Sumter, April 12, 1862. He was born in St. Bernard Parish and married a prominent Creole woman.

Beluche, Renato (1780-1860). Served as a privateer under Jean Lafitte and gunner alongside Dominique You on Battery Three during the Battle of New Orleans. Served as an admiral under Simon Bolivar in the Independence of Gran Colombia. Born in Chalmette, died in Puerto Cabello, Venezuela. Buried in Caracas in the Pantheon of Heroes of Venezuelan Independence.

Benjamin, Judah P. (1811-84). Wealthy New Orleans lawyer and slave owner. U.S. senator from Louisiana who resigned his office when Louisiana seceded from the Union. Confederate secretary of war and state, who, after having been exiled, lived in England and gained international fame as a commercial lawyer.

Boggs, Corrine C. "Lindy" (1916-2013). Congresswoman from Louisiana since 1973, after the disappearance of her husband, Congressman Hale Boggs, in a plane over Alaska in October 1973. A descendant of Louisiana's first governor, William. C. C. Claiborne, she was one of New Orleans's outstanding citizens and leaders.

Bolden, Charles "Buddy" (1877-1931). One of the creators of New Orleans jazz. Attributed with the creation of "Big Four" rhythm. Born in New Orleans, buried in a pauper's grave in Holt Cemetery.

Cable, George Washington (1844-1925). Gained international recognition as a novelist and short-story writer of works based on Louisiana. His uncomplimentary characterizations aroused the bitter animosity of Louisiana Creoles. Born in New Orleans of wealthy slave owners, he fought in the Civil War for the Confederacy.

Calvé, Julie (1815-98). French native and star of New Orleans French Opera production of *Les Huguenots*. Married Charles Boudousquié, director of the French Opera House on Bourbon Street. Listed in 1882 City Directory as music teacher at Holy Angels Academy.

Capote, Truman (1924-86). Bestselling author. Wrote *In Cold Blood*. Recipient of many literary awards. Born in New Orleans.

Carrollton, William (1788-1844). General in the War of 1812. Had camp on the site of the McCarty Plantation.

Chase, John Churchill (1905-86). Noted cartoonist, historian, and author. Designer of many logos. Well known for his book, *Frenchmen, Desire, Good Children*.

Chopin, Kate (1850-1904). Born Katherine O'Flaherty. Married Oscar Chopin of Natchitoches Parish. Lived in New Orleans after her marriage. Author of *The Awakening* and forerunner of feminist authors in the twentieth-century South.

Claiborne, William Charles Cole (1775-1817). Oversaw the transfer of Louisiana to the Americans after the Louisiana Purchase. First non-colonial governor of Louisiana.

Clark, Daniel (1766-1813). Irish-American merchant and landowner who assisted Thomas Jefferson in negotiations leading to the Louisiana Purchase and later wounded Governor Claiborne in a duel brought about by his implication in the Aaron Burr conspiracy.

Danna, Dr. Joseph Anthony (1877-1954). Graduated from Tulane Medical School in 1901 and was both intern and resident at Hotel Dieu (1908). Later became senior surgeon at Charity Hospital and Hotel Dieu. Left money to Loyola for Danna Student Center, dedicated in 1964. Knighted by the king of Italy. Appointed by Pope Pius XII as a Knight of St. Gregory.

de Boré, Etienne (1741-1820). Sugar manufacturer in Louisiana. Developed a way to granulate sugar on a commercial scale. First mayor of New Orleans.

Delgado, Isaac (1839-1912). Philanthropist to whom New Orleans owes its art museum and former boy's trade school (now Delgado Community College).

de Sedella, Antonio, "Père Antoine" (1730-1829). Expelled from the colony of Louisiana for attempting to set up office of the Spanish Inquisition. He later returned as a loving pastor who endeared himself to the people.

Deutsche, Hermann B. (1889-1970). One of the deans of New Orleans journalism. Served on newspapers operated by the Times-Picayune Publishing Company for forty-seven years.

Dibert, Eve Butterworth (1864-1938). Philanthropist who made gifts to Dibert Tuberculosis Hospital, residence of Sisters of Charity, and John Dibert School, among others, in memory of her husband.

Dillard, James (1856-1940). Son of a slaveholder, advocate for black education. Dillard University is named in his honor.

Dix, Dorothy (Elizabeth Meriwether Gilmer) (1861-1951). Crime reporter and columnist specializing in "advice to the lovelorn." Supporter of women's suffrage and working women.

Dixon, Dave (1923-2010). Conceived and originated plan to build the Superdome. Organized the U.S. Football League.

Dufour, Charles L. "Pie" (1903-96). Newspaperman for forty years. Known for his column "Pie Dufour's A la Mode" for the *States-Item.* One of the unofficial historians of New Orleans. Author of *Ten Flags of the Wind.*

du Pratz, Antoine-Simon Le Page (1695-1775). Born in Holland and came to Dauphin Island in 1718. His three-volume work, *Histoire de la Louisiane,* tells of plantation life on Bayou St. John and in Natchez.

Faulkner, William (1897-1962). American writer, Nobel laureate, and Pulitzer Prize winner for fiction. Resided in New Orleans when his first novel, *Soldiers' Pay,* was published.

Fitzmorris, James Edward "Jimmy" (1921-). Lieutenant governor of Louisiana 1972-80. Assistant for economic development to Gov. Dave Treen.

Fortier, Alcée (1856-1951). Teacher and historian noted for his Creole studies and historical works.

Francis, Norman C. (1931-). First layman and black man to be president of Xavier University, elected in 1968. He retired in 2015.

Gaines, Myra Clark (1805-85). Principal and ultimate victor of a sensational fifty-year lawsuit against the city of New Orleans for the estate of her wealthy father, Daniel Clark.

Gallier, James, Jr. (1827-68). Continued his father's architectural work. Designer of the French Opera House.

Gallier, James, Sr. (1798-1866). Architect who designed City Hall and many Garden District homes in New Orleans. Exponent of Greek Revival style of architecture.

Galvez, Bernardo de (1746-86). Spanish governor of Louisiana who distinguished himself by wresting East and West Florida from the British (1780-83). Later became viceroy of Mexico.

Gandolfo, Henri A. (1897-1990). Author of *Metairie Cemetery: An Historical Memoir.* Connected with Metairie Cemetery for sixty-five years, a student of memorial architecture, and a repository of history and lore on the statesmen and rogues buried there.

Gayarré, Charles Etienne (1805-95). Dabbled in politics while writing several histories of Louisiana and two novels. Led Creoles in bitter controversy against George Washington Cable.

Gottschalk, Louis Moreau (1829-69). Considered leading pianist-composer of his day; gave concerts throughout the world. *La Morte* and *Tremole Etude* are his best-known works.

Grau, Shirley Ann (Mrs. James Kern Fiebleman) (1929-). Author of *The Keepers of the House,* which won the Pulitzer Prize for fiction in 1965.

Hannan, Archbishop Philip Matthew (1913-2011). Born in Washington, D.C. Held administrative offices in many national organizations. Served in the United States Army Air Forces as chaplain 1942-46 and known as the Parachute Priest. Presided over the funeral of Pres. John F. Kennedy at St. Matthew's Cathedral in Washington, D.C. Archbishop of New Orleans 1965-89.

Hellman, Lillian (1907-84). Scenario writer, editor, and award-winning and bestselling author. Her outstanding works include *The Little Foxes* and *Watch on the Rhine,* among others. Political activist.

Herman, Peter Gulotta "Pete" (1896-1973). Held the bantamweight title 1917-20, regained it in 1921. Retired in 1922 with seventy-one career wins. He was elected to the Boxing Hall of Fame in 1960.

Higgins, Andrew (1886-1952). Founded Higgins Industries, a company based in New Orleans. Manufactured the Higgins LCVP (Landing Craft, Vehicle, Personnel) for use in World War II, which allowed soldiers to land on open beach. He also built larger land crafts, patrol torpedo boats (PT boats), torpedo tubes, gun turrets, and smoke generators.

Huber, Leonard V. (1903-84). Civic worker, collector, traveler, lecturer, and writer. Works include *New Orleans, A Pictorial History* and *Louisiana: A Pictorial History*.

Jackson, Andrew (1767-1845). Called the Savior of New Orleans during the Battle of New Orleans in the War of 1812. A popular Louisiana hero. Seventh president of the United States, 1829-37.

Jackson, Mahalia (1911-72). Queen of gospel singers, Civil Rights spokeswoman, and recording star. Born in the Black Pearl community of Carrollton. Her name and legacy are honored today at the Mahalia Jackson Theater of the Performing Arts in New Orleans.

Kane, Harnett T. (1910-84). Reporter, bestselling author, lecturer, and historian. Author of *Louisiana Hayride*.

Kenner, Duncan Farrar (1813-87). Active supporter of Confederate cause. After the war, he was instrumental in ridding the state of carpetbaggers and scalawags. Born in New Orleans. He also served as president of the Louisiana Sugar Planters Association.

Keyes, Frances Parkinson (Mrs. Henry Wilder Keyes) (1885-1970). Author of numerous novels and short stories, many of which are set in New Orleans. World-traveler and owner and restorer of the Beauregard House at 1113 Chartres Street, which was the birthplace of Paul Morphy and the home of P. G. T. Beauregard after the Civil War.

King, Grace Elizabeth (1851-1932). Student of Creole life and manners. Author of *New Orleans: The Place, the People* and *Creole Families of New Orleans,* which have enriched Louisiana literature. Student of Charles Gayarré.

Lafitte, Jean (1780-1825). Famous smuggler and pirate who was pardoned because of his participation on behalf of the United States at the Battle of New Orleans.

Lafon, Thomy (1810-93). Black philanthropist and businessman, whose donations to charities in New Orleans won him the distinction of having a public school named after him.

Laveau, Marie (1783-1881). Mulattress and voodoo queen. Dealer in charms, remedies, and advice.

Le Moyne, Jean Baptiste, Sieur de Bienville (1680-1768). French-Canadian explorer, three-time governor of Louisiana under French domination, founder of New Orleans, and promulgator in Louisiana of celebrated *Code Noir*.

Livingston, Edward (1764-1836). Represented both New York and Louisiana in Congress. Served as secretary of state under Andrew Jackson and later as minister to France.

Long, Huey Pierce (1893-1935). Creator of the Share Our Wealth program. Assumed a prominent place in national affairs as U.S. senator and presidential aspirant. He was assassinated at the height of his career.

Longstreet, James (1821-1904). Brigadier general in the Confederate Army who, after the war, became a republican. A resident of New Orleans, he became unpopular with the people of his state for his role in politics of the Reconstruction period. Pres. Ulysses S. Grant appointed him minister to Turkey.

McDonogh, John (1779-1850). Wealthy merchant whose bequest formed the foundation for the New Orleans public school system.

McMain, Eleanor Laura (1868-1934). Progressive reformer on social issues, including child labor legislation, and a leader in the establishment of a School of Social Work through Newcomb College. A secondary school is named in her honor.

Maestri, Robert (1889-1974). Mayor of New Orleans 1936-46. Reorganized fiscal policies of the city and improved municipal facilities.

Matas, Dr. Rudolph (1860-1957). Pioneer in the field of vascular surgery and recipient of medical decorations from many European and Latin American countries. A giant of medicine.

Mayo, Dr. Sara T. (1869-1930). New Orleans physician. Founded a hospital for women that bore her name (Sara Mayo Hospital).

Morial, Ernest "Dutch" (1929-89). First black mayor of New Orleans, elected in 1977. In early political life, he was the first black assistant in the U.S. attorney's office, the first black member of the legislature since Reconstruction, the first black juvenile court judge, and the first black Circuit Court of Appeals judge. He was the first mayor to live on the historic Bayou St. John during his administration.

Morphy, Paul Charles (1837-84). Considered to be one of the greatest chess players of all time. Born in the house his grandfather built, later called the Beauregard House because of the general's term of residence there.

Morrison, deLesseps S., Sr. (1912-64). Mayor of New Orleans 1946-61, when he resigned to take the post of ambassador to the Organization of American States, to which he was appointed by President Kennedy. Morrison and his son were killed in a plane crash en route to Mexico in May 1964.

Morton, Ferdinand La Mothe "Jelly Roll" (1885-1941). Reputed inventor of jazz. One of the jazz immortals. Played piano in Storyville for one dollar per night plus tips. His life is documented more than that of any other musician in jazz history. Jelly Roll and His Red Hot Peppers has been considered the peak of jazz-band excellence.

Newcomb, Josephine Louise Le Monnier (1816-1901). Founded Sophie Newcomb College as a memorial to her daughter, Sophie Newcomb. She provided contributions totaling $2.8 million.

Ochsner, Alton (1896-1981). Professor at Tulane 1927-61. Served on staff of several hospitals and founded Ochsner Foundation Hospital. Spearheaded drive against smoking as a cause of lung cancer.

Pauger, Adrien de (1670-1726). Designed the city of New Orleans (at that time, it only consisted of the Vieux Carré).

Pinchback, Pinckney Benton Stewart (1837-1921). Mulatto politician who became lieutenant governor of Louisiana during Reconstruction and acted as governor 1872-73. He was the only black to serve as governor of Louisiana during that period.

Plimsoll, Samuel (1824-98). Became the leading advocate for safe loading conditions for ship operations in 1867. The Plimsoll mark, which he created, is a series of lines to be placed on both sides of ships, signifying the Load Line allowed for Tropical Water, Fresh Water, Tropical Zones, Summer, Winter, and Winter North Atlantic.

Pollock, Oliver (1737-1823). Irish-born merchant who spent many years in New Orleans and rendered financial assistance to the American cause during the Revolutionary War. Later, he became a U.S. commercial agent with diplomatic standing.

Poydras, Julien de Lallande (1746-1824). Trader, philanthropist, and poet whose charitable works included the establishment of dowry funds for impoverished Pointe Coupee and West Baton Rouge Parish women. He was active in politics and represented Louisiana in the legislature.

Prima, Louis (1911-78). Nationally known bandleader, singer, trumpet player, composer, recording artist, and television and movie performer.

Ripley, Eliza Moore (1832-1912). Wrote entertainingly about life in New Orleans in the 1840s and 1850s.

Rivers, Pearl (Mrs. George Nicholson) (1849-96). First woman in New Orleans to earn her living on a newspaper, the *Picayune,* and the first woman publisher of an important newspaper in the United States. Founded the organization that grew into the Society for the Prevention of the Cruelty to Animals.

Rummel, Archbishop Joseph Francis (1876-1964). Born in Baden, Germany, he first served as papal chamberlain. In 1935, he was appointed archbishop of New Orleans. Buried in crypt of St. Louis Cathedral.

Saxon, Lyle (1891-1946). Started writing short stories in 1926. Wrote books about New Orleans, beginning with *Father Mississippi*. Born in Baton Rouge, Saxon was a bon vivant, typical plantation gentleman, conversationalist, artist with a jigger of vermouth, and writer without an enemy.

Schulte, Archbishop Francis Bible (1926-2016). Born in Philadelphia. Appointed member of President Bush's Education Policy Advisory Committee in 1989, member of Vatican Congregation for Catholic Education in 1989, and twelfth archbishop of New Orleans in 1988.

Slidell, John (1793-1871). U.S. senator and member of Congress. Prominent in state and national affairs in the 1850s. Minister to France under the Confederacy. City of Slidell named in his honor.

Soulé, George (1834-1926). Mathematician and educator. Established first commercial college in New Orleans.

Stern, Edgar B. (1886-1959). Member of the Board of Administrators of Charity Hospital, the State Welfare Board, the Louisiana Development Commission, and the Board of Administrators of Tulane University. Founder of the Bureau of Governmental Research.

Stern, Edith Rosenwald (Mrs. Edgar B.) (1895-1980). Along with her husband, named outstanding philanthropists in New Orleans in 1977 for the first century of the *States-Item*'s existence. Since her death in 1980, Longue Vue, her home, has operated as a museum of decorative arts and horticulture.

Tallant, Robert (1909-57). Author who wrote on subjects concerning New Orleans and Louisiana, including *Gumbo Ya-Ya* and *The Pirate Lafitte and the Battle of New Orleans*, which won the Literary Award of the Louisiana Library Association in 1952. Revised the New Orleans City Guide.

Taylor, Patrick F. (1937-2004). Chairman, president, and CEO of Taylor Energy, the only independently owned oil company. Created and funded the Taylor Plan, which gives all students the opportunity to attend college. The Taylor Plan became Louisiana law in 1989.

Taylor, Zachary (1784-1850). Migrated from Kentucky to Louisiana and achieved fame in the Mexican War. Became the twelfth president of the United States.

Toole, John Kennedy (1937-69). Author who won the Pulitzer Prize for *A Confederacy of Dunces*, set in New Orleans and published ten years after his suicide, which is believed to have been brought on by his failure to obtain literary recognition.

Touro, Judah (1775-1854). Gave liberally to numerous charities and buildings during his lifetime, many of which now bear his name, including Touro-Shakespeare Home, Touro Infirmary, and Touro Synagogue in New Orleans.

Treigle, Norman (1927-75). Considered to be one of the great actors in opera. Made his operatic debut with the New Orleans Opera Association. Was a leading male star of the New York Opera with more than fifty roles to his credit. Frequent co-star with Beverly Sills. Born in New Orleans.

Tulane, Paul (1801-87). Donated more than one million dollars to the University of Louisiana (now Tulane University).

Vaccaro, Joseph (1855-1945). With his brothers, established the Standard Fruit Company, whose ships sailed the Gulf and Caribbean between New Orleans and Central America.

Vaudreuil-Cavagnal, Pierre de Rigaud, Marquis de (1698-1778). Referred to as the Grand Marquis. Governor of Louisiana from 1743 to 1753. Made New Orleans a center of culture and gaiety.

Warmoth, Henry Clay (1842-1931). Dominated carpetbag regime as Reconstruction governor 1868-72. Author of *War, Politics, and Reconstruction: Stormy Days in Louisiana*.

White, Edward Douglass, Jr. (1844-1921). Entered Confederate Army at age eighteen. Served as associate justice of the Louisiana Supreme Court, U.S. senator, and chief justice of the U.S. Supreme Court.

Wilson, Samuel, Jr. (1911-93). Architectural historian and coauthor of *New Orleans Architecture, Volumes I and IV; Louisiana Purchase; The St. Louis Cemeteries of New Orleans;* and other publications.

Wood, Albert Baldwin (1879-1956). Electrical engineer. Invented twelve-foot screw pumps capable of draining 10 million cubic feet of water out of below-sea-level New Orleans every year, which ultimately prevented flooding and made swamps habitable.

Wright, Sophie Bell (1866-1912). Teacher and humanitarian responsible for night schools and many social-service agencies in New Orleans. First woman to win the *Daily Picayune's* Loving Cup.

You, Dominique (1775-1830). A member of Lafitte's "hellish banditti." Distinguished himself in the Battle of New Orleans and settled down to become a law-abiding citizen.

Chronology

1541	Hernando De Soto discovers the Mississippi River.
1543	*July.* Luis Moscoco and the survivors of De Soto's expedition, descending the river on their way to Mexico, are the first white men to view the site of the future city of New Orleans.
1682	*April 9.* De La Salle claims all land drained by the Mississippi River for France, erects a cross near the mouth of the Mississippi, and names the territory Louisiana in honor of Louis XIV.
1699	*March 2.* Iberville and his expedition stop at the present site of New Orleans and erect a cross. Later, Bayou Mardi Gras named by Iberville. Ocean Springs settled. *March 9.* Indians show Iberville the portage between Lake Pontchartrain and Mississippi River. Bienville encounters the English frigate *Carolina Galley* and keeps it from entering French Louisiana.
1700	Bienville founds Fort de Mississippi (Fort de la Boulaye) near what is now Phoenix in Plaquemines Parish.
1702	Government moved from Fort Maurepas to Mobile settlement just north of present-day Mobile.
1708	Some Mobile colonists are given land grants at Bayou St. John.
1711	Mobile relocated to its present site.
1712	Antoine Crozat is given Louisiana as a commercial enterprise.
1715	King Louis XIV dies; grandson, Louis XV, becomes king at the age of five with Philippe, duc d'Orleans acting as regent.
1716	King of France issues edict regulating land grants in Louisiana. This edict establishes the arpent system. One arpent equals approximately 192 feet. Land situated along the river is surveyed into long, narrow lots, measuring approximately 2-4 arpents wide by 40-60 arpents deep. "French long lots" demarcate much of southeastern Louisiana today.
1717	Crozat's venture fails. Scottish John Law takes over the enterprise, establishes the Company of the West, and recruits investors to Louisiana.

1718	*Spring.* Bienville, with the assistance of Pauger and de La Tour, lays out the streets and founds *La Nouvelle Orléans* as trading colony for the Company of the West.
1719	First African slaves arrive in Louisiana.
1719-21	Company of the West signs up thousands of settlers from France, Germany, and Switzerland.
1720	John Law's "Mississippi Bubble" bursts.
1720s	Germans settle upriver from New Orleans in *Côte des Allemands.*
1721	*December 23.* Company of the Indies transfers headquarters of the Louisiana colony from Biloxi to New Orleans.
1722	*September.* Hurricane destroys much of the city. First artificial levees are erected.
1723	Under Governor Bienville, New Orleans becomes capital of Louisiana.
1724	*March.* Bienville promulgates the Code Noir, regulating slavery and religious worship.
1727	*August 6.* The Ursulines arrive and establish a convent school for girls.
1728	*December.* The first company of Filles à la Cassette (Casket Girls) arrives in Mobile.
1729	*December.* Refugees arrive with news of Indian massacre at Fort Rosalie (Natchez), and Governor Périer begins construction of first defense works (ditches and stockade) against a possible Indian attack.
1731	Louisiana becomes a Royal Colony of France again.
1736	Charity Hospital founded.
1743	Under Governor Vaudreuil, New Orleans becomes a lively social center.
1745	Ursuline Convent designed and built (1749-53) in what is now the 1100 block of Chartres Street. It remains the oldest complete structure from French colonial Louisiana.
1754-63	French and Indian War (also known as Seven Years' War). France is defeated and the colonial world is realigned. Louisiana east of the Mississippi is ceded to England. Land west of the Mississippi and the city of New Orleans was ceded to Spain in 1762 and did not fall into English hands.
1755-85	French settlers are expelled from Acadie (now Nova Scotia) by the English. Many settle in Louisiana, west of New Orleans.
1762	*November 3.* Louisiana transferred to Spain by Treaty of Fontainebleau.
1763	*July 9.* The Jesuits are expelled from Louisiana by the French authorities and their property confiscated.

1768   *October.* Opposition to Spanish rule breaks into open rebellion. Superior Council is abolished; Cabildo is established.

1777   Under Governor Galvez, Americans are allowed to establish bases in New Orleans and send aid to revolutionary forces.

1779-82   After war declared between Spain and England, Galvez, in a series of campaigns, drives the English out of the country.

1788   *March 21.* Fire destroys more than 800 houses and necessitates rebuilding a great part of the city. Madame John's Legacy was built on Dumaine Street right after the fire. It is an example of a French Creole house.

     December 5. Padre Antonio de Sedella, later known as Père Antoine, is appointed commissary of the Inquisition and sent back to Spain by Governor Miró.

     Faubourg Ste. Marie is laid out on the Gravier Plantation. This area is now the Central Business District.

1789   St. Louis Cemetery No. 1 is laid out.

1791   French Market founded along the riverfront.

1792   The Henry brothers from Paris stage the first professional theatrical performances held in New Orleans.

1794   First regular newspaper, *Le Moniteur de la Louisiane,* begins publication. Fire destroys 200 buildings in New Orleans.

1795   Carondelet Canal, connecting the city with Bayou St. John, is opened. Etienne de Boré succeeds in refining sugar in commercial quantities. Almonester rebuilds Cathedral, Cabildo, and first floor of Presbytère. Spain and the U.S. sign the Treaty of San Lorenzo, which grants Americans access to the Mississippi River and the right of deposit in New Orleans.

1796   Yellow fever outbreak in New Orleans.

1800   *October 1.* Spain retrocedes Louisiana to France.

1803   *November 30.* France takes formal possession of the colony from Spain in the Place d'Armes. French commissioner de Laussat arrives.

     December 20. William C. C. Claiborne and Gen. James Wilkinson take possession of the city in the name of the United States.

1805   *February 22.* The city of New Orleans is incorporated, and the first municipal officials arrive shortly afterward.

     Plantation of Bernard de Marigny is subdivided for urban development.

1806-10   Delord-Sarpy (Duplantier), Saulet, Robin, and Lividais plantations are subdivided for urban development.

1809   More than 9,000 refugees from Saint Domingue arrive in New Orleans.

1810	Claude Tremé's plantation is subdivided for urban development.
1812	*January 10.* The *New Orleans,* the first steamboat to descend the Mississippi, arrives from Pittsburgh.
	April 30. Louisiana is admitted to the Union and New Orleans becomes the capital of the state.
1815	*January 8.* The American forces under Gen. Andrew Jackson defeat the British in the final decisive action of the Battle of New Orleans.
1816	Crevasse at McCarty's plantation; part of the city floods.
1823	*May 9.* James H. Caldwell opens the first American Theater on Camp Street, introducing the use of gas lighting.
1824-28	First Jewish congregation established, Congregation Shangari Chassed (Gates of Mercy).
1825	*April 10.* Lafayette arrives in New Orleans for a five-day visit.
1827	All Catholic funerals held in Mortuary Chapel (now Our Lady of Guadalupe Church).
1830	Esplanade Avenue called Promenade Publique.
1830s-50s	Irish immigration period.
1831	*April.* The Pontchartrain Railroad, the first railroad west of the Alleghenies, offers freight and passenger service to Milneburg.
1832-38	New Basin Canal is excavated.
1833	J. H. Caldwell granted exclusive privilege for street illumination by gas. Incorporation of the city of Lafayette.
1834	The first house in the town of Carrollton is built. The Medical College of Louisiana, which eventually becomes the University of Louisiana (1847) and Tulane University (1884), is established. U.S. Mint is built on Esplanade at the river. It will operate as a mint from 1838 to 1862 and from 1878 to 1910.
1836	*March 8.* New charter divides city into three municipalities, each with its own board of aldermen.
1837	*January 25.* The *Picayune,* now the *Times-Picayune,* begins publication.
	Shrove Tuesday. First Mardi Gras parade held.
1838	The first house in the Garden District and the first on Esplanade are built. New Basin Canal opened for traffic.
1840s-50s	German immigration period.
1849	Crevasse in the levee at Sauvé Plantation in what is now Jefferson Parish diverts river water into lowlands between the natural levees of the Mississippi River and the Metairie/Gentilly ridges.
1850s	Newspaper Row forms in the 300 block of Camp Street. Cotton District forms around Gravier and Carondelet streets.
1853	10,000 inhabitants perish in the most severe yellow fever epidemic in the history of New Orleans.

	May 10. The City Hall, now Gallier Hall, designed and built by James Gallier, Sr., is dedicated.
1855-58	Three prominent churches are built in close proximity to one another, representing the multiethnic nature of the city: St. Alphonsus (Irish), St. Mary's Assumption (German), Notre Dame de Bon Secours (French).
1857	Krewe of Comus founded.
1859	*December 1.* The French Opera House opens its doors with a production of *Guillaume Tell.*
1861	*January 26.* Louisiana adopts the Ordinance of Secession.
1862	*April 30.* The city surrenders to David E. Farragut and his Federal forces.
	May 1. Gen. Benjamin Butler assumes command of the city.
1864	*May 1.* Constitution of Louisiana amended to abolish slavery.
1864-66	Small Greek community founds the first Eastern Orthodox church in Western Hemisphere.
1866	*July 30.* Riot occurs in Mechanics Institute in which large numbers of blacks and whites are killed and wounded.
1869	Dillard University opens its doors.
1870s-90s	Orthodox Jewish community forms with immigrants from Poland and Russia. They settle between Dryades Street and St. Charles Avenue.
1870s-1900s	Sicilians arrive by the thousands, last large wave of immigrants to the city.
1872	*Shrove Tuesday.* Rex parades for Grand Duke Alexis of Russia.
1874	The St. Louis Hotel is purchased by the state of Louisiana to serve as the state capital until the capital is moved from New Orleans to Baton Rouge in 1882.
	September 14. The White League forces defeat the Metropolitan Police in a pitched battle at the foot of Canal Street.
1880	*August.* Capt. James B. Eads completes the jetties at South Pass, deepening the channels and saving the port.
1882	Chinese Mission is founded on Liberty Street, draws Chinese immigrants to the area.
1884	With an endowment by Paul Tulane, the University of Louisiana becomes Tulane University.
	December 16. The Cotton Exposition opens in Audubon Park.
1886	*October 11.* Newcomb College founded.
1890	Board of Commissioners of Orleans Lakefront (the Levee Board) organized and put in charge of 129 miles of levee, 27 miles of the river, and 94 miles of inner-city levees.
1891	*March 14.* Eleven Italian prisoners, alleged assassins of Police Chief Hennessy, killed in parish prison by outraged mob of citizens. Two are dragged outside and hung.

1892	*September 7.* James J. Corbett defeats John L. Sullivan in a 21-round knockout victory in New Orleans.
1894	Leprosarium at Carville, Louisiana, established. Tulane University moves uptown.
1896	Board of Commissioners of the Port of New Orleans (the Dock Board) created to have authority over all water frontage in Orleans Parish and considerable portions of river and canal frontage in adjacent parishes.
1898-1917	Storyville thrives.
1900	Race riot breaks out after Robert Charles, a black "back to Africa" advocate, fatally shoots a white police officer. Often described as the city's last major race riot, attesting to the relatively peaceful race relations in New Orleans.
1901-20s	Dock Board modernizes port facilities.
1905	Last of yellow fever epidemics occur.
1910	Last coins minted in New Orleans.
1911	Loyola, founded by the Jesuits, becomes a college.
1912	*July 10.* Loyola becomes a university. *August 12.* The commission form of city government adopted.
1915	Xavier College established at Washington and Pine streets. *September 29.* Major hurricane inflicts serious property damage throughout the city.
1918-21	Industrial Canal constructed.
1919	French Opera House burns.
1920s-40s	Carondelet and New Basin canals are determined to be obsolete and filled in. New Basin Canal bed used for the Pontchartrain Expressway.
1921	Vieux Carré Commission established. The federal government takes over the Leprosarium at Carville, and it becomes the only public-health leprosarium in North America.
1923	Industrial Canal connected to the river by locks. Notre Dame Seminary built.
1925	Xavier becomes full-fledged university. Orleans Club founded.
1927	Major flood threatens New Orleans.
1928	U.S. Engineers take over responsibility for flood control.
1930	Municipal Auditorium built to the rear of Old Congo Square facing Rampart.
1934	Industrial Canal becomes link in newly fashioned Intracoastal Waterway, which now leads from Rio Grande River in Texas to Florida coast.
1935	*September 8.* Huey P. Long assassinated in State Capitol Building in Baton Rouge, allegedly by Dr. Carl A. Weiss, who was then shot by Long's bodyguards.

	December 13. Bonnet Carré Spillway dedicated.
	December 16. Huey P. Long Bridge across the Mississippi completed and dedicated.
1936	Vieux Carré Commission authorized by state legislature to regulate architecture through building permits for the preservation of the French Quarter.
1940	Moisant Airfield established in the farming community of Kenner. Today it is the Louis Armstrong International Airport.
1942	German U-boat sinks *Robert E. Lee* near mouth of Mississippi River, kills 25.
1945	International House opens.
1947	*May 6.* International Free Trade Zone established.
	September 16-19. Hurricane kills hundreds in Louisiana, Mississippi, and Florida.
1950	Louisiana Landmarks Society is founded.
1954	Brown vs. Board of Education Supreme Court decision reverses 1896 Plessy vs. Ferguson ruling on "separate but equal" public schools.
1956	Causeway Bridge built over Lake Pontchartrain.
1957	*April 15.* First span of the Greater New Orleans Mississippi River Bridge completed.
1958	*September.* UNO, originally LSUNO, opens on the lakefront as the States' first racially integrated public college. First Mississippi River bridge built downtown.
1959	City Hall relocates from Gallier Hall on Lafayette Square to Duncan Plaza Civic Complex.
1960-61	Civil Rights movement comes to a head with the integration of public schools.
1960s-70s	Hispanic immigrants begin to arrive in the city.
1963	Mississippi River Gulf Outlet officially opened, cutting 40 miles off of the distance to the Gulf.
1964	The nationwide trend of replacing rail transportation with buses hits the city, leaving only the St. Charles Avenue streetcar line.
1965	*September 9.* Hurricane Betsy hits New Orleans.
1966	Poydras Street widened, anchors the corporate corridor in the Central Business District.
1967	Second Lake Pontchartrain Causeway built, creating twin spans. Saints NFL franchise arrives in the city.
1969	*August 17.* Category 5 Hurricane Camille hits New Orleans.
1970	First Jazz and Heritage Festival held at Congo Square.
1970s	French Market renovated.
1972	Last Mardi Gras parades roll through the French Quarter.
1973	Theater of Performing Arts completed in what would later be

Armstrong Park. Disastrous fire at Howard Johnson's Motor Hotel. Second-worst Mississippi River flood; Bonnet Carré Spillway opened to relieve pressure on levees.

1975   *August.* Superdome opens with a football game at a building cost of $161 million.

1976   Moonwalk opens on the riverfront in the French Quarter.

Late 1970s   Vietnamese refugees arrive in New Orleans at the invitation of the Catholic Church.

1980   Armstrong Park opens at a building cost of $30 million on a space of 10 acres at the site of Old Congo Square.

1982   *July 9.* Pan Am Jet 759 crashes moments after takeoff from New Orleans International Airport, killing 153.

1983-84   Oil bust hits the city.

1984   *May 4-November 11.* Louisiana World Exposition in New Orleans. Mississippi Aerial River Transit (MART; gondola from World's Fair) is a part of New Orleans skyline (until 1994).

Mid-1980s   Jax Brewery and Riverwalk marketplaces developed

1987   *September 12.* Pope John Paul II visits New Orleans and says Mass on the UNO Arena grounds at the lakefront.
Fall. The New Orleans Saints, under owner Tom Benson and coach Jim Mora, are in the NFL playoffs for the first time in their 20-year existence.

1988   *May 11.* Seven-alarm fire on the third floor of the Cabildo.
August. Republican National Convention held in New Orleans.
September 30. Second span of the GNOMR Bridge opens. Both spans now called the Crescent City Connection.
Streetcar line returns to the Riverfront to connect French Quarter with Jax Brewery and Riverwalk.

1990   Aquarium of the Americas opens.

1990-91   Coastal Wetlands Planning and Protection Act brings federal funds to Louisiana for much-needed coastal restoration.

1990s-2000s   Archdiocese of New Orleans closes churches due to lack of congregants.

1993   *December 17.* Fair Grounds grandstand burns down.

1995   *March 8-9.* Greater New Orleans area floods and shuts city down for two days. Rivergate Convention Center is demolished to make way for land-based casino.

1996   *December 14.* The bulk cargo ship *MV Bright Field* crashes into the Riverwalk.

2000   *June 6.* D-Day Museum opens, later renamed the National World War II Museum.

2003	*December 20.* 200th anniversary of the Louisiana Purchase celebrated.
2004	Streetcars return to Canal Street and Carrollton Avenue. State-of-the-art containerized shipping facility opens at Napoleon Avenue Wharf.
2005	*August 29.* Hurricane Katrina hits New Orleans. Federal levees breach.
2006	Bring New Orleans Back Commission unveils initial recommendations for consideration by Mayor C. Ray Nagin.
2010	*February 7.* New Orleans Saints win Super Bowl XLIV in Miami, defeating Indianapolis Colts 31-17.
	April 20. Deepwater Horizon oil well explodes in the Gulf of Mexico.
2012	*July 21.* The U.S. Department of Justice and the New Orleans Police Department announce plans to cut corruption from the police force and improve safety in the city.
2015	*January.* Over 10,000 people attended the 200th anniversary observance of the Battle of New Orleans.
	August. The 10th anniversary of Hurricane Katrina is marked by visits from Pres. Barack Obama and former presidents Bill Clinton and George W. Bush.
2017	*Spring.* By order of the City Council and upheld by the courts, four monuments were removed: the Battle of Liberty Place Monument, commemorating a White League protest; statue of Confederate president Jefferson Davis; statue of Confederate general P. G. T. Beauregard; and statue of Confederate general Robert E. Lee. The actions drew crowds for and against the removals, and some violence resulted.
	July. Saints and Pelicans owner Tom Benson purchased the 110-year-old Dixie Brewing Company, intending to restart the local brewery.
2018	New Orleans celebrates the 300th anniversary of the founding of the city.

Glossary

allée: French, alley. A double row of trees leading from the road or river to a plantation home.

ancienne population: The indigenous Latin inhabitants, also known as Creoles.

armoire: A cabinet closing with one or two doors, having rows of shelves and used for keeping clothes.

arpent: A historic land measure in Louisiana. A linear arpent is equal to 191.835 feet; a square arpent is approximately 85 percent of an English acre.

backswamp: Lowland, a section of a floodplain where deposits of fine silts and clays settle after a flood. Backswamps usually lie behind a stream's natural levees.

banquette: French, low bench. A sidewalk, so called because the early wooden sidewalks were elevated, or banked up, above the muddy streets.

batture: French, from *battre,* to beat. The land built up by the silting action of a river.

bayou: American Indian, from *bayuk,* creek or river. A distributary coming out of a river or lake, not contributing to it.

blanchisseuse: French, from *blancher,* to whiten or clean. A washerwoman.

bouillabaisse: Provençal, from *bouis-baisso,* boiled down. A stew of red snapper and redfish, with various kinds of vegetables, seasonings, and spices.

briquette entre poteaux: French, brick between posts. A method of construction in vogue in the eighteenth century in which bricks were filled in between the spaces of a framework of cypress timbers.

café au lait: Black coffee with milk. Slang expression indicating presence of black heritage.

café noir: Black coffee.

Cajun: Acadian, corruption of *Acadien.* French immigrant from Acadia, now Nova Scotia, or descendant of one who came to live in Bayou country of Louisiana.

cedula: A permit or order issued by the government.

Charivari: Medieval Latin, from *carivarium.* A serenade of "rough music" with kettles, pans, and the like, originally given in derision of unpopular marriage. Often spelled *chivari.*

Chef Menteur: Big Liar, chief among liars. River so called because currents are deceptive, running both ways. Governor Kerlérec so called by Indians for obvious reasons.

Code Noir: Code of behavior governing conduct of slaves and masters.

Congo: A man from the Congo nation. Slang, very black man.

contraflow: When traffic on both sides of the interstate flows in one direction.

courtbouillon: Redfish cooked with highly seasoned gravy.

crawfish bisque: French, *bisque,* thick soup. A rich soup made with crawfish, whose heads are stuffed and served on top.

Creole: Spanish, from *criollo,* native born. In New Orleans, referred to native born of French or Spanish parents. Also used in referring to native grown, e.g., Creole tomatoes.

dix: French, for ten. Ten-dollar banknote printed in 1880, only usable in New Orleans.

fais-dodo: French, from *dormir,* to sleep, and *fais dodo* (children), go to sleep. A country dance.

faubourg: French, literal, plantation, suburb.

F.M.C. or F.W.C.: "Free Man of Color" or "Free Woman of Color." Initials found in old documents that refer to freed slaves.

gallery: French, from *galerie,* or Latin, from *galleria,* gallery. A porch or balcony.

garçonniere: French, from *garçon,* boy, bachelor. Bachelor's quarters, usually separate from the principal part of the house.

gris-gris: Amulet, talisman, or charm, worn for luck or used to conjure evil on enemies by voodoo devotees. Presumably of African origin.

gumbo: Louisiana French, from *gumbo,* or Angolan or Bantu, *ki ngombo.* A soup thickened with the mucilaginous pods of the okra plant and containing shrimp, crabs, and often chicken, oysters, or other meat varieties.

gumbo-des-herbes: French, from *herbe,* herb. Gumbo made of herbs and greens, including spinach, mustard greens, etc., instead of okra.

gumbo-filé: A condiment made of powdering leaves of the redbay tree in swampy areas, often containing powdered sassafras root. Used in place of okra for thickening gumbo.

jalousie: French, literal, vertical or Venetian blind. In Louisiana, the common two-battened outdoor blind.

jambalaya: A Spanish-Creole dish made with rice and some other core ingredient, such as shrimp, oysters, chicken, or sausage.

lagniappe: French, from *la nappe,* tablecloth (in particular, one that catches remaining grains of rice), or Spanish, from *la napa,* small gift. A trifling gift presented to a customer by a merchant.

levee: French, from *lever,* to raise. An embankment on the Mississippi or smaller streams to prevent floods. Natural or manmade.

make ménage: French, from *faire le ménage,* to clean the house. Local expression. To clean the house.

mamaloi: French, from maman, mother, and *roi,* king. The voodoo priestess.

Mardi Gras: French, literal, Fat Tuesday. Shrove Tuesday, the last day of Carnival.

maroon: African refugees who escaped from slavery.

marraine: French, literal, a godmother.

mulatto: Spanish, from *mulato,* a young mule. One of mixed race. In particular, the offspring of a black and a white individual.

nainaine: Creole diminutive of *marraine.*

neutral ground: Median strip of land on a roadway, especially one planted with grass.

octoroon: Latin, from *octo,* eight. The child of a quadroon and a white person. A person having one-eighth African blood.

papillotes: French, from *papillon,* butterfly, or literal, curl paper or foil parcel. Curl papers (for the hair). Also, buttered or oiled paper in which fish, especially pompano, is broiled to retain flavor.

parish: In Louisiana, the equivalent of county. Parishes here were originally ecclesiastical, not civil divisions.

parrain: French, literal, a godfather.

perique: Local term. A unique kind of tobacco grown only in St. James Parish. Said to have been the nickname of Pierre Chenet, an Acadian who first produced the variety of tobacco.

picayune: Formerly the Spanish half-real, worth about 6¼ cents. Now out of use, except to refer to something small and unimportant.

Ponchatoula: Choctaw, from *pasha,* hair, and *itula (itola),* to fall or hang. A term used to describe the Spanish moss that hangs or falls off trees.

porte-cochère: French, from *porte,* gate or door, and *carosse,* carriage or coach. The gateway that allows vehicles to drive into a courtyard.

praline: A bonbon made of pecans browned in sugar. It is said to have been invented by Marechal du Plessis Praslin's cook.

quadroon: Spanish, from *cuarteron,* a quadroon. The child of a mulatto and a white person. A person having one-fourth African blood.

quartee: Local. Half of a five-cent piece in colonial New Orleans.

soirée: French, from *soir,* evening. An evening party.

sugar-house: Local. A sugar mill or factory.

tignon: Middle French, from *tignon* or *chignon,* nape of the neck. Bandana-like headdress required for free women of color after 1786.

vamoose: Spanish, from *vamos,* let's go. Get out!

Vieux Carré: French, literal, old square. The original walled city of New Orleans, bounded by Canal Street, North Rampart Street, Esplanade Avenue, and the Mississippi River.

voodoo: Fon, *vôdu,* a deity. An African religion, commonly perceived as a cult of witchcraft imported into America by slaves from the present-day Republic of Benin, Haiti, and the Caribbean.

Bibliography

Andersen, Christine, and Hurricane Katrina External Review Panel. "The New Orleans Hurricane Protection System: What Went Wrong and Why." *American Society of Civil Engineers* (2007).

Associated Press. "Name Game: Sports Teams Wrestle with Getting Right Name." June 18, 2016, accessed October 4, 2016. http://apnews.com/8f228add7b76478d33dd09515da4a.

BBC News. Television News Report (2010).

Berg, Robbie. "Isaac Tropical Cyclone Report." National Hurricane Center. January 28, 2013, accessed September 17, 2016. www.nhc.noaa.gov/data/tcr/AL092012_Isaac.pdf.

Blackstone, William. *Commentaries on the Law of England*. Vol. 1. Oxford: Oxford University Press, 1769.

Bohrer, Becky. "Mayor: Crime Part of New Orleans 'Brand.'" *Washington Post,* August 10, 2007.

Butler, Benjamin Franklin. *Autobiography and Personal Reminescences of Major General Benjamin Butler*. Boston: A. M. Thayer, 1892.

Campanella, Richard. "Addressing New Orleans East's Core Problem." Nola. com. December 10, 2013, accessed September 16, 2016. http://nola.com/homegarden/index.ssf12013/12/addressing_new_orleans_easts_c.html.

Chase, John C. *Frenchmen, Desire, Good Children*. Reprint, Gretna: Pelican,2015.

Christovich, Mary Louise, and Roulhac Toledano. *New Orleans Architecture*. Vol. 2, *The American Sector*. Gretna: Pelican, 1972.

Claiborne, William Charles Cole. *Official Letter Books of W. C. C. Claiborne 1801-1816*. Edited by Dunbar Rowland. Vol. 7. Jackson, MS: State Department of Archives and History, n.d.

Davis, Edwin Adams. *Louisiana: A Narrative History*. Baton Rouge: Claitor's Law Books, 1971.

Davis, John H. *Mafia Kingfish: Carlos Marcello and the Assassination of John F. Kennedy*. New York: McGraw Hill, 1989.

Davis, William C. *The Pirates Laffite: The Treacherous World of the Corsairs of the Gulf*. Boston: Houghton Mifflin Harcourt, 2005.

Deiler, J. Hanno. *The Settlement of the German Coast of Louisiana and the Creoles of German Descent*. Philadelphia: Americana Germanica Press, 1909.

Derbes, Robin Von Breton. "The WPA Saved New Orleans and Destroyed It Too." *New Orleans Magazine* (July 1976): 75-78.

Evans, Clement Anselm. *Confederate Military History: A Library of Confederate States History*. Vol. 10. Atlanta: Confederate Publishing, 1899.

Fitzmorris, Tom. "New Orleans Menu." August 8, 2016, accessed September 9, 2016. http://nomenu.com/?page_id=39897.

Fraiser, Jim. *The French Quarter of New Orleans*. Jackson: University Press of Mississippi, 2003.

French, B. F. *Historical Collections of Louisiana*. Vol. 5, *The Memoirs of M. Dumont*. New York: New York, 1853.

Frieberg, Edna B. *Bayou St. John in Colonial Times, 1699-1803*. New Orleans: Harvey Press, 1980.

Gadbois, Karen. "Landrieu Letting the Sun Shine on City Contracting Process." June 3, 2010, accessed September 17, 2016. http://thelensnola.org/2010/06/03/landrieu-contracting-changes.

Gayarré, Charles. *History of Louisiana: The French Domination*. Vol. 2. New York: William J. Widdleton, 1851.

———. *History of Louisiana: The Spanish Domination*. Vol. 3. New Orleans: F. F. Hansell & Bro., 1903.

Gruesz, Kristin Silva. *Ambassadors of Culture: The Transamerican Origins of Latino Writing*. Princeton: Princeton University Press, 2002.

Grummond, Jane Lucas de. *Renato Beluche: Smuggler, Privateer, and Patriot*. Baton Rouge: Louisiana State University Press, 1983.

Haas, Edward F. "Victor H. Schiro, Hurricane Betsy and the Forgiveness Bill." *Gulf Coast Historical Review* (Fall 1990): 66.

Hammer, David. "Verify: Louisiana Is *Not* Losing a Football Field of Land Every Hour." May 12, 2017, accessed August 20, 2017. http://www.wwltv.com/news/local/investigations/david-hammer/verify-louisiana-is-not-losing-a-football-field-of-land-every-hour/439310241.

Historic District Landmarks Commission. "Irish Channel Historic Ddistrict." New Orleans: 2011.

Howell, Brian. *New Orleans Saints*. Edina, MN: ABDO, 2011.

Jewell, Edwin. *Jewell's Crescent City Illustrated*. 1873.

Kazek, Kelly. "When French Orphans Called Casket Girls Came to Alabama as Wives for Colonists." AL.com. September 14, 2015, accessed October 3, 2016. http://al.com/living/index.ssf/2015/09/when_french_orphans_called_cas.html.

Kendall, John. *History of New Orleans*. Chicago: Lewis, 1922.

"Key Moments in Saints History." 2015, accessed September 5, 2016. http://www.neworleanssaints.com/team/history/key-moments.html.

King, Grace. *Creole Families of New Orleans*. Macmillan Company, 1921.

Le Gardeur, René J., Jr. *The First New Orleans Theatre 1792-1803*. New Orleans: Leeward Books, 1963.

Lomax, Alan. *Mister Jelly Roll: The Fortunes of Jelly Roll Morton, New Orleans Creole and Inventor of Jazz*. New York: Grove Press, 1956.

Lossing, Benson. *A History of the United States*. New York: James Sheehy, 1881.

Louisiana State Museum. "The Cabildo. Two Centuries of Louisiana History, Antebellum Louisiana I: Disease, Death, and Mourning." 2016.

mafia.wikia.com. N.d., accessed October 5, 2016. http://mafia.wikia.com/anthony_carolla.

Martin, François. *History of Louisiana from the Earliest Period*. New Orleans: Lyman and Beardslee, 1827.

Merrill, Ellen C. *Germans of Louisiana*. Gretna: Pelican, 2005.

Merrit, Kennedy. "Louisiana's Governor Declares State of Emergency Over Disappearing Coastline." April 20, 2017, accessed August 20, 2017. http://www.npr.org/sections/thetwo-way/2017/04/20/524896256/louisianas-governor-declares-state-of-emergency-over-disappearing-coastline.

Monteverde, Danny, Frank Donze, and Michelle Krupa. "Mayor Mitch Landrieu Fires Back at New Orleans Corruption Critics." Nola.com. May 6, 2011, accessed September 13, 2016. http://nola.com/politics/index.ssf/2011/05/mayor_mitch_landrieu_fires_bac.html.

Moore, Anne Chiecko. *Benjamin Harrison: Centennial President*. New York: Nova Science, 2006.

Navarro, Alyssa. "New NASA Map Shows How Fast New Orleans Is Sinking." Tech Times. May 19, 2010, accessed September 5, 2016. http://www.techtimes.com/articles/159568/20160519/new-nasa-map-shows-how-fast-new-orleans-is-sinking.htm.

New Orleans Bee. 1853.

New Orleans Crescent. "Down." 1853.

———. "Mid-Summer." 1853.

New Orleans Regional Planning Commission. *History of Regional Growth of Jefferson, New Orleans and St. Bernard Parishes*. New Orleans: New Orleans Regional Planning Commission, 1969.

Nola.com. "New Orleans Tourism by the Numbers." May 2016, accessed August 27, 2016. http://nola.com/business/index.ssf/2016/05/new_orleans_tourism_by_the_num.html.

———. "Transcript of Nagin's Speech." January 16, 2006, accessed

September 12, 2016. http://nola.com/news/t-p/stories/o11706_nagin_transcript.html.

Nonprofit Knowledge Works. "New Orleans East." The Data Center. N.d., accessed August 3, 2016. http://www.datacenterresearch.org/data-resources/neighborhood-data-district-9/.

"Official: Astrodome Can't Take More Refugees." September 2, 2005, accessed June 17, 2016. http://www.foxnews.com/story/2005/09/02/official-astrodome-cant-take-more-refugees.html.

Orrell, John. "Hurricane Katrina Response: National Guard's 'Finest Hour.'" U.S. Army. August 27, 2007, accessed June 17, 2016. https://www.army.mil/article/44368/Hurricane_Katrina_response__National_Guard__039_s___039_finest_hour__039_/.

"Port of New Orleans." 2015. www.portno.com.

Reckdahl, Katy. "The Dark Side of Katrina Recovery." *Politico Magazine* (August 31, 2015).

Rightor, Henry. *Standard History of New Orleans, Louisiana.* Cambridge: Lewis, 1900.

Rose, Al. *Storyville, New Orleans: Being an Authenic, Illustrated Account of the Notorious Red-Light District.* Birmingham: University of Alabama Press, 1978.

Roth, David. "Louisiana Hurricane History." National Weather Service. January 13, 2010, accessed September 17, 2016. www.wpc.ncep.noaa.gov/research/lahur.pdf.

Salvaggio, John E. *New Orleans' Charity Hospital: A Story of Physicians, Politics, and Poverty.* Baton Rouge: Louisiana State University Press, 1992.

Saxon, Lyle. *Fabulous New Orleans.* New York: Century, 1928. Reprint, Gretna: Pelican, 2004.

Schott, Arthur O. "Pelicans Baseball." N.d., accessed June 3, 2016. http://www.milb.com/content/page.jsp?ymd=20070130&content_id=41061416&sid=t588&vkey=team4.

Sewerage and Water Board of New Orleans. "Drainage System Facts." 2016. https://www.swbno.org/history_drainage_facts.asp.

Shankman, Sabrina, and Tom Jennings. "New Orleans Cops Say They Got Orders Authorizing Them to Shoot Looters in the Chaos After Hurricane Katrina." Nola.com. August 27, 2010, accessed June 17, 2016. http://nola.com/crime/index.ssf/2010/08/new_orleans_cops_say_they_got.html.

Stahls, Paul F. *Jefferson Parish: Rich Heritage Promising Future.* San Antonio: Historical Publishing Network, 2009.

Stanforth, Deirdre. *Romantic New Orleans.* Gretna: Pelican, 1992.

Taylor, Joe Gray. *Louisiana: A Bicentennial History.* New York: W. W. Norton, 1976.

————. *Louisiana: A History.* New York: W. W. Norton, 1984.

Terrage, Mark de Villiers du. "A History of the Foundation of Louisiana, 1717-1722." *Louisiana Historical Quarterly* 3 (April 1920): 174.

Texada, David Ker. *Alejandro O'Reilly and the New Orleans Rebels.* Lafayette: University of Southwestern Louisiana, 1970.

U.S. Census. March 2016, accessed September 5, 2016. http://factfinder. census.gov/faces/tableservices/jsf/pages/productview.xhtml?src=bkmk.

U.S. Department of Veterans Affairs. "Southeast Louisiana Veterans Health Care System." 2016. http://www.neworleans.va.gov/about/index.asp.

U.S. Streetcar Systems. "U.S. Streetcar Systems—Louisiana." August 31, 2011, accessed September 6, 2016. http://www.railwaypreservation. com/vintagetrolley/neworleans.htm.

University Medical Center. "Our History." 2016. http://www.umcno.org/ history.

Weiss, Toni. "Economic Impact of the Mardi Gras Season 2014." Tulane University, 2015.

Wernick, Adam. "Louisiana's Coastline Is Disappearing at the Rate of a Football Field an Hour." Public Radio International. September 23, 2014, accessed June 10, 2016. http://www.pri.org/stories/2014-09-23/ louisianas-coastline-disappearing-rate-football-field-hour.

Wharton, George M. *The New Orleans Sketchbook.* Philadelphia: A. Hart, 1853.

About the Authors

Joan Boudousquié Garvey retired in 1997 after twenty years in the New Orleans public-school system as a teacher and administrator. She was a guide for Smithsonian Institution Southern Tours and lectured on New Orleans and Louisiana history for the Louisiana Tourist Promotion Association and the Friends of the Cabildo. A native New Orleanian, she received a BA from Loyola University of the South and MA from UNO. She was married to the late Walter Garvey. They had seven children, fourteen grandchildren, and nine great-grandchildren. A paternal ancestor, Antoine Boudousquié, printer in New Orleans in the service of the Spanish in 1795, and Charles Boudousquié, a paternal great-grandfather, the impresario of the French Opera before the Civil War, provided credentials for her membership as a Louisiana Colonial. She died in 2016.

Mary Lou Schultis Widmer is a novelist-historian and native New Orleanian. She graduated from Loyola University. After teaching for sixteen years, she retired to devote her time to writing. She was married to the late Albert F. Widmer, Sr., and has two children, four grandchildren, and six great-grandchildren. She is the past president of Romance Writers of America's Southern Louisiana Chapter and a member of the Daughters of 1812 and Louisiana Colonials organizations, having certified her descent from ancestors living in Louisiana before 1803.

Index